833.914   Reid
B691re   Heinrich Boll

GLENDALE COLLEGE LIBRARY
1500 N. VERDUGO RD.
GLENDALE, CA   91208

Heinrich Böll
A German For His Time

J.H. REID

Heinrich Böll
A German for His Time

OSWALD WOLFF BOOKS
BERG PUBLISHERS
Oxford / New York / Hamburg

Distributed exclusively in the US and Canada by
St. Martin's Press, New York

833.914
B691re

First published in 1988 by
Berg Publishers Limited
Market House, Deddington, Oxford 0X5 4SW, UK
Room 400, 175 Fifth Avenue, New York, NY 10010, USA
Schenefelder Landstr. 14K, 2000 Hamburg 55, W.-Germany

© J.H. Reid 1988

All rights reserved.
No part of this publication may be reproduced
in any form or by any means without the permission
of Berg Publishers Limited.

British Library Cataloguing in Publication Data

Reid, J.H.
  Heinrich Böll: a German for his time.
  1. Böll, Heinrich—Criticism and
  interpretation
  I. Title
  833'.914   PT2603.0394

  ISBN 0–85496–533–5

Library of Congress Cataloging-in-Publication Data

Reid, J. H. (J. Hamish)
  Heinrich Böll, a German for his time.

  "Oswald Wolff books."
  Bibliography: p.
  Includes index.
  I. Böll, Heinrich, 1917–   . 2 Authors, German—
20th Century—Biography. I. Title.
PT2603.0394Z7297   833'.914   87–15783
  ISBN 0–85496–533–5

Printed in Great Britain by Billings of Worcester

12/88

Contents

For my parents

Preface

All translations, including the titles of works by Böll and others, are by myself. For convenience the translations of titles have been placed in the Index. References are to the editions listed in the Bibliography, where the code letters and names are also identified.

Some of the material in this book is based on work which I have published elsewhere. Again details can be ascertained from the Bibliography. I am grateful to the editors of *Forum for Modern Language Studies* for their permission to draw extensively on my article on *Fürsorgliche Belagerung* for parts of Chapter 8.

I am especially grateful to the Carnegie Trust for the Universities of Scotland for the generous travelling scholarship which enabled me to carry out my initial research on Heinrich Böll in the early 1960s, when I developed an interest in the writer and his work which has lasted for more than a quarter of a century. I remember the patience and humorous understanding with which he discussed his work with me then in spite of the after-effects of a bout of influenza. It is a matter of great sadness for me that shortly after I had embarked on this monograph Böll died, not yet seventy.

My thanks are due to Hinrich Siefken and Rhys Williams for their helpful comments on the manuscript, to the numerous friends and colleagues, students, teachers and sixth-formers with whom I have discussed Böll's works, and not least to my sons, who allowed me the use of 'their' computer with which to process the words of this book.

J.H.R.

1

Passionately of His Time

I believe that one of the most important principles
when judging literature is that one has to go back into
the time when it was written — completely. One has
also to imagine the way it was at that time, what was
happening when it was written. I can't read any other
way.

(Ich glaube, das ist eines der wichtigsten Prinzipien
bei der Beurteilung von Literatur, daß man in die
Zeit, in der sie geschrieben ist, zurückgehen muß,
und zwar ganz. Sich auch vorstellen muß, wie war das
damals, was passierte damals, als das geschrieben
worden ist. Ich kann gar nicht anders lesen.)
                                        (Vormweg, p. 112)

These were Böll's words in a conversation in December 1982 and
published a few months before he died in 1985. Böll himself was not
only a writer, but also a voracious reader, whose interests latterly
embraced not only the literature of his contemporaries in the
German-speaking countries, but also that of South America and
especially of the Soviet Union. His parents had been devout — if
anti-clerical — Catholics who introduced him to the novelists of the
renouveau catholique in France: Bloy, Bernanos and Mauriac; to their
English and German counterparts: Chesterton, Reinhold Schneider
and Gertrud von Le Fort; and also to older foreign writers, notably
Dickens and Dostoevsky. After the liberation of German culture
from Nazi censorship in 1945 he read everything that he could get
hold of. Joyce and Kafka were revelations, but there was also the
great influx of American realists: Hemingway, Jones, McCullers,
Mailer, Steinbeck and Faulkner, together with their European
contemporaries Sartre, Camus and Greene. One of his convictions
was 'that literature provides better information than politics, economics and whatever. How do I know America? From its literature.
How do I know Spain, when I've only been there once in my life for
a short time? I know it because I know Cervantes; and not only him'
('daß die Literatur die besseren Auskünfte gibt als die Politik, die

1

Wirtschaft und was immer. Woher kenne ich Amerika? Aus der Literatur. Woher kenne ich Spanien, wo ich erst einmal im Leben kurz gewesen bin? Ich kenne es, weil ich Cervantes kenne; und nicht nur ihn') (I, p. 598). Literature provided information on a country's society and culture, but the act of reading also required the ability to set what was being read in its historical context. This was not least true of that literature one might imagine to be 'contemporary'. In 1975 he wrote: 'In the meantime novels are becoming "historical" more quickly even than in the nineteenth century and already one would almost need to provide the appropriate background for a novel that appeared in the Fifties of our century if one wanted to interpret it today' ('Inzwischen sind Romane schneller "historisch" als noch im neunzehnten Jahrhundert, und man müßte schon fast einem Roman, der in den fünfziger Jahren unseres Jahrhunderts erschien, wenn man ihn heute interpretieren wollte, den entsprechenden Hintergrund mitgeben') (E 3, p. 235). One of the purposes of the present study is to place the novels and stories of Böll in their historical context, both in terms of the events of the time and in terms of the way in which writers were dealing with these events.

This is particularly appropriate in Böll's case as for him person- ally the act of *writing* was a means of taking part in the history of his own times. This was one of the topics he discussed with Christian Linder in 1975:

C.L. You view writing not so much as something autobiographical but as biographical, in the sense of taking part in the history of your times?
H.B.: Yes. Within a particular constellation, within a particular milieu, for example.

(**C.L.**: Sie verstehen Schreiben nicht so sehr als autobiographisch, son- dern biographisch, im Sinne von Teilnahme an Zeitgeschichte?
H.B.: Ja. Innerhalb einer bestimmten Konstellation, innerhalb eines bestimmten Milieus etwa.)

(I, 376)

And as he was a man who from his earliest days took a passionate interest in everything that was happening around him, the contem- porary world was the material from which he constructed his novels, short stories, plays and radio plays. 'I am of my times, passionately of my times' ('Ich bin ja Zeitgenosse — leidenschaftlicher Zeitge- nosse') (I, p. 401). The term 'Zeitgenosse' (contemporary) is the key to his outlook, to be found in 1953 in the essay 'Der Zeitgenosse und die Wirklichkeit' ('The contemporary and reality') (E 1, pp. 71ff.) and in December 1982 in the two conversations on the topic

2

'Schreiben als Zeitgenossenschaft' ('Writing as contemporaneity') (Vormweg, pp. 103ff.). His criticism of his Church proceeded, he said in 1983, from his 'being of his times', from the fact that he had observed the Church's development from 1933, when it signed a concordat with Hitler, to the post-war years when it dashed his hopes for a more progressive stance (Limagne, p. 187). In 1961 when the *Frankfurter Allgemeine Zeitung* organised a questionnaire on whether the paintings of Pablo Picasso would stand the test of time Böll replied with the words: 'I am not interested in whether art will last; I believe that art is made by contemporaries for contemporaries; there are unrecognised contemporaries and recognised ones, there is fleeting and there is permanent contemporaneity; I consider Picasso a permanent contemporary' ('Für die Frage nach der Beständigkeit der Kunst interessiere ich mich nicht; ich glaube, Kunst wird von Zeitgenossen für Zeitgenossen gemacht; es gibt verkannte, gibt erkannte Zeitgenossen, es gibt flüchtige und andauernde Zeitgenossenschaft; Picasso halte ich für einen andauernden Zeitgenossen') (*Frankfurter Allgemeine Zeitung*, 21.10.1961).

In 1964 he described himself as one who had never felt alone, but always 'gebunden', tied, involved, committed:

Tied to time and times, to what a whole generation has experienced, digested, seen and heard, which in autobiographical terms has only rarely been anything like significant enough to be articulated in language; tied to the restlessness and homelessness of a generation which suddenly finds itself transferred into grandparenthood and still has not reached — how do they call it — maturity.

(Gebunden an Zeit und Zeitgenossenschaft, an das von einer Generation Erlebte, Erfahrene, Gesehene und Gehörte, das autobiographisch nur selten annähernd bezeichnend genug gewesen ist, um in Sprache gefaßt zu werden; gebunden an die Ruhe- und Heimatlosigkeit einer Generation, die sich plötzlich ins Großvateralter versetzt findet und immer noch nicht — wie nennt man das doch — reif geworden ist.)

And in 1975 in his address on the occasion of the award of the Georg Büchner Prize to Manès Sperber he said that 'contemporaneity, observing and enduring time' was 'our only settlement . . . impatience in a present which does not seem to exist, whose essence appears to be transience: transient, in search of a home, on this earth and in this age, sceptical of a future into which the seconds hand is constantly thrusting us' ('Zeitgenossenschaft, das Beobachten und Erdulden der Zeit . . . unsere einzige Niederlassung, . . . Ungeduld in einer Gegenwart, die es gar nicht zu geben, deren Wesen Flüchtigkeit zu sein scheint: flüchtig, auf der Suche nach einer Heimat, auf dieser Erde und in dieser Zeit, mißtrauisch gegenüber einer Zukunft, in die uns der Sekundenzeiger immer wieder hineinschiebt') (E 3, p. 272). His experiences, his contemporaneity were, Böll believed, not only his own but those of a whole generation. They were part of the transience of humankind, and literature was always a 'writing against death' (E 1, p. 327).

Heinrich Böll was an intellectual of the European rather than the British variety. It is true that he tried to discount this. Unlike France's Jean-Paul Sartre, who was in the first place a philosopher and an intellectual, Böll regarded himself in the first place as a writer of fiction and only secondarily as one who wrote political essays or gave political speeches (I, p. 402). But many of the controversies described in this book would be unlikely in a British context, simply because British writers do not usually intervene in the day to day business of politics. There are of course exceptions. Böll thought highly of Graham Greene, who had, for example, publicly objected to the severe prison sentences meted out to the train robbers (Kesting, p. 84). But on the whole British writers since the war have tended to avoid involvement in controversial issues of the day, and the media have not sought to ascertain their attitudes on, say, the question of Northern Ireland, birth control, or even the plight of their counterparts in the Soviet Union or Czechoslovakia. The situation is quite different in France and Germany. However, the German intellectual finds himself in an ahistorical situation, in view of the vilification of intellectuals by the Nazis and their forerunners both in the Second Empire and in the Weimar Republic. Indeed Dietz Bering has pointed out that intellectuals, what Karl Mannheim called the 'free-floating intelligentsia' ('freischwebende Intelligenz'), faced almost as much hostility from the socialists as they did from the nationalists (Bering, 1978). To be sure, intellectuals played a vital role in the years 1918 to 1933: the writer Heinrich Mann — whose journalism has been compared to Böll's (Vogt, 1978, p. 75) — was even proposed as candidate for the German presidency in 1932; a proposal echoed in 1984 when Luise Rinser stood for the presidency of the Federal Republic as the candidate for the Greens Party. But the Weimar Republic was brutally ended by the Nazis, large numbers of intellectuals emigrated, and when democracy was restored in 1945 the intellectual tradition had been broken. Moreover, the division of Germany into two opposing political and social systems, each cemented into the two mutually hostile power blocs under the hegemony of the United States and the Soviet Union respectively, brought with it demands

4

from politicians on both sides that writers should support the decisions of their leaders, anything less being regarded, according to context, as a betrayal of freedom or of socialism. The cold war, as manifested by the militant anti-Communism of Konrad Adenauer and his American patrons, created an atmosphere in West Germany which was hostile to independent expressions of criticism. A pertinent example is the uproar over the building of the Berlin Wall by the East German authorities in August 1961 to stop the outflow of citizens to the West. Twenty-three West German intellectuals wrote to the President of the United Nations, Mongi Slim, refusing to make one-sided accusations but asking for his intervention; almost at the same time Georg Ramseger asked in *Die Welt* why the West German writers were silent on the issue, and in the *Frankfurter Allgemeine Zeitung* Ernst-Otto Maetzke mocked the letter to Mongi Slim, suggesting that it was time these writers wrote 'another nice book' (Richter, 1961, pp. 123ff.). When the East German poet Wolf Biermann was attacked by the Communist Party leadership in December 1965 and ultimately prevented from publishing his works in his own country, Böll protested, but he also reminded his readers that only a short time previously the West German Chancellor Ludwig Erhard had attacked the writer Rolf Hochhuth as a 'Pinscher', a little dog snapping at the heels of his master; the difference was that Erhard's words, unlike those of Erich Honecker, held no dangers for those they were directed at, a distinction which in view of his experiences in the autumn of 1977 Böll might later not have wished to sustain (*Die Zeit*, 17.12.1965, p. 17).

The most comprehensive attack on West German intellectuals came in 1975 from the conservative sociologist Helmut Schelsky in his book *Die Arbeit tun die anderen*. Schelsky's thesis was that in all the advanced Western democracies the traditional class struggle between workers and capitalists had been virtually eliminated; the new class struggle was that between those who produce wealth and those who 'interpret' the production process: the journalists, writers and media-people, the 'intellectuals', whom he described as the new 'priest-caste', concerned not for the welfare of those they claimed to represent but rather for their own power, decrying all that West German society had achieved in the forty years since the end of the war, devaluing the very virtues that their own wealth depended on, namely industriousness and achievement, and claiming that traditional exploitation still existed in order to disguise their own striving to subject society to their will. The main targets of his polemic were the psycho-sociologist Alexander Mitscherlich, the journalist Rudolf Augstein — and the writer Heinrich Böll, to whom

5

he devoted a twenty-eight page diatribe entitled 'Heinrich Böll — Cardinal and Martyr' (Schelsky, 1975, pp. 460–77). Schelsky's book is a document of the New Right, fighting back after the setbacks of the years 1967 to 1972; what gives it its interest is not least the element of personal invective. Böll's response was remarkably calm. He accepted some of Schelsky's points, but declared that West German intellectuals had had the role of 'conscience of the nation' forced upon them by others; West Germany lacked a political culture such as France possessed, and writers were being thrust into the gap (I, pp. 417ff.). Elsewhere he contrasted the honour accorded to Sartre by de Gaulle, even when the philosopher was critical of the government's behaviour (Kesting, pp. 77f.), and spoke of his envy for the Poles in this regard, whose writers and intellectuals had always been respected (Riese, p. 31).

If Böll regarded himself only secondarily as the writer of political essays and speeches, this did not mean that his fiction was any less 'topical' or 'committed' than his non-fiction. Indeed in his address to the city fathers of Cologne, who gave him the freedom of the city in 1983, he suggested that the former was more subversive than the latter — and that this was true of most literature. Goethe could hardly be regarded as 'wholesome reading' ('heilende Lektüre'), when his works conveyed 'chaos, misfortune, pain, fear, adultery, suicide'; Kleist's plays did not inspire confidence in authority; even the apparent utopias of Stifter left one with the feeling that catastrophe was just around the corner (EZ, pp. 85ff.). For this reason Böll felt that the debate over whether literature should be 'committed' or not was unfruitful — the division of literature into 'engagé' or 'not' was 'bourgeois presumptuousness' ('bürgerliche Anmaßung') (I, p. 606). It is true that on occasion he attacked writers (seldom by name) who knew allegiance only to their art (E 1, p. 356), but that was exceptional; even the phenomenon of 'new inwardness' which marked German literature in the later 1970s he defended as not a 'retreat', but merely a return to an 'eternal stream' in literature (Riese, p. 21). He regarded himself as 'committed', without being able to say to what he was committed (I, pp. 22f.). Some of his commitments will become clear in the course of this study. One fundamental belief was in the importance of the freedom of the artist, a freedom which was the litmus paper for civil liberties in general (I, pp. 22f.; E 1, pp. 301ff.). At other times he stressed the 'corrosive' function of literature (I, p. 408; Vormweg, p. 113). There was a strong existentialist or anarchist element in Böll's outlook which made him suspicious of all rigidities in social life, whether structures of authority in Church or State, or patterns imposed on personal life from without. Literature had the function of 'corroding', calling into question these structures. One of the negative qualities attributed to intellectuals by the Nazis and their predecessors was precisely their 'corrosive' ('zersetzend') attitude (Bering, 1978, p. 125). In using the term Böll was consciously accepting the challenge.

Böll's passionate concern for his own times means that his birth date is of more than usual importance: 'I believe this: that you have to work out very exactly what kind of biographical times an author comes from' ('Ich glaube folgendes: daß man sehr genau unterscheiden muß, aus welcher Zeitbiographie ein Autor stammt') (Lenz, p. 31). Born in December 1917, he was only four years younger than, for example, Alfred Andersch, but these four years were decisive. In 1933 when Hitler came to power, Andersch was nineteen and already the organiser of a Communist youth group, for which he was temporarily interned in a concentration camp. In January 1933 Böll was only fourteen. While in the post-war years he and Andersch were to develop in similar ways, it was the older man who became involved in political journalism even as a prisoner of war; Böll was in this respect a late starter. In the other direction, Günter Grass, born in 1927, belonged to a different generation altogether; six at the time of the Nazi takeover, he was a member of the Hitler Youth and was still only eighteen when the war ended, whereas Böll was twenty-seven. While Böll had experimented with writing before the war it was only in 1946 that he began to publish. Thereafter his works were to accompany the development of West Germany in the first forty years of its life, and they did so in a quite direct way.

In his 1953 essay 'Der Zeitgenosse und die Wirklichkeit' Böll distinguished between that which is merely 'topical' and that which is 'real', the significant events which shape our lives. He went on to insist that it was only through the topical that the writer could find the 'key to reality' (E 1, pp. 71ff.). He gave as an example a report on the Japanese fishermen who were exposed to radiation during an American nuclear test in the Pacific. The report alarmed everyone who read it at the time; it was topical, but a few days later the fishermen were forgotten. The *reality* of the event, however, was the reality of a new form of death, the possibility that from now on the very air that we breathe may unbeknown to us be polluted with deadly poison. The example is revealing for what it tells us of Böll's interests, and the threat of nuclear disaster was one to which he returned at the end of his life; as a statement of his *ars poetica* the essay is equally important. Probably without knowing it, Böll was echoing Charles Baudelaire's words on the artist almost a century earlier: 'Il s'agit pour lui de dégager de la mode ce qu'elle peut

7

contenir de poétique dans l'historique, de tirer l'éternel du transitoire' (Baudelaire, 1863, p. 892). One of the most characteristic and influential poetics of the 1950s was Hugo Friedrich's *Die Struktur der modernen Lyrik*, in which modernist, hermetic, elitist poetry is traced back to Baudelaire; by contrast Bertolt Brecht, whose poetry is popular, interventionist and 'useful' is mentioned by Friedrich only once — and then only for his theory of drama (Friedrich, 1956). Brecht's poetry was appreciated only from the more socially-oriented 1960s onwards. Böll's early literary theory was thus in line with 'modernism'. His later pronouncements, as his statement on Picasso suggests, were less concerned with 'the eternal'. Nevertheless his point of departure was always the particular, the today, even if this meant that his works did *not* take on the appearance of having been written for eternity — later readers may well be puzzled by allusions to events or people long since forgotten. Instead they provide a fascinating documentation of the development of West Germany out of the collapse of the Reich from 1943 onwards, so that Manfred Durzak can describe all his novels as 'Zeitromane', novels which concern themselves with their immediate times (Durzak, 1971, p. 40). This documentation even includes the more or less exact dating of the time at which the events described in the novels occur: *Der Zug war pünktlich* (1949) takes place at the end of September 1943; *Wo warst du, Adam?* (1951) from 1944 to the end of the war in 1945; *Und sagte kein einziges Wort* (1953) in September 1952; *Haus ohne Hüter* (1954) in the autumn of 1953; *Das Brot der frühen Jahre* (1955) in March 1955; *Billard um halbzehn* (1959) on the 6 September 1958; *Ansichten eines Clowns* (1963) in March 1962; *Gruppenbild mit Dame* (1971) in 1971; *Fürsorgliche Belagerung* (1979) in November 1978; and *Frauen vor Flußlandschaft* (1985) in the late summer of 1984.

This preoccupation with the immediate present might seem to imply that Böll disregarded Germany's past history. Not so. The past plays a vital part in all his major works. This is as true of the war novel *Wo warst du, Adam?*, in which the pre-war lives of such characters as Bressen and Filskeit help to explain their enthusiastic embracing of the Nazi cause, as it is of a work like *Billard um halbzehn*, where Heinrich Fähmel's career as an architect from before the First World War onwards is conveyed in some detail and is of similar importance for our understanding of his present standpoint. In an essay on Tolstoy's *War and Peace* Böll declared that all literature was an 'approach' to history: 'Every novel is, if not utopian, historical, even the so-called novel of the present-day' ('Jeder Roman ist, wenn nicht utopisch, historisch, auch der sogenannte Gegenwartsroman'). Literature did not compete with history-writing any more that it did with psychology; it approached its material in a different way, 'by loading onto the historical material people who "did not make history"' ('indem sie dem geschichtlichen Stoff Personen auflädt, die "keine Geschichte gemacht haben"') (E 2, p. 414). His own novels were 'all approaches to the inexplicabilities of recent German history' ('lauter Annäherungsversuche an die Unerklärlichkeiten der jüngeren deutschen Geschichte') (E 2, p. 418). However, elsewhere he also confessed himself incapable of writing either historical or utopian, that is futuristic, novels, always finding himself thrown back into the present-day (I, p. 507; cf. also I, p. 268). Part of the reason for this inability may have been his conviction that the National Socialist domination and debasement of German culture and society between 1933 and 1945 caused a complete break in historical continuity, with the result that all that preceded it seemed relegated to a 'museum' and was no longer an immediately relevant reality (I, p. 26). Direct representation of the past was therefore not congenial to him. On the other hand he was acutely aware that many of his compatriots were refusing to face up to their past. There was a tendency to forget what happened before 1945. Germans were usually well-informed on the consequences of the war, but preferred not to think of its causes (E 3, p. 293); they were indignant about the behaviour of the Soviet army of occupation, but forgot the appalling crimes which the Germans themselves had committed on Soviet territory (E 3, p. 327). 'We are living in a country which has repressed its history, the war, the persecution of the Jews' ('Wir leben in einem Land, das seine Geschichte verdrängt hat, den Krieg, die Judenverfolgung') (I, p. 575). There was a strong temptation 'to drop out of German history' but Böll was determined to participate again and again (E. 3, p. 503).

The past could not be undone. The phrases 'Bewältigung der Vergangenheit' ('coming to terms with the past') and 'Wiedergutmachung' ('making good') were 'barbaric'; he could not imagine that there could ever exist a natural, spontaneous relationship between a Jew and a German of his generation: 'We are living in a present which contains the whole of the past' ('Wir leben in einer Gegenwart, die alles Vergangene enthält') (E 2, p. 338). Böll's passionate concern for his times necessarily embraced the analysis of how these times came about. It is therefore wholly appropriate that this study should begin with an account of Böll's perception of the historical development of his own country in the twentieth century as he himself experienced it in the crucial years between 1918 and 1945.

2

The Disintegration of Bourgeois Society (1917–1945)

Heinrich Böll's biography is known almost exclusively through what he himself reported. His biography is his autobiography. In recent years there have been numerous studies of the art of autobiography; all agree that it is an art rather than a science. The most famous autobiography in the German language is that of Goethe, who entitled it *Dichtung und Wahrheit* — 'poetry and truth' in the sense that it is the story of a poet, but also 'fiction and truth' in that Goethe was tracing patterns in his life, interpreting it, presenting it as he wished it to be seen. As a writer of fiction Böll was interpreting history, creating patterns of meaning, ordering his material to enable his reader to make sense of it. Writing about himself he was performing a similar task. Hans Werner Richter describes an occasion on which he was due to present a television discussion of 20 July 1944, the day of the unsuccessful attempt by army officers to assassinate Hitler. Each of the participants was to relate what he was doing that day; Böll had told him beforehand how he had been in a hospital in Romania and had been selling army trousers to civilians, an interesting, self-critical, entertaining story, but when the moment came for him to speak to the cameras he told a quite different, more trivial story. Afterwards Richter asked him why he had changed his mind and received the reply: 'I'm not going to spoil my biography' ('Ich werde mir doch nicht meine Biographie verderben'). Böll, to Richter's surprise, was during his lifetime manipulating, 'doctoring', his biography (Richter, 1986, pp. 74f.). But in another sense too his autobiography is related to his fiction: both are part of his 'Zeitgenossenschaft', his taking part in history. Purely private experiences are rigorously exluded from Böll's autobiographical statements; there are no love stories; Annemarie, his wife for over forty years — 'the lady to whom I am married', as he liked to put it (FT, p. 302) — is scarcely present at all (Wallmann, p. 133).

Böll left no autobiography in the traditional sense, no account of his life from birth to the time of writing. In 1975 he said that he wished he could write a 'classical autobiography' but found it impossible, perhaps because his whole literary output was 'a transformation of autobiography' (I, p. 379). Ten years previously he had remarked on the difficulty he had had with a contribution for an anthology in which various people described their experiences of the year 1945; for days he had searched for a beginning, writing ten different versions of one incident, until he gave up, realising that it could not be retold as it was, it needed to be 'transformed' otherwise it would read like a cheap novelette (E 2, pp. 145f.). One difficulty he had was with the very use of the first person: he felt greater distance towards the first person narrators of his novels than to characters described in the third person (Lengning, 1972, p. 102); stylistic problems of this kind made it 'incredibly difficult to write autobiographically' (I, p. 321). Many of the details of his life must be gleaned from his conversations; he evidently was less inhibited in speaking spontaneously about his life than he was when writing about it. Prior to 1981 he had written a few brief accounts of his life for particular occasions: 'Selbstvorstellung eines jungen Autors', first published in French as 'Présentation d'un jeune auteur par lui-même' in 1953; the 'Biographische Notiz' of 1956; and 'Über mich selbst' in 1959. Other essays relate specific autobiographical episodes: 'Raderberg, Raderthal' (1965), places connected with his early childhood; 'Kümmelblättchen, Spritzenland, Kampfkommandantur' (1965), the eventual outcome of his wrestling with the year 1945; 'An einen Bischof, einen General und einen Minister des Jahrgangs 1917' (1966) on some aspects of the war years; 'Suchanzeigen' (1972) on his mother; and 'Am Anfang' (1973) on the immediate post-war years. What Böll meant by 'transformation' ('Verwandlung') in terms of his autobiography can be grasped from a study particularly of the middle three items listed here. 'Kümmelblättchen' is a montage of incidents, recollections, statistics, ending characteristically with a reference to two madonnas which survived the bombing of Cologne; 'An einen Bischof' has three fictitious narratees (Rimmon-Kenan, 1983, pp. 103–5) and again does not narrate in any linear way; the third is a 'search' for the real person who was his mother, by one who is acutely aware of the danger of turning her into 'literature' (E 2, p. 529). All are highly self-conscious artefacts.

In the 1980s, however, Böll wrote two more substantial autobiographical essays. The first was inspired by a series in the *Frankfurter Allgemeine Zeitung* in which authors, among them Peter Rühmkorf and Günter Kunert, were invited to describe their schooldays in the Third Reich; Böll's contribution was entitled 'Den Nazis verdanke ich mein Abitur' ('I owe my school certificate to the Nazis'); an expanded version appeared under the title *Was soll aus dem Jungen bloß werden?* *Oder: Irgendwas mit Büchern* in 1981. Jürgen P. Wallmann suggested that its informal tone might cause critics to accuse him of carelessness. Böll replied that it was a very carefully composed piece of work, one which had gone through several versions; there was scarcely a work over which he had taken as much trouble (Wallmann, p. 130). Nor was it quite a self-portrait; even here he denied that he as author was identical with the first person of the narrative (p. 133). Clearly there were incidents which he could not invent and these were the most difficult parts of the work; otherwise, however, it was a construct. Two aspects of *Was soll aus dem Jungen bloß werden?* may be singled out in this respect. The first is the cyclical form of the narrative. In musical terms it is a rondo, marked by its constant digressions, the conversational tone leading the narrator away from any consistent linear narrative, but always returning to the main theme: schooldays under the Nazis. And secondly it uses two literary models: the Böll family is made to resemble the Micawbers of Dickens's *David Copperfield*, and their progress is the 'decline of a family' ('Verfall einer Familie') of Thomas Mann's *Buddenbrooks*. Similar features can be detected in Böll's other major autobiographical work of the 1980s, his contribution to an anthology to celebrate the fortieth anniversary of the end of the war, the thirty-three page long 'Brief an meine Söhne oder vier Fahrräder'. Here too we note the specified narratees. The narrator speaks of the dangers of autobiography, of projecting oneself as a hero: '"Story-telling" is a perilous activity, in the "story-teller" there lies always concealed the boaster, the braggart who, if you look at him closely, is always a hero after all or at least a sufferer' ('"Erzählen" ist eine gefährliche Tätigkeit, im "Erzähler" verbirgt sich immer der Bramarbaseur, der Angeber, der ja doch, genau betrachtet, immer ein Held ist oder doch wenigstens ein Dulder') (FT, p. 80). The literary patterns referred to here are those of the *Odyssey*, the *Märchen* and the thriller. In these ways Böll was fictionalising his autobiography.

Conversely there is the question to what extent Böll's fiction is autobiographical. Christian Linder describes Böll as primarily an autobiographical author. Linder's approach is psychoanalytical. His thesis is that Böll's writing was motivated by the desire to preserve the values of his childhood; his impulses were never political but personal (Linder, 1986, pp. 36ff.). Böll himself did not fully agree with this analysis (Wallmann, p. 131), although some of the statements which he made during their conversations in 1975 might bear it out. Elsewhere he spoke of the importance of the formative years up to the age of twenty-one for a writer's development. It was what one experienced then naïvely, the 'elements of human life', that counted; influences thereafter were too conscious to be useful (I, p. 15). The 'basic experience' of his early years was, he said, not so much the war as the 'disintegration of bourgeois society' ('Zerfall der bürgerlichen Gesellschaft') in the 1920s and 1930s (I, p. 377). The *Angst* which accompanied him throughout his life went back to his experience of the international economic crisis of 1929 and the Nazi terror which followed it (I, pp. 368f.). He frequently criticised the 'clumsy autobiographical approach' to his novels: 'I believe that an author is present in the whole of his work and that one has to keep the whole work in front of one in the whole of its development, including its contradictions' ('Ich glaube, daß ein Autor im gesamten Werk vorhanden ist und daß man das ganze Werk immer vor Augen haben muß, in seiner ganzen Entwicklung, auch in seinen Widersprüchen'). For example, he rejected the identification of Hans Schnier, the central figure of *Ansichten eines Clowns*, with the author: 'I am not the clown, perhaps I am even rather the clown's father, you understand' ('Ich bin nicht der Clown, vielleicht bin ich sogar eher der Vater des Clowns, verstehen Sie') (I, p. 565). He suggested that there was an analogy between his novels and the films of Rainer Werner Fassbinder or Helmut Käutner, in which the director sometimes plays a minor role (I, p. 566); thus the mysterious B.H.T. of *Gruppenbild mit Dame* was Böll himself (Durzak, 1972, p. 189). And yet it is not difficult to find statements made by Hans Schnier which correspond to what Böll said in a non-literary context: the artist never has time off, says Schnier (R 4, pp. 141ff.), and Böll repeated these words to Linder (I, p. 359). A great many of the details in Böll's fiction set in the Third Reich and the war are based on autobiography. In *Gruppenbild mit Dame* the impatience of the inhabitants of Cologne waiting for the Americans to invade the city at the end of the war, while the American strategy was to leave Cologne to the South and make across Germany towards Kassel, reflects Böll's and his family's experience as presented in the 'Brief an meine Söhne'. Leni's annoyance at being fobbed off with a story of 'strawberries and cream' in the sex education class in the same novel is based on what happened in Böll's own school class (J, pp. 92f.). Both Fred Bogner's tutoring in Latin and mathematics and his mother's inability to turn anyone away who came to her door in the opening chapter of *Und sagte kein einziges Wort* draw on details of Böll's own life as described in *Was soll aus dem Jungen bloß werden?* *Entfernung von der Truppe* uses motifs from his wartime experiences (I, p. 618). The story 'Als der Krieg ausbrach' is included in Böll's fiction, but it is 'almost autobiographical' (I, p. 619). Robert Fähmel's wanderings in the neighbourhood of Cologne with poems of Hölderlin in his pocket are similar to Böll's own activities as an eighteen-year-old, described in his autobiography. Indeed *Billard um halbzehn* is possibly the most autobiographical of all Böll's longer works: Heinrich and Johanna Fähmel are largely based on Böll's own parents, albeit 'transposed' into a higher social class.

Heinrich Böll was born on 21 December 1917. His father Viktor Böll had three children by his first wife Katharina, only one of whom, Grete, survived childhood. Katharina died in 1901 and in 1906 Viktor married Maria Hermanns, who had been his house-keeper. They had five children, two daughters, Mechthild and Gertrud, and three sons, Alois, Alfred and Heinrich. Although the youngest, Heinrich had the ancestral name. His paternal grand-father was a Heinrich Böll who was born in Xanten in 1829 and had nine children by his first marriage — three more by a second — the eldest of whom was likewise called Heinrich and gave the name in turn to his eldest son.

In an autobiographical sketch of 1959 Böll reported that his ancestors had emigrated from England to escape the persecution of Roman Catholics by Henry VIII: Böll's own uncompromising moral standpoint is thus given ancestral significance, although emigration from Nazi Germany was not an option that ever occurred to him (J, p. 37). These *émigrés* were ship's carpenters, but they 'always preferred to live in towns rather than in the country' — a hint of the indifference, even hostility towards the countryside to be found in his own early works — and eventually became joiners. His mother's ancestors were peasants and brewers: 'one generation was wealthy and diligent, then the next one would produce the profligate, the following generation would be poor, producing the success again, until in the final branch, from which my mother came, there gathered utter contempt for the world and the name was ex-tinguished' ('eine Generation war wohlhabend und tüchtig, dann brachte die nächste den Verschwender hervor, war die übernächste arm, brachte wieder den Tüchtigen hervor, bis sich im letzten Zweig, aus dem meine Mutter stammte, alle Weltverachtung sam-melte und der Name erlosch') (E 1, pp. 284f.). His maternal grand-father was a civil servant (I, p. 538). Elsewhere Böll described him as 'easy-going, spoiled', with an unfortunate love of the bottle behind the crumbling façade of respectability (I, pp. 528f.). His son Heinrich Hermanns was a grammar-school-teacher, an atheist, to his mother's dismay, and an anti-monarchist. It is reported that on the occasion of the Emperor's birthday he once hoisted a chamber-pot to the top of the flagpole, and it was probably for this that he was disgraced and relegated to Wyk on the island of Föhr. He was married, but had no children — not, however, by choice, according to Böll's brother Alfred. His wife committed suicide when she discovered she was suffering from an incurable disease, and he followed suit shortly after (Alfred Böll, 1981, pp. 118–27). This pattern of the decline of the family's social status, however, is one which Böll traces again and again in his autobiographical utterances — and he does so with a certain amount of complacency, as when he emphasises his own family's classless status in the 1930s (J, p. 86).

Böll's paternal grandfather was a master-joiner, 'a very successful man in the petty-bourgeois sense' ('ein sehr erfolgreicher Mann im kleinbürgerlichen Sinne') (I, p. 540), who had invested his money in property. His eldest son Heinrich was likewise a joiner. Another son, Alfred, became a priest, whose parish later included the mansion of the Krupp family, where he was a frequent guest (Alfred Böll, 1981, p. 28). Another, Alois, was a successful architect, who designed a number of churches and public buildings in and around Cologne (ibid., pp. 31ff.). Viktor Böll was born in Essen, just across the road from Krupp's factory (I, p. 538). He too was a joiner by trade, moving to Cologne to set up his own business at the age of twenty-five. There he went up market in the artistic sphere, specialising in wood-carving for churches and gaining something of a reputation in this field — his advertising leaflet mentions work done for churches in Salonika in Greece and Theux in Belgium, as well as for places nearer home (Alfred Böll, pp. 60f.). He was an enterprising and very largely a self-educated man, who had developed an interest in art history at evening classes which he liked to share with his children. He used to take them to the many art galleries in Cologne and explain to them the development of the history of painting from the Middle Ages to Picasso (I, p. 531). On the outbreak of the First World War he was judged not robust enough for immediate conscription — and when he was eventually put on a transport train for Verdun he pretended to have appendicitis and was operated on (J, p. 75). He was an anti-militarist. Alfred Böll reports how he would not allow him to receive an airgun for Christmas (p. 146) and both he and Heinrich document his scorn for Kaiser Wilhelm's heroic posturings (Alfred Böll, 1981, p. 158; E 1, p. 284). The Schweik myth, the anti-militarist strain in Böll's outlook, is another ancestral feature. The text published by his children on his death is revealing: 'Three daughters, three sons, three daughter-in-laws and sixteen grandchildren mourn him who taught them to honour God and not to fear earthly rulers. Up to his death he retained a child-like heart and the independence of mind which he instilled into his children' ('Drei Töchter, drei Söhne, drei Schwiegertöchter und sechzehn

Enkelkinder betrauern ihn, der sie lehrte, Gott zu ehren und die irdischen Herren nicht zu fürchten. Bis zu seinem Tode bewahrte er sich ein kindliches Herz und den unabhängigen Sinn, in dem er seine Kinder erzog') (Alfred Böll, 1981, p. 239).

His wife, Böll's mother, was if anything an even greater influence. Böll described her once as the 'only genuine left-wing Catholic' ('die einzige echte Linkskatholikin') he had ever met, 'a marvellous, a great woman' ('eine großartige, eine große Frau') (Selbstinterview, p. 601). She was a highly intelligent, sensitive person, a kind-hearted woman who could never bear to send anyone away from her door empty-handed, no matter how struggling her own family was (J, p. 64). Böll's 'feminism' was to a large extent born out of indignation at the upbringing of his mother, the way in which she as a woman was deprived of educational opportunities by society and by the Church (I, p. 541). She was evidently the model for such characters as Fred Bogner's mother, Johanna Fähmel, and Käte Tolm. Böll wrote very affectionately of his parents, indeed of his whole family, stressing again and again how fortunate he was to have been protected against the Nazi virus. Perhaps unusually in writers, the antagonism between son and parents does not form a motivating impulse in his literary output. At least in his autobiography the immediate surroundings of his family appears as a haven of kindliness, reasonableness, warmth, a place where anti-Nazi sentiments could be expressed with impunity.

Two other elements in the parental background were important. The one is Catholicism, the other the Rhineland. Böll once described his Catholicism as being as much part of him as the colour of a black man's skin (E 2, p. 174); Catholicism was the 'material' from which he was made, and every author had to take up a critical distance to the material from which he was made (Q, p. 187). His parents and his ancestors as far back as he could trace were Roman Catholics with a strong 'Jansenist' streak; their origins were on the Dutch border where Jansenism, the puritanical brand of Catholicism, still has a powerful hold; his parents themselves rejected this puritanism without being able completely to free themselves of it (Limagne, p. 185). As a girl his mother had had to go to church twice a day. His father and uncles were forced to go on pilgrimages on which they had to carry a cross through the night and to fast into the following morning (I, p. 539). By contrast they brought their children up in a more liberal, although still devout, manner. The memory of Bismarck's attacks on the independence of the Catholic Church was still strong — they both had had to be confirmed in secret (Limagne, p. 191). When Böll temporarily ceased to practise his religion in the 1930s his parents put no pressure on him to return to the fold.

Pressed for a definition of 'rhenishness' Böll found it impossible to hit on a formula which would apply to such diverse Rhinelanders as Friedrich Engels, Konrad Adenauer, Heinrich Heine, Karl Schurz and Walter Scheel, to whom he felt he could justifiably add Karl Marx from Trier (E 3, p. 109). The Rhineland background is related to the issue of Catholicism. For historical reasons the Rhineland is predominantly Catholic; in 1814, however, it was annexed by Protestant Prussia — Böll compared the arrogance of the Prussian officials who came to inspect it with the traditional arrogance of the Germans towards the Poles (EZ, p. 218). Böll's family distrusted the Prussians. An ancestor of Viktor Böll's first wife wrote in his diary that the French during their occupation from 1794 to 1814 had treated the Rhinelanders like barbarians, but the Prussians who replaced them had been much worse (Alfred Böll, 1981, p. 67). As Catholics the Bölls were against Bismarck, and regarded the unification of Germany under Bismarck as a 'kind of swindle' (I, p. 582). Berlin, from which the united German state was ruled from 1871 onwards, was Protestant. After the First World War the Rhineland was occupied by the French and, under the Treaty of Versailles, declared a demilitarised zone. When the Nazis marched into the Rhineland in 1936, Böll and his family viewed it as an invasion by the Prussians: 'The Nazis disguised as Prussians, the Prussians disguised as Nazis in the Rhineland! We — I at least — would have rather had the French . . . or the English invade from the other side' ('Die Nazis als Preußen verkleidet, die Preußen als Nazis verkleidet im Rheinland! Uns — mir jedenfalls — wär's lieber gewesen, wenn die Franzosen . . . oder Engländer von der anderen Seite her einmarschiert wären') (J, p. 75). One possibly unfortunate result of this anti-Prussian stance was that the Böll family found no access to the critical, left-wing literature of the Weimar republic, which was primarily associated with Berlin (J, p. 79). Cologne was 'never militaristic' (E 2, p. 151). Böll claimed that it was the city where Hitler felt least at ease (E 1, p. 116), where people threw flowerpots at Hitler and ridiculed Göring (E 1, p. 284). Thus another part of Böll's family myth is that of an independent, liberal Catholic anti-Prussianism.

When Böll was born Germany was still ruled by an emperor; something which seemed to him in 1960 as remote as the Punic Wars (E 1, p. 366). Like the character of an early short story, he was 'as old as the Russian Revolution . . . as old as the dirt and the hunger' ('so alt wie die russische Revolution . . . so alt wie der Dreck

17

und der Hunger') (R 1, p. 218). It was the time of the worst famine of the war — the infamous 'turnips winter', in which thousands died of hunger (E 2, pp. 247f.). The war ended the following year and his earliest memory was of the return of Hindenburg's defeated army (E 1, p. 285). The Kaiser was deposed, and there followed the fifteen years of Weimar democracy, with their twin poles of inflation at the one end and unemployment at the other. In 1921 the family was prospering enough to be able to move from the suburbs of Cologne to a house which an enterprising uncle had built on the outskirts. Böll was four years old and regretted the move; he had liked the proximity to the Rhine as well as the urban environment. He remembered throwing sand at the jeeps of the forces of occupation and asking for 'Tschokelät pliehs' when the drivers stopped and got out in a fury (E 2, p. 121). Two years later, in December 1923, inflation reached its peak: on Böll's sixth birthday the dollar price reached 4,210,500 million marks. The first money he held in his hand consisted of a banknote valued at one billion marks, for which he bought a stick of barley sugar; his father had to fetch the money to pay his apprentices from the bank in a wheelbarrow (E 1, p. 285). This experience of total inflation was to be one reason for contemporary Germans' preoccupation with a stable currency (E 3, pp. 352ff.). It meant at the time 'total bankruptcy' for the bourgeoisie (I, p. 540) and marked the beginning of his parents' economic decline, which the world crisis of 1929 merely confirmed and accelerated. The collapse of a bank for tradesmen in which his father was financially involved (I, p. 362) forced them to sell their house in the suburbs and move into rented accommodation in the city, accommodation which was too expensive for them and necessitated further moves (I, p. 612).

His childhood in the 1920s was a happy one, 'a very free and playful childhood' ('eine sehr freie und verspielte Kindheit') (I, p. 363). The house on the outskirts of Cologne was in a new estate which included representatives of the professional and of the working classes, the bourgeoisie and the 'Reds'. Böll preferred to play with the children of the latter, who had the more interesting games, and, unlike the professors, bank managers and architects, his parents tolerated this. The class divisions became clearer to him, if still incomprehensible, when he was sent to the Roman Catholic primary school while his friends went to the 'free school', and later, when at the age of ten he went on to grammar school and they did not (E 2, pp. 123ff.).

The collapse of world trade and its effects on the European economy was the first crisis with which Böll was faced. It helped to strengthen the family's solidarity — indeed it may have been the reason that the break with his parents never occurred: the 'recognition that success and failure did not simply depend on my parents . . . but that outside the family economic and political events were taking place — and even outside Germany' ('Die Erkenntnis, daß Wohl und Wehe nicht nur von meinen Eltern abhingen . . . Sondern daß außerhalb der Familie ökonomische und politische Ereignisse stattfanden — und sogar außerhalb Deutschlands') (I, p. 365). The second crisis had a similar effect — the Nazi takeover in January 1933: 'After the experience of the trade crisis, of being at the mercy of economic forces, now came the experience of being at the mercy of political forces, which was almost worse, since you could get used to the former and somehow do something for yourself, but there was nothing you could do about the other' ('Nach der Erfahrung der Wirtschaftskrise, des ökonomischen Ausgeliefertseins, nun die Erfahrung des politischen Ausgeliefertseins, die fast noch schlimmer war, weil man sich in dem anderen einrichten und irgendwie helfen konnte, aber dagegen gab es fast nichts') (I, p. 366). By turning in upon itself the Böll family was able to survive the Nazis and the war intact. That this had its questionable aspects is admitted by Böll himself: his family turned into a 'proper clan', developed 'an arrogance mixed almost with hysteria with regard to the world about us' ('Fast eine mit Hysterie gemischte Arroganz gegenüber der Umwelt') (I, p. 365). Family life, its strengths and its weaknesses, was to become a major literary theme for Böll from *Und sagte kein einziges Wort* down to *Fürsorgliche Belagerung*.

Between 24 October 1929 and the 30 January 1933 Germany collapsed into chaos. Unemployment soared from 2 million in the winter of 1928/9 to 4.4 million at the end of 1930, and to over 6 million (27.5 per cent of the working population) at the end of 1932. Bankruptcies were legion, banks collapsed, unemployment benefit was reduced, social security contributions were raised, and the reparations which Germany still owed to the victors of 1918 could no longer be paid. Pitched battles were fought in the streets and in public houses between Nazi storm-troopers and the paramilitary brigades of the Communist Party. Böll's daily route to school took him through what were 'partly classical Communist working-class areas' ('zum Teil klassische kommunistische Arbeiterviertel') where as a fourteen-year-old he frequently witnessed street-fighting (Lenz, p. 42); occasionally the police had to reroute the school-children for their own safety (E 1, p. 255). In elections to the Reichstag in 1930 the National Socialists increased their representation from 12 to 107 seats; in new elections in 1932 they gained a further 123 seats to become the strongest party in parliament. As they had never attempted to conceal their contempt for democratic institutions there seemed no question of their being asked to form a government. Nevertheless, first Kurt von Schleicher and then Franz von Papen carried out secret negotiations which were designed to enable them to do just that. In the Reichstag they frequently came to blows with the Communist deputies, who had also gained seats. From 1930 onwards Germany was governed not by democratic coalitions as hitherto, but by a minority government backed up by the power of the President to sign emergency decrees and to dissolve the Reichstag if it rejected these decrees.

The major factor which Böll emphasised in his analysis of the reasons for Germany's collapse into fascism was what he called the 'blindness of the middle classes' ('Blindheit des Bürgertums') (I, pp. 518f.): their inability to perceive the true nature of the Nazis until it was too late and their belief that they were serving their own interests by flirting with Hitler. In this connection Böll's own anti-bourgeois stance, his claim that his family dropped out of the bourgeoisie, is significant; but it was a diagnosis which was to affect Böll's attitude to post-war developments too. He found it especially distressing that those people who could best have afforded to resist the rise of fascism, the university professors, for example, did so little (Kesting, p. 70). The meeting which von Papen arranged between Hitler and top industrialists on 4 January 1933 anticipated Hitler's formal accession to power on 30 January (E 1, pp. 496f., 545). President Hindenburg, the East Prussian landowner, the Kaiser's field marshal, the monarchist president, stood for everything that Böll and his family distrusted: militarism; the lie that Germany had not been defeated in the war but 'stabbed in the back' by the socialists and liberals at home; Prussianism; and the interests of the rich at the expense of the poor (I, p. 549). At a time when the unemployed were finding their support reduced, subsidies were flowing to the landowners in East Prussia (the so-called 'Osthilfe'), and, although it was never proved, Hindenburg himself appeared to be involved in a shady deal designed to avoid paying tax on his estates (J, p. 15). Hindenburg, the nationalists and the financiers were those 'truly responsible' for Hitler's gaining power (I, pp. 546f.). The first Reichstag of 1932 lasted only a few weeks. Parliament was dissolved and new elections took place in November. In these second elections of 1932 the Nazis actually lost votes and it looked as if their momentum had been lost; at that very moment the nationalists together with the industrialists and the bankers stepped in and brought Hitler to power (I, p. 547).

When at the end of January 1933 it was announced that Hindenburg had invited Hitler to become chancellor, Böll's mother at once declared: 'That is war' ('Das ist der Krieg') (J, p. 14). Her family contradicted her, believing that Hitler could not last (J, p. 16). However, throughout Böll's account of his boyhood in the Third Reich runs the theme of his awareness that he was living under the threat of a war, one in which his generation would be inextricably involved. War was to be the inevitable consequence of the blindness of the middle classes which had brought Hitler to power. And war was connected in another way with Nazi ideology: dying for a cause. When one of his former schoolmates was killed fighting for the Condor Legion in the Spanish Civil War there was a school service in his honour. Böll was uneasy and interpreted his unease a quarter of a century later as the realisation that school was a preparation for death. From 1936 onwards he and his schoolmates were in the eyes of his teachers 'Morituri' and were given sympathetic treatment accordingly (J, p. 44). Böll, however, was determined to be a 'student for life . . . not a student for death' (J, p. 72).

Helped by his family he observed events with a sceptical eye. The burning of the Reichstag building, blamed by the Nazis on the Communists, took place rather 'punctually' (J, p. 16). Concentration camps were established near Cologne; Social Democrats, Communists and members of the Catholic Centre Party 'disappeared'; some of them returned, silent and terrified. His brothers' friends were among those arrested (Q, p. 27). In March 1933 the last relatively free elections took place in Germany, when, in spite of their control of the media and their terrorist methods, the Nazis still did not obtain an absolute majority; in Cologne, although they were the strongest party, they obtained only one-third of the votes cast (J, p. 19). The books of liberal and radical authors were publicly burned in Cologne as in other German cities (E 2, p. 29); an act of symbolic barbarity which Böll found less impressive in view of the physical barbarity that was happening all around him. The 'Day of Potsdam', 21 March 1933, when Hindenburg and Hitler celebrated the merging of the old Prussian militarist traditions with the new National Socialist ideals, was 'one of the most embarrassing performances of German history' ('eine der peinlichsten Veranstaltungen der gesamten deutschen Geschichte') (I, p. 615).

Two other events of 1933 were of especial importance to Böll and his family: the signing of the Concordat between the Vatican and Germany on 20 July and the execution in Cologne on 3 November of seven young Communists accused of having murdered two SA men. In his memory Böll associated the latter event with the 'night of the long knives', 30 June 1934, when Hitler, fearing his rival Ernst Röhm, the commander of the storm-troopers, stamped his authority on the Party by ordering his SS to liquidate the leaders of the SA. Böll recalled looking at his collection of cigarette cards and noting the prominent members of the Nazi party who had been liquidated (J, p. 38). From then on, Böll said, there could be no doubt about the nature of Hitler nor that he was more durable than many had assumed. Almost a year previously, however, the trial had taken place in Cologne of seventeen members of the Communist Red Front organisation, who were accused of murdering two renegade Communists. The evidence was unsatisfactory, but Göring was determined to set an example and seven were condemned to death by beheading. One of the condemned men affected Böll especially deeply. He was nineteen, and in the condemned cell he wrote poems, in one of which he thanked a friend for praying with him, was grateful for all the candles that had been lit for him in the churches and asked for the Lord's Prayer to be said at his grave. This combination of Communism and Catholicism — Böll called it the 'Italian' aspect of the Cologne brand of Communism — had a lasting effect on Böll himself. On the day of the execution: 'It grew quiet, ever quieter; I ceased to make frivolous remarks about Hitler, except at home and even there not in everyone's presence' ('Es wurde still, stiller; ich machte keine frivolen Bemerkungen über Hitler mehr, nur noch zu Hause und auch dort nicht in jedermanns Gegenwart') (J, p. 32). *Billard um halbzehn* was partly inspired by this event (I, p. 16).

The Concordat, signed at about the time of the trial, had a lasting effect on Böll's relations with his Church. Even before the signing, Catholic politicians had played an ominous role in the rise of Hitler. It was the Catholic Franz von Papen who had persuaded Hindenburg to accept Hitler. Together with Monsignor Kaas, the chairman of the Catholic Centre Party, which in company with all the other parties apart from the Social Democrats had voted in the Reichstag for Hitler's Enabling Legislation, he engineered the Concordat, and it was the fact that the Vatican was the first state to afford Hitler diplomatic recognition that gave the Nazis respectability among Catholic Germans (E 1, p. 541). Böll and his family at first contemplated leaving the Church in protest; however, as so many Germans were leaving the Church and joining the Nazis they in the end decided to remain (J, p. 26). Soon afterwards he noticed Catholics going to communion in their SA uniforms (E 1, p. 273). Looking back, he felt the Concordat had stopped the movement towards Catholic renewal which had been beginning in the 1920s

22

under French influence; loyalty to the State, under whichever government, led to the Church's failure to set any moral example after the war (Wallmann, p. 129). The recognition that the Church was in the first place concerned for its worldly influence is something which runs through Böll's presentation of the dichotomy between Church and religion from *Und sagte kein einziges Wort* to *Ansichten eines Clowns* and beyond.

One feature of the Third Reich and National Socialism which is almost completely missing in Böll's account of his schooldays is the persecution of the Jews. The first official anti-Semitic actions took place as early as 1933; the Nuremberg Laws of 1935 prohibited marriages between 'Germans' and Jews and excluded Jews from all forms of public service; the 'Reichskristallnacht' of November 1938 witnessed brutal pogroms against Jews, their businesses and their synagogues. Everybody in Germany was aware that Nazism was a 'terrorist regime' ('Regime des Terrors'); but only a few knew of the 'perfect, dreadful, bureaucratic method of killing millions of people' ('perfekte, fürchterliche, bürokratische Art, Millionen Menschen umzubringen') (I, p. 243). Böll himself never encountered anti-Semitism based on religious grounds, that is the Jews' crucifixion of Christ, either in the Church or at school; but he pointed out that anti-Semitism was a strong component of Hitler's thinking and that this was clear to anyone who had read *Mein Kampf*. His family knew Jews who had been able to emigrate to escape internment; he personally had seen no transports of Jews to the concentration camps (I, p. 635f.). According to his earliest autobiographical sketch, however, at the beginning of the war there had still been Jewish families in the house where his parents lived and they had been forbidden to use the air-raid shelters during bombing raids. His parents had allowed them to use their hall and telephone, and he recalled long-distance calls to Lisbon whose meaning they understood only later, in 1942, when the Jews were herded into furniture vans and driven off to the extermination camps (E 1, p. 115).

That Hitler transformed the German economy overnight, creating jobs and prosperity for all, Böll described as an illusion. For his family at any rate the financial problems remained acute. His father had contacts in the administration in Cologne, who occasionally were able to get him renovation jobs in old offices. Of the three houses that he had built as an investment for his old age, only one remained, but it was almost constantly under the bailiff since the Bölls were unable to pay their own rent, taxes and debts. They took in lodgers — Böll describes one occasion on which they persuaded the lodgers to play cards, hoping to make some money out of them, only to discover that the lodgers were as hard up as themselves (J, p. 65). One of the important motivations for Böll's writing was this experience of social distress in the 1920s and 1930s (I, p. 139). It is in this connection that the anti-bourgeois stance of the family is stressed once more. For the family's economic decline did not mean that they drew in their horns and tried to live within their means. On the contrary, they bought books (J, p. 71), they went to concerts, they even moved in 1936 to a flat in a better area and dispensed with lodgers (J, p. 61). In the bourgeois sense they were 'unreasonable' (J, p. 71). On the other hand, it has to be said that the books they read were scarcely 'unbourgeois', almost all of them came from the Catholic publishing house of Jakob Hegner; Böll's early reading has been described as 'arch-conservative' (Schröter, 1982, p. 47). 'We had the mad, perhaps criminal desire to *live* and to survive. We managed' ('Wir hatten den verrückten, vielleicht sogar kriminellen Wunsch, zu *leben* und zu überleben. Wir schlugen uns durch') (J, p. 62). When the electricity was cut off his mother would regularly reconnect it illegally, otherwise they had to read by candlelight, which they did intensively (J, p. 87). They even took to drugs, in their bohemian way. He, his mother and his older sister were for a time hooked on pervitin, a powerful stimulant, which was at that time freely available from chemists (J, pp. 86f.).

The crisis of Hitler's seizure of power consolidated the family bonds, especially when Böll was allowed to take part in illegal meetings of Catholic youth groups in his parents' flat: 'that was an enormous demonstration of trust, there really was a lot at stake. All these things naturally strengthened our inner resistance' ('das war ein ungeheurer Vertrauensbeweis, es ging ja wirklich um einiges. Alle diese Dinge haben natürlich den inneren Widerstand verstärkt') (I, p. 366). The question of resistance is one which has to be posed at this point. Böll's family, especially his mother, detested the Nazis. However, emigration appears to have been an option which never occurred to them, any more than taking a taxi to the moon (J, p. 37). Like the vast majority of ordinary German families they were not directly threatened. 'I functioned without conforming', Böll told Vonnegut (Vonnegut, p. 16). Their resistance remained an inward one, apart from the examples of humanity already mentioned. Böll refused to join the Hitler Youth. Membership did not become compulsory until 1936; Böll was old enough to avoid it, although pressure was put on him to join (Wallmann, p. 128). But in any case Böll was never a 'club-person'. He was briefly a member of a Catholic youth group, but left when they began to practise marching (E 2, p. 20). On the other hand, in the hope that the family business might win orders from official quarters it was felt opportune that one of the brothers should join the SA. The choice fell on brother Alois; they included in their rosaries the slightly blasphemous invocation 'Thou who hast joined the SA for us' ('Der du für uns in die SA eingetreten bist') (J, p. 46), which later, when the family fortunes continued to be depressed, became 'Thou who hast joined the SA for us *in vain*.' ('Der du für uns *umsonst* in die SA eingetreten bist') (J, p. 60). After the war Germans liked to stress that they had had no choice in whether to join the Nazis or not; the corollary was the 'collective guilt' thesis. Böll refused to accept the latter and he insisted that the system had contained numerous loopholes (Wallmann, p. 128).

Although one myth to which he does not subscribe is that of the writer whose schooldays were unhappy, Böll was hardly a model schoolboy. By his own account his real place of learning was the street, the city (E 1, pp. 255f.) His parents were prepared to make considerable sacrifices to allow all of their children to go on to grammar school and university: Grete studied economics and became a social worker; Mechthild became a teacher; Alfred a doctor; while both Gertrud, who according to Alfred was the cleverest next to Heinrich (Alfred Böll, 1981, p. 200), and Alois chose not to go on to sit the *Abitur* in spite of parental pressure. Nevertheless, both father and mother did not regard school attendance as essential: his mother was known for the corner of her kitchen where her coffee-grinder stood and where those — not only from the family — who were afraid of bad marks at school could find refuge (ibid., p. 224), while his father went so far as to have a supply of blank excusal notes which could be filled in by whichever truant it happened to be (ibid. p. 237). Heinrich's secondary-school days were marked by frequent truancies. His excuse was a chronic sinusitis, which enabled him to be permanently excused from gymnastics, which he hated. 'Schlagball' on the other hand, a form of baseball which plays a central role in *Billard um halbzehn*, was a sport which he enjoyed and in which his two brothers were notable stars (J, p. 57). Much of the time he would go for walks through the streets of Cologne past the shop window displays, markets and cinemas and observe the behaviour of his fellow-citizens, the cigarette smugglers and the whores. When the Nazis took over the streets with their parades, he began to explore the countryside around Cologne by bicycle. In the summer of 1936 he went on a long cycle tour on his own from Cologne to Bamberg and back. According to his brother Alfred he had few friends (Alfred Böll, 1981, p. 208), and he himself wrote that long before he was eighteen he was 'well on the way to developing from outsider into eccentric' ('auf dem besten Wege, vom Außenseiter zum Sonderling zu werden') (J, p. 58). What emerges from his autobiography, however, is not so much the loner as someone who abhorred mass activities, precisely those activities that the Nazis emphasised, the training camps designed to foster community spirit by the singing of songs round the campfire, the parades and the assemblies (J, p. 79ff.). His discovery of the opposite sex was one thing which kept him 'normal', and incidentally prevented him from seriously considering the priesthood as a career; celibacy was not for him and there were too many relatives and acquaintances in the priesthood for him not be aware of the pitfalls (J, p. 58f.).

Since he evidently had no academic ambitions, his parents considered removing him from school when he was sixteen and finding him a job. He resisted this for two reasons. The first was that the jobs he seemed destined for, i.e. surveying or working in a wholesale coffee business, would have robbed him of his freedom: 'That smelled of being forcibly organised' ('Das roch nach erzwungener Organisiertheit') (J, p. 35). Already the notion of becoming a writer was in his mind. The other was that his school was 'almost completely non-Nazi and therefore a good cover — cover against Nazi organisations, professional organisations and so on' ('fast völlig unnazistisch und insofern eine gute Deckung — Deckung gegenüber Nazi-Organisationen, Berufsorganisationen und so weiter') (I, p. 367). He was later grateful to his teachers and to his school, 'that quiet, Catholic school which radiated passive resistance' ('diese stille, katholische Schule, die passiven Widerstand ausstrahlte') (E 3, p. 227). The headmaster was a nationalist, but not a National Socialist, and although he tried to persuade Böll to join the Hitler Youth, he respected his refusal to do so. It was the 'nationalist' element in National Socialism that seduced him and his generation and enabled them to overlook the true brutality of the Nazis (I, p. 615). Böll's favourite subjects were mathematics, Latin and history — not German literature. Two anecdotes may serve to illustrate in what sense his school consolidated his resistance to National Socialism. Hitler's *Mein Kampf* was one of the compulsory texts; but the German teacher carried out his obligation to treat it by getting the class to reduce a given passage of thirty pages to ten, excising the bombast and the repetitions (I, p. 615f.). And the classics teacher concentrated on texts by Juvenal in which 'arbitrariness, despotism, depravity, corruption of political morals' ('Willkür, Despotismus, Korruption, Verderbnis der politischen Sitten') were castigated and in which even parallels to the Röhm affair could be drawn (J, pp. 88f.).

Böll sat his *Abitur* in February 1937. It was a formality, at which the teachers practically told him the topics in advance. He himself treated it with such indifference that he did not bother to turn up to the final ceremony. His brother Alfred collected the certificate for him (J, p. 96) and it was not until two years later that he noticed that his date of birth had been misprinted (J, p. 7). In all the discussions with his parents it had been agreed that his future profession should have 'something to do with books', and he began, not very enthusiastically, an apprenticeship in a bookshop in Bonn. As with school he regarded it as a place where he was safe from the Nazis. The bookshop had a very large second-hand department containing books which were otherwise unobtainable, which indeed could be purchased only by special permission from Goebbels's Ministry but which he was able to read on the spot. In this way he encountered works by Freud as early as 1938, something which was unusual for these times, as Freud's books had been among the first to be burned in 1933 (I, pp. 616f.).

Nevertheless he did not complete his apprenticeship. After less than a year he left to spend the next six months working for his father in the office and in the workshop, reading and especially writing. Even while still at school he had begun writing; his brother Alfred reports how annoyed Heinrich would get if one of the family crept up on him while he sat at the family typewriter and tried to read what he was writing (Alfred Böll, 1981, pp. 208f.). It was 'a kind of inner withdrawal' ('eine Art innere Zurückziehung') (I, p. 617). The times were so unsettling. He knew that he was due to be called up for 'labour duty', the war was coming closer and closer, there seemed no point in settling down to a 'bourgeois profession'. In this sense too the 'disintegration of the bourgeoisie' was a defining experience, the lack of permanence, of the ability to see a future. Between the spring and autumn of 1938 he wrote short stories, poems, even a novel, all of which were destroyed in a bombing raid in May 1942 (E 1, p. 179). (Elsewhere he spoke of up to six novels, which were still in a cellar in his house in Cologne in 1961: I, p. 14.) He did not even attempt to have any of them published, mainly because he did not think much of them, but he would probably not have wished them to appear under the Nazi regime (I, p. 136) — in 1959 he described the worst fate that could befall him as having to publish a single sentence which his conscience as a 'free writer' could not answer for (E 1, p. 305). Dostoevsky was an early influence (I, p. 137). He had first encountered the Russian novelist in 1934 or 1935 in a course of lectures in Cologne and bought a second-hand copy of *Crime and Punishment* in

1935; thereafter he acquired a cheap edition of the complete works. Dostoevsky put everything else that he had read in the shade, not least because simultaneously he was being forced to read Hitler's *Mein Kampf* (I, pp. 181ff.). In this respect at least, Böll's reading was less conservative than has been suggested (Schröter, 1982, p. 47), nor did it consist solely of 'second-rate authors' (Vogt, 1978, p. 12). Léon Bloy was a later influence; at the end of 1936 he read *Le sang des pauvres*, which was 'like a bombshell' (J, p. 79). One of the novels Böll wrote astonished his wife when she was shown it later, as its hero had two wives (J, p. 65) — perhaps Böll had been influenced by Goethe's early play *Stella*, but it may also be an early indication of his opposition to what he later attacked as the reduction to love to a legal institution by marriage (I, p. 551).

Labour Duty (*Arbeitsdienst*) was a product of youth unemployment in the 1920s. It was initiated by voluntary organisations to give young people the opportunity to work and live together, usually in the country, learn a trade and contribute something to the community. For this they were paid little more than a subsistence wage. In 1930 it was institutionalised by the government of Heinrich Brüning but remained voluntary. In 1935 the Nazis made it compulsory for all young men and women to spend six months in the 'Reichsarbeitsdienst'. It was no longer the social and personal value of learning a trade that was stressed. The participants were issued with uniforms and were given a paramilitary training until in the end it became a preparation for the army. Böll appreciated the positive inspiration of its initiators; when he encountered it, however, it had become 'a terrorist organisation'. Discipline was harsh, living conditions were primitive, the work was hard, the pay very poor, so that when he was later drafted into the regular army he found it almost a relief by contrast. The work involved clearing and draining forests near Kassel. It was here that for the first time he encountered people of the working classes and below: criminals, illiterates, for whom he sometimes composed letters, a milieu he had not dreamed existed (I, pp. 617ff.).

When it was over, in the spring of 1939 he matriculated at the University of Cologne. In his earliest accounts he said he had been a student of German literature (E 1, pp. 114, 179). The professor of German literature at Cologne was Ernst Bertram, a disciple of Stefan George, who at least temporarily supported the Nazis and was for this reason removed from his post in 1946. Böll later described him as 'an enormously subtle, very sensitive and even highly-strung person, who stumbled completely blindly into this catastrophe' ('ein ungeheuer subtiler, sehr sensibler, auch sehr empfindsamer Mensch, der vollkommen blind in diese Katastrophe reingetappt ist') (Lenz, p. 47); the narrator of *Entfernung von der Truppe*, which contains autobiographical motifs, has studied for a semester under Bertram (R 4, p. 290). Later Böll said he had studied classics; in his lectures to students at Frankfurt university he even described it as a 'short but relatively intensive' study (E 2, p. 49), but he told Wintzen that he had seldom attended classes, preferring to spend his time reading in the park; academic studies had been another stop-gap occupation. The crisis over the Sudetenland had taken place in the autumn of 1938 while he was on Labour Duty. Hitler had already annexed Austria earlier that year without registering much protest from the other European powers. He now demanded that the German-speaking parts of northern Czechoslovakia should be given autonomy and threatened to invade. Chamberlain and Daladier gave in to his demands at the Munich conference in September, but war had merely been postponed by a year. In July Böll was called up for military service and when war broke out he was in a barracks near Osnabrück (I, pp. 618f.).

Hitler's invasion of Poland on 1 September 1939 was preceded for several months by newspaper and radio reports of Polish attacks on German-speaking people in the Polish Corridor, as described in the semi-autobiographical story 'Die Postkarte' (R 2, p. 70). In spite of this propaganda effort, and in contrast to the mood of 1941, Böll could not remember a single person who was enthusiastic about the outbreak of war, neither among the civilian population (Wallmann, p. 128) nor among the soldiers themselves (I, pp. 619f.). He was not immediately sent to the front, as he had still to complete his training, and by the time he had arrived in Poland, in Bromberg, the war there was over and the war on the French front had begun. In Bromberg he made friends with some Polish civilians and also 'encountered terrorist actions' by the SS against Poles. Böll's fortune held in France — not until after the French had capitulated was he sent there, in July or August 1940, when he was posted to a village in Picardy, developed dysentery and had to return to Germany, where he spent a year on guard duty in various barracks between Cologne and Bielefeld. By now the mood in Germany had changed. While the population at large had remained sceptical after the defeat of Poland, the collapse of France led to euphoria both at home and at the front. Hitler's position was enormously strengthened; the atmosphere, Böll reported, was a true test of those who had been infected by Nazism and those who had not. For those who were posted to France the experience was a revelation. Germany between the wars was one of the poorer countries of Europe, France one of the richest;

suddenly they encountered unimagined luxury, the opportunity to eat, drink and be merry and to enrich themselves at the expense of the captive population (I, pp. 620ff.). In a review of Erich Kuby's *Mein Krieg* Böll pointed at the hypocrisy of so many 'decent, respectable citizens, who today defend till their voices break every kind of private property, and smugly "knocked off", "requisitioned" the property of other people as if it was the most natural thing in the world when occupied France was plundered' ('ordentliche, anständige Bürger, die heute bis zum Überschnappen jegliche Art von Privateigentum verteidigen, in verschmunzelter Selbstverständlichkeit anderer Leute Eigentum "organisiert", "requiriert" haben, wie das besetzte Frankreich ausgeplündert wurde') (E 3, p. 288). This is one of the central experiences of Böll's life which led to his contempt for middle-class values. In war man is taught to kill and to steal — 'as a soldier you really are trained, for example, to steal, they only call it differently, there are these bourgeois expressions like "knocking off" or stuff like that' ('als Soldat wird man ja wirklich etwa zum Diebstahl erzogen, das nennt man dann nur anders, da gibt es so bürgerliche Ausdrücke wie Organisieren oder so einen anderen Quatsch') (I, p. 407). For example, his commanding officer in France embezzled millions of francs in shady deals with French building firms and even raced his own horses at Longchamps (I, p. 624); for years a sergeant enriched himself on the wages he received for fictitious labourers on fictitious jobs (E 1, p. 268) — a motif which Böll was to use in *Gruppenbild mit Dame*. Later on, in the Soviet Union and Romania Böll encountered even more grotesque instances of corruption and cynicism: the trade in 'Verwundetenzettel', official documentation that one had been wounded and was on one's way to hospital; the selling of army coats, shirts, socks to the civilian population — 'The whole of the Russian population was running around wearing German army socks . . . those grey ones with the white rings' ('Die ganze russische Bevölkerung lief mit den deutschen Wehrmachtssocken herum, . . . diese grauen mit den weißen Ringen') — ; even the sale of weapons including complete flak batteries to the partisans, which Böll witnessed at Odessa (I, pp. 629f.).

The mood changed again when Hitler invaded the Soviet Union in June 1941. Not immediately, for initially the German army continued to appear unstoppable, but once it became plain that Moscow was not going to fall in a 'Blitzkrieg' and the German armies were caught in the Russian snow, the Germans became sceptical once again. Stalingrad was the turning-point (I, p. 623). Of 284,000 German soldiers encircled by the Red Army at Stalingrad between November 1942 and February 1943, only 34,000 escaped by air; 90,000 were taken prisoner; the rest died. Hitler ordered three days of public mourning. For Böll and many others the war was lost (I, p. 508). For the occupied French it was equally clear. After his illness had been cured Böll was sent back to France, where he remained for over a year, stationed in a village on the Channel coast between Saint-Valéry and Le Tréport. On the fall of Stalingrad there appeared overnight on the walls of all the houses the one word 'Stalingrad' (I, p. 623).

Throughout the war Böll remained a private, which for someone of his intellectual calibre indicated at least one kind of resistance to Hitler. He described the army in terms of society at large with its class distinctions. In these terms he had the status of worker and along with the other workers he was employed building bunkers in the Western defence system (Q, pp. 33f.). Among them he encountered some Berlin Communists and for a time he was friendly with a Marxist who taught him the rudiments of dialectical materialism (I, p. 138). However, he was also used as an interpreter for electricians, carpenters and other tradesmen who were required by the Germans. It was depressing if understandable that he was never able to develop any kind of friendship with French civilians. The only moments of humanity came when he had to visit the brothels in the early morning to fetch the articles dropped there by the German officers and NCOs the previous night. At nine in the morning a brothel was anything but erotic, and he was sometimes even offered a cup of coffee and able to converse quite naturally with the girls and their madame (I, pp. 624f.). Otherwise his sojourn in France was the most tedious and, he felt, absurd episode of his life. His 'Brief an einen jungen Katholiken' describes the 'moral dangers' — they had little to do with the brothels, however, but lay 'in the absolute despair, in the realisation of the meaninglessness of such an existence' ('in der absoluten Verzweiflung, in der Erkenntnis der Sinnlosigkeit einer solchen Existenz'). One could escape only through culture, cynicism or corruption (E 1, p. 267). From time to time he would feign illness and get leave to visit Paris and its bookshops.

On 6 March 1942 on one of his leaves he married Annemarie Cech in Cologne. They had known each other since before the war (Q, p. 41). She was a secondary-school-teacher. They wrote to each other every day while he was away; her letters were frequently delayed and would arrive in bundles which he arranged chronologically and read like a novel (E 1, p. 116). He also telephoned her as frequently as he could at the expense of the German army (I, p. 626). He could visit her at home only occasionally; two successive flats in Cologne were destroyed by bombs (E 2, pp. 240ff.).

In August 1943 he was sent to the Soviet Union. As an expert malingerer he could have avoided it, but he was simply curious: all his teachers had had the 'front experience' in the First World War and he wanted to find out what it was really like. His transport train was blown up by French partisans, many of his companions were killed, but he escaped with minor injuries. Late in 1943 he arrived in the Crimea, which by then was completely cut off by the Red Army; for three months he experienced positional warfare with all its frustrations, bitterly regretting his curiosity; he was wounded, sent back home, returned to the Crimea, wounded again, flown out to Odessa and then transported back to Germany where henceforth he did everything he could to avoid being sent back to the front. For some months he succeeded in persuading doctors that he had an eye disease, until he was found out and sent to Romania in May or June 1944. For the first time he experienced a real battle as they attempted to drive back the Soviets. It was a terrifying experience, full of privations; an 'abstract experience', in which it was impossible to make out what was happening. The German army was demoralised — there was no question for Böll that the morale of the troops remained intact to the end. He was wounded, this time, to his relief, more seriously, and transferred eventually to a military hospital in Hungary (I, pp. 626ff.).

The rest of his wartime experiences is like something out of a cheap adventure story — 'almost colportage', he called it (I, p. 632). In a number of respects it contrasts with the image of the war conveyed in his fiction. In the army hospital a friendly doctor told him that if he wanted his wound to heal slowly he should drink lots of alcohol. In this way he was able to postpone his reposting to the front. Meantime on 20 July 1944 a group of officers attempted to assassinate Hitler; not only did Hitler exact a terrible revenge on the immediate conspirators, but throughout the army political discipline was intensified and careless talk could lead to summary execution. 'Germany between 20 July 1944 and the war's end — that was *total* terror exercised by the Interior Minister, Himmler' ('Deutschland zwischen dem 20. Juli 1944 und *Kriegsende* — das war *totaler* Terror des Herrn Innenministers Himmler'). More than 30,000 members of the army are estimated to have been executed (FT, p. 92). In August 1944 Romania, one of Germany's allies, changed sides. Böll had managed to keep a map of Europe in his possession, illegally, as the troops were not supposed to be able to follow what was going on. He realised that he was likely to be sent to the Romanian front once his wound had healed and that the confused political situation there would make life especially precarious as it would be impossible to know who was fighting whom. He resolved to change the path that fate had intended for him (I, p. 370). He had a supply of stolen papers, blank authorisation forms for leave of absence or for official journeys, and even an official stamp. When he was declared fit for active service once more he persuaded the girl in the hospital office to leave open the name of the regional headquarters to which he was to report; once on the train to Debreczin he filled in the blank space with the name of the town of Metz, as far to the west as the German armies now were stationed. He then changed trains. On the way to Metz he was able to visit his wife and arrived eventually in September or October 1944. From now on he lived mainly with false papers, sometimes without any papers, from time to time feigning a fever in order to be in the safety of a military hospital again (I, pp. 631f.).

In November 1944 his mother died of a heart attack during a bombing raid. She had been in poor health for a number of years. The family, including Böll's older sister and his wife, had been bombed out of their home in Cologne and were living at the time in a hotel in Ahrweiler in the Eifel, south of Bonn and west of the Rhine. By chance Böll himself was in an army hospital a few miles away, malingering once again. The whole family left the hotel after the funeral, going to live with his brother Alois, who took his military duties even less seriously, Alois's wife and three children in a church hall in the village of Marienfeld near Cologne — shortly after their departure the hotel was destroyed by bombs. Böll had a certificate of convalescence from the hospital, the date of which he continually altered until it became almost illegible and unusable. For some months he lived with his family in the cold and hunger of Marien-feld, stealing wood for their fires, dependent on the salary of his wife Annemarie, in constant fear of the military police from whom from time to time he had to hide in cupboards in case they should find out that he had forged his papers, hoping and praying that the Americans would arrive and liberate them. Although the Allied attacks were serious enough, Böll describes these months as ones of 'fear and hunger, hunger and fear of the Germans' ('Angst und Hunger, Hunger und Angst vor den Deutschen'). From this time on he was filled with a lasting suspicion of anything that reeked of fascism, and constantly made sure that his petrol tank was filled, he had at least enough money in his pockets to survive a week and that he insisted on living in the proximity of the Dutch and Belgian borders (FT, p. 87).

At the beginning of 1945 he could stand the strain no longer and reported to his regiment of 'reservists', for the most part cripples who had lost a leg, both legs, an arm and so on. No questions were asked and he was given legal papers, a fortnight's leave, and, almost as important, an army coat. All the time deserters were being shot, and anyone who appeared in any way fit for action could count himself lucky if he was merely picked up by the military police and attached to a platoon. In February 1945 he managed to persuade an officer in Mainz to give him a fortnight's leave on the pretext that he had to attend his mother's funeral and see to the papers he needed for his graduation. The leave expired on 2 March; with the help of the family typewriter Böll extended it to the 25th, by which time he assumed the war would be over. On 2 March he watched the cloud of smoke and dust which marked the final destruction of Cologne; five days later the city had surrendered to the Americans. Böll and his family, however, were not to be liberated for some time yet, as the Americans continued north-eastwards. When 25 March came, the Americans had still not overrun them and Böll decided that the safest place was the army, reported for duty at the nearest headquarters and tricked the officer on duty into not inspecting his forged papers. For the following fortnight he was once more on the front line, although with strict instructions not to fire at the Americans, who would have retaliated by destroying them all. By 8 April his platoon had disintegrated and he was on his way home when a lieutenant forced him at the point of a machine-gun to join another unit. The following day they surrendered to the Americans (FT, pp. 99ff.).

Even in a prisoner of war camp his adventures were not over. Some, such as Alfred Andersch, Hans Werner Richter, Gustav René Hocke, had been able to make plans for a future socialist Germany even when still prisoners (Peitsch/Reith, 1983, p. 131). Böll found no such solidarity, only the secret courts run by the most fanatical of the Nazi prisoners, who were quite capable even now of drowning 'defeatists' in the latrines (FT, p. 106); the slogan in his camp was still 'Final Victory' ('Endsieg') (Riese, p. 17). There was also the question of how to get out and home most quickly. Those who were prepared to work were given extra rations; Böll resolved to endure the hunger in the hope of early release, reckoning that those who agreed to work would most likely have to spend years in captivity. His calculations paid off. Of the 200,000 prisoners in his camp only sixty were categorised 'unfit for employment in their own profession'; one of them was Heinrich Böll. He was given special treatment and later passed on to the British, who eventually released him in September 1945, much earlier than he could have hoped (FT, pp. 106f.). The one fault that he found with the British was that they, unlike the Americans, allowed prisoners to retain their military decorations (E 1, pp. 114f.). He summarised his captivity in these words: 'American soldiers had taken me prisoner, Britons had finally held me in custody, I was guarded by Belgians, who had been allotted the district of Cologne as their area of occupation within the British zone. But I was released on the 15.9.1945 from German captivity' ('Gefangengenommen hatten mich amerikanische Soldaten, zuletzt in Obhut gehabt Briten, bewacht war ich von Belgiern, denen innerhalb der britischen Zone der Regierungsbezirk Köln als Besatzungsgebiet zuerkannt worden war. Entlassen wurde ich am 15.9.1945 aber aus deutscher Gefangenschaft') (E 2, p. 148). The end of the war was for Böll a liberation, a liberation from German fascism, from German terror. One could accurately tell a German's political stance according to whether he described 8 May 1945 as the 'day of defeat or of liberation' (FT, pp. 98f.).

Remarkably, with the exception of his mother, Böll's whole family had survived the war. Some 4 million German soldiers are believed to have been killed in the war; to this figure must be added a further half a million civilians who died in air-raids. Of those Germans taken prisoner by the Soviet Union, about 37 per cent did not return. In 1945, Böll pointed out, there were as many 75-year-olds as those of his own generation, many more 66-year-olds and twice as many 56-year-olds (E 2, p. 234). If the story of the Bölls in the inter-war years was one of the 'decline of a family', that of the author in the war was an 'Odyssey' (FT, p. 80) in which the hero returned home after many wanderings to find his Penelope (FT, p. 109). It is difficult not to find his account of his wartime experiences fascinating in a conventional way. The Schweik is always present, the plot is full of twists and turns. One can thus understand why he was so reluctant to make a novel of it. However unpleasant it was at the time, the happy end, the successful deceptions inevitably make the experience appear bearable, not to say exciting.

In this latter respect it contrasts distinctly both with the image of war he gave in his fiction and with the commentaries on war he provides in his conversations and essays. There it is the 'bloody boredom' ('blutige Langeweile'), the 'infinite boredom' ('unendliche Langeweile') that he stressed (I, p. 369; E 1, p. 116), the senselessness and absurdity of war. 'Basically war, when it is war, is a great deal of stupid fooling about, a lot of pretending. Stupidity, bloody stupidity, senseless, totally senseless actions everyone knew to be senseless' ('Im Grunde ist der Krieg, da wo er Krieg ist, viel viel dumme Spielerei, viel Angabe. Dummheit, blutige Dummheit, sinnlos, vollkommen sinnlose Aktionen, von denen jeder wußte, daß sie sinnlos waren') (Q, p. 39). The war experience intensified Böll's outlook on life rather than changing it. The experience of death was an extension of the insecurity caused by inflation and unemployment (I, pp. 369f.). The arbitrariness of events which he saw as the keynote of war (I, p. 524), the recognition that the railway waiting-room was a symbol of existence (I, p. 372) were features of the instability of bourgeois society as he experienced it in the inter-war years. If Böll was to take up the stance of a non-conformist outsider in his attitude to political developments in the 1950s, it was his negative experiences of mass activities under the Nazis and his failure to find any positive solidarity in these same years that made him do so. One other component of his wartime experiences, however, loomed ever larger in his later discussions of them, his diagnosis of war as a male, not to say macho phenomenon. In 1969 he described the 'male experience of the "front"' ('Männererlebnis "Front"') as 'something ridiculous' ('etwas Lächerliches')' (Q, p. 39). In 1975 he was more explicit:

> The war taught me how ridiculous manliness is. If there had not been a war, then I should probably have discovered this ridiculousness in some profession or other. . . . That sounds very nasty now, because after all in war men put up with quite a lot, they die, they get wounded. And yet in its ridiculousness, its absurd ridiculousness, war may well have made me despise men.

> (Der Krieg hat mich gelehrt, wie lächerlich die Männlichkeit ist. Hätte es keinen Krieg gegeben, dann hätte ich wahrscheinlich diese Lächerlichkeit in irgendeinem Beruf entdeckt. . . . Das klingt jetzt sehr böse, weil ja Männer im Krieg auch einiges mitmachen, sie sterben, sie werden verwundet. Und trotzdem hat mich der Krieg in seiner Lächerlichkeit, in seiner absurden Lächerlichkeit, möglicherweise zum Verächter des Mannes gemacht.)

> (I, p. 542)

Here is one explanation for the dominant role played by women in his novels and stories.

3

An Almost Classless Society?
(1945–1949)

When Böll was released from captivity he was a sick man (I, p. 636).
Shortly after his reunion with his wife their son Christoph died. At
first they lived in a village east of Cologne, but they moved to the
city as soon as possible, where his wife took up her teaching duties
again; for two years Böll himself was almost incapable of work. His
brother Alois had taken over their father's joinery business and he
helped out there. He registered as a student at the University of
Cologne, but only in order to obtain a rations card. While he did join
in repairing the house in which he and his family were living, he
refused to help to clear the rubble-strewn streets of Cologne, although that was the declared civic duty of every returning soldier.
Why he refused he could not say — the sight of rows of people
leaning on pickaxe and shovel reminded him too vividly of the war
(E 2, p. 152; Lenz, p. 59). For a time he worked in the statistical
department of the city administration of Cologne, eking out his
earnings by giving private tuition in mathematics and Latin. But his
principal concern was to fulfil the ambition he had nurtured since
before the war: the liberation was not least a liberation of his
creative energies and three weeks after his release he had already
begun to write.

These immediate post-war years were ones of considerable deprivation and poverty. Seven years later Böll described how in 1945 he
would sometimes go to Cologne railway station, buy a platform
ticket and walk up and down the international trains, looking
through the windows at the prosperous foreigners who smelt of
expensive soap, could afford to extinguish half-smoked cigarettes
under their well-shod feet and seemed like millionaires (E 1, pp.
17f.). The winter of 1946/7, when temperatures dropped to twenty
degrees below zero, was especially hard and long. His wife's
monthly earnings were the equivalent of 15 kilograms of bread or 10
to 15 hundredweight of briquettes. If he sold a short story to a
publisher he received between 100 and 400 marks for it, enough to
buy between 2 and 10 hundredweight of briquettes. In order to

survive they had to steal firewood and coal or buy and sell on the black market (E 3, p. 53). A signed copy of Thomas Mann's *Buddenbrooks* was especially lucrative (J, p. 89). His wartime experiences with the black market stood him in good stead in the economic chaos of post-war Cologne and his expertise was used by others who were too proud to stoop to such illegalities (I, p. 385). Like his mother in the 1930s he learned to 'doctor' the electricity meter (E 2, p. 149). From 1947 onwards they received food parcels from friends in England, although there was food rationing in England too (FT, p. 56).

By the end of the war 70 per cent of the buildings of Cologne had been destroyed or damaged. 20,000 people had died in the Allied bombing raids. A city of 768,000 now numbered only 40,000, although by the end of the year this figure had increased to 400,000. When in July 1945 the primary schools re-opened, of 2,176 pre-war classrooms only 212 were left. A committee of the United Nations estimated that a daily minimum of 2,550 calories was necessary to maintain health and vitality; official rations consisted of 1,500 calories; in many cases one was fortunate to receive even 1,000. At the end of 1946 it was calculated that only 12 per cent of children in Cologne were of normal weight. Whole families were forced to live in subterranean cellars, without light and without water. The problem was compounded by the need to resettle the thousands of refugees who had been expelled from the Eastern territories. There were no clothes and no medicines. Money was worthless — a packet of cigarettes would buy as much food as the week's wages of a tram-conductor. The affluent American troops of occupation were a source of food and cigarettes and by 1949 there were 15,000 prostitutes in Cologne, ten times the pre-war figure (Grosser, 1974, p. 87). The destruction of Germany was not merely physical — the 'inner destruction' was 'almost more important' (Lenz, p. 57). The war had taught men to steal and to kill. Moreover, the totalitarian claims of National Socialism meant that there was scarcely an area of social, intellectual or cultural life that had not been debased and discredited by association with Hitler.

Germany's defeat was a total one, the surrender was unconditional. In accordance with the agreements reached at the Yalta and Potsdam Conferences of 1945, the Eastern frontier of Germany was shifted westwards to the line of the rivers Oder and Neisse. What remained of the old Reich was divided into four zones of occupation, controlled respectively by the Americans, the British, the French and the Russians. Berlin, the former capital, was in the middle of the Soviet zone and received special status, being divided itself into four sectors mirroring the division of Germany as a whole. One result of the division was that each occupying power tried to create a new Germany in its own image, not only politically — ultimately a capitalist Federal Republic reflected the American model and a socialist Democratic Republic the Soviet one — but also culturally. Cologne was in the British zone of occupation. Böll found the British 'very pleasant' (Riese, p. 15), 'very unobtrusive, we hardly saw them, scarcely noticed them' ('sehr zurückhaltend, wir haben sie kaum gesehen, kaum bemerkt'). Their cultural information centre 'Die Brücke' ('The Bridge') was important and useful in bringing writers together and conducting discussions (I, pp. 593f.). The French, however, were much more active in organising meetings between French and German writers and disseminating both French and German post-war culture by means of periodicals and conferences (E 3, pp. 137f.).

The end of the war was a liberation. It was a liberation from the Nazi terror and from the hated army uniform. It was also a liberation from responsibility, and this, as Böll later realised, was unfortunate for the development of post-war Germany. There was something 'nihilistic' about his feelings at the end of the war: Germany was an occupied country — let the forces of occupation get on with running it (Lenz, p. 55). The trials of the major war criminals were conducted by the victorious allies at Nuremberg in 1946. De-Nazification in the Western zones tended to be a mechanical operation. Anyone who had been a member of a Nazi organisation — SA, SS or the Nazi Party itself — was initially excluded from public office. But since this included practically all civil servants, teachers and legal officers, the regulations had to be loosened and many Nazi criminals slipped through the net. The alternative to de-Nazification, the thesis that the Germans were collectively guilty of the crimes committed in the name of the German people, was similarly unproductive. If all were equally and collectively guilty, then nobody was personally responsible and ultimately nobody was guilty at all. Böll found the notion of collective guilt understandable but ultimately inhumane, and it helped to instil a lasting hatred of global judgments, such as anti-Americanism or anti-Communism (I, pp. 243f.). He, and others like him, did not feel especially guilty: the end of the war found him 'without any great personal contrition and also without any great personal feeling of guilt' ('ohne große persönliche Reue und auch ohne großes persönliches Schuldgefühl') (I, p. 506); to be continually addressed in the POW camp as a 'fucking German Nazi' (I, p. 595; E 3, p. 298) paradoxically strengthened his sense of national identity — 'Because this people was so despised I too wished to belong to it' ('Weil dieses Volk so verachtet wurde, wollte ich auch dazugehören') (I, p. 244). Resistance to the Nazis in the Third Reich had come largely from Communists operating illegally in underground organisations. The development of the cold war meant that these men too were not called to serve the new democracy in West Germany (I, p. 637). Böll's own generation might have seemed the most appropriate one for the future. But not only had it been decimated in the war, it was 'profoundly indifferent to politics' ('politisch von einer tiefen Gleichgültigkeit') (ibid.). The post-war intellectual mood has been described as one of a 'total suspicion of ideology' ('der totale Ideologieverdacht') (Mayer, 1967, pp. 300ff.). Without Hitler and Stalin, Böll once said, he might well have become a Communist; as it was, however, he and his generation had no opportunity to become Communists (I, p. 61). There remained the older generation, those who had been too old to be active in the war and had kept their distance from the Nazis, the sixty-year-olds and upwards, and these were the people who were selected by the Allies to administer Germany (I, p. 637). Konrad Adenauer, for example, was born in 1876; Mayor of Cologne until he was deposed by the Nazis in 1933, he spent the Third Reich in seclusion, avoided involvement in the plot to assassinate Hitler, became Mayor of Cologne again after the war and first Chancellor of the Federal Republic in 1949. The result of this unfortunate age constellation was a gulf between the intellectuals of Böll's generation and the emergent politicians who were to mould the new Germany (I, pp. 640f.).

Böll's description of his generation's indifference to politics in the immediate post-war period may be questioned. It was no doubt his personal experience, but, as in the POW camps, he was out of touch with developments elsewhere. He had, for example, no contacts with the contributors to the journal *Der Ruf* prior to 1950 (I, pp. 139f.). *Der Ruf* had been a journal edited by prisoners of war in an American camp from 1944 onwards; it was refounded in 1946 by Alfred Andersch and Hans Werner Richter as a mouthpiece for the younger generation, but after only sixteen issues it was banned by the American authorities because it was taking a political line of which they disapproved, namely one of an albeit non-Marxist 'socialist humanism' (Schwab-Felisch, 1962, p. 32). It was therefore not entirely the case that Böll's contemporaries were unpolitical, nor was the 'liberation' that Böll felt a total one — the Allies operated a strict system of censorship (Peitsch, 1982, pp. 165ff.). It is in any case not clear to what extent Böll was politically aware at this time, since we have no direct contemporary evidence and his later pronouncements are sometimes contradictory. In 1977 he stated that it was not until the issue of German rearmament was being discussed in the mid-1950s that he awakened from his apolitical mood (Lenz, p. 56). But in 1974 he had claimed to have been 'long politicised' and to have observed the Currency Reform of 1948 'very critically' (Q, p. 138). In his last major interview he was more precise. Up to 1947 he had no interest in politics, he was too exhausted and interested only in writing. Thereafter he was in touch only with Catholic circles, people he had known before the war, anti-fascists and survivors (Limberg, p. 9).

The years up to the foundation of the Federal Republic in 1949 were ones of ferment and experimentation. It was a period when, in spite of the distress and discomfort, there was hope that the *tabula rasa* created by the war might produce a new and more just society. Böll like many of his contemporaries (Scherpe, 1982, pp. 46ff.) believed that the society which was beginning to emerge out of the chaos was almost classless, anarchistic:

> something remarkable was forming, at bottom it was a society of have-nots and potential thieves. I tell you loud and clear: the things that were stolen, that we stole — windows, doors, bricks, firewood, books we found in ruined cellars — it was classless to a certain extent; there was something classless, let's say in Cologne between 1945 and even 1949, . . . something — I don't want to call it anarchist, that would be too self-conscious —, but something of getting by from day to day, you went to the black market if you had money, you sold something or bought something, you just managed to get by.

> (da bildete sich ja etwas sehr Merkwürdiges, im Grunde auch eine Gesellschaft von Besitzlosen und potentiellen Dieben. Ich sag's laut und deutlich: Was da alles geklaut worden ist und was wir geklaut haben — Fenster, Türen, Ziegelsteine, Brennholz, Bücher, wenn wir sie in zerstörten Kellern fanden — , das war ja klassenlos bis zu einem gewissen Grad; es hatte etwas Klassenloses, sagen wir, so in Köln zwischen 1945 und noch 1949, . . . war etwas — ich will das nicht anarchistisch nennen, das wäre zu bewußt —, aber etwas vom Tag-auf-Tag-Leben sich so durch-schlagen, da ging man mal auf den Schwarzmarkt, wenn man Geld hatte, verkaufte was oder kaufte was, schlug sich so gerade durch.)

> (Lenz, p. 57)

This 'classlessness' imposed on Germans bore within it a hope, one which was shared by wide sections of the community. The CDU's first manifesto, the Ahlen Programme of 1947, which made an 'enormous impression' on Böll (Limberg, p. 9), declared that capitalism had failed the German people and that at least the coal-mining and other monopoly industries must be nationalised. There were discussions between Catholics and Marxists aimed at reconciling their standpoints (Wirth, 1968, pp. 16ff.). In 1985 Böll described his outlook in the immediate aftermath of the war as one of a Christian Socialism (Vonnegut, p. 17). The powerlessness of Germany immediately after the war did not only lead to nihilism; it also implied possibilities of moral regeneration (I, p. 41). The betrayal came almost at once.

A major watershed of these years was the Currency Reform of 1948. According to Alfred Grosser it was the one measure taken by the Allies which received the general support of the population (Grosser, 1974, p. 100). Böll was more critical. As early as 1953 he described the time before the Currency Reform as one which people appeared determined to forget, 'although it contained lessons which would have been worth preserving' ('obwohl sie Lehren enthielt, die zu bewahren sich gelohnt hätte') (E 1, p. 119). In 1956 he was particularly outspoken:

> We were ripe for a new brotherliness after the catastrophe, after the famine, we had a kind of birthright for this new brotherliness, for we were neither collectively guilty nor collectively innocent — but we sold this birthright, not for a mess of pottage but for a cracker, one which contained really pretty surprises. We didn't incur our collective guilt on 30 January 1933, nor on any of the dates up to 8 May 1945, our collective guilt dates back only to the day of the Currency Reform, from that day onwards the signal has been constantly at green for the strong, red for the weak, those who can never traverse the jungle.

> (Wir waren reif für eine neue Brüderlichkeit nach der Katastrophe, nach der Hungersnot, wir hatten eine Art Erstgeburtsrecht für diese neue Brüderlichkeit, weil wir weder kollektiv schuldig noch kollektiv unschuldig waren — aber wir haben dieses Erstgeburtsrecht verkauft, nicht für ein Linsengericht, sondern für ein Knallbonbon, in dem es recht hübsche Überraschungen gab. Unsere Kollektivschuld nahmen wir nicht am 30. Januar 1933 auf, nicht an einem der Daten bis zum 8. Mai 1945, eine Kollektivschuld gibt es erst seit dem Tag der Währungsreform, seit diesem Tage stehen die Signale immer auf Grün für die Starken, immer auf Rot für die Schwachen, die den Dschungel nie durchqueren können.)
> (E 1, p. 177)

On 20 June 1948 all the money circulating in the Western zones of occupation was declared invalid; every individual had the right to receive the sum of 40 marks in the new currency, the Deutsche Mark, which thereby replaced the old Reichsmark. Stocks and shares were devalued by 90 per cent, cash and bank deposits by even more, so that for 100 Reichsmark one received about 6.50 DM. On the face of it the measure was reasonably egalitarian, but for the fact that property and goods were not affected. News of the impending event leaked out to the lucky few in advance, so that on the day itself the shops were suddenly full of goods which a day earlier had been unobtainable. Share prices on the stock-market rose sharply. Fortunes were made by some, the small savers were ruined. Shortly before 20 June publishers were suddenly willing to give Böll cash advances for manuscripts: in this way they were unloading money which was about to become worthless and at the same time gaining the right to publish works which they would not have to pay for in hard currency (E 3, p. 54; FT, pp. 53ff.). Böll's 1956 polemic against the Currency Reform has implicit socialist undertones. It represented the end of socialist hopes, the return to the old system of capitalism, the law of the jungle. This was the 'Restoration'. The 'Restaurationszeit' is a term originally applied to the period between 1815 and 1830 when throughout Europe regimes were attempting to return to the feudal conditions which had pertained prior to the French Revolution of 1789. At least as early as 1952, however, the term was being used in left-wing circles in Germany to refer to the reaction against the 'revolutionary' years of 1945 to 1948 (Bauer, 1952; Mannzen, 1952).

In 1975 Böll spoke of the opportunity that Germans had had in 1945:

After that war, quite apart from questions of de-Nazification . . . we ought to have started something which might have been called socialism, links between Christian and social or socialist ideas. And they did exist, in a rudimentary way, even in the CDU's programme there were notions of this kind, even in the CSU, notions one reads today with astonishment; this hope or this opportunity was even expressed in political terms, for example in the Ahlen Programme. But in the end it turned out that what we call Restoration, what has to be called Restoration, almost unavoidably recreated the old structures: family egoism again, striving for possessions again, middle-class values again.

(Man hätte . . . nach diesem Krieg, ganz unabhängig von Entnazifizierungsgeschichten, etwas anfangen müssen, was man möglicherweise Sozialismus genannt hätte, Verbindungen von christlichen mit sozialen Ideen oder sozialistischen. Und das gab es ja auch, ansatzweise, es gab ja im Programm der CDU sogar Vorstellungen dieser Art, sogar in der CSU, die man heute noch mit Erstaunen lesen kann; diese Hoffnung oder diese Chance hat sich sogar politisch ausgedrückt, etwa im Ahlener Programm. Aber es hat sich letzten Endes eben gezeigt, daß das, was wir Restauration nennen und was man so nennen muß, die alten Formen fast zwanghaft wieder kreiert hat: wieder Familienegoismus, wieder Besitzstreben, wieder Bürgerlichkeit.)

(I, p. 394)

In the atmosphere of the cold war such dreams had been unrealistic. The Americans would have admitted socialism in their sphere of influence just as little as the Soviets capitalism in theirs. The Currency Reform itself consolidated the final division of Germany, as the Soviets refused to participate and their zone of occupation subsequently developed independently of the three Western zones. It was only logical that in 1949 the three Western zones united to form the Federal Republic of Germany, while a few months later the Democratic Republic was set up in the East.

Such were the material and social circumstances in which Böll began to write. The literary and intellectual climate was no less interesting and confused. For a long time it was widely held that the twelve years of Nazi rule had cut Germany off from the progressive literature of the twentieth century, whether one defines this in terms of 'modernism' or in terms of radical, liberal or socialist content. More recently it has been shown that this was at best a half-truth, propagated in part in order to disguise the cultural continuities between the Third Reich and the post-war period (Schäfer, 1981, pp. 7–54). Böll himself read Proust before the war, and his short term of employment in the second-hand bookshop in Bonn introduced him to some banned authors; but Kafka, Joyce, Hemingway, Faulkner and Sartre were all authors whom he did not encounter until after 1945 (I, p. 591). As he himself pointed out, in order to take advantages of the loopholes in Nazi cultural policies one had to know that the writers who might interest one actually existed, and this he did not — older people, those who came from a more culturally aware milieu had opportunities not afforded to the majority of Germans (Lenz, pp. 36ff.). In 1961 he described the difficulty for the young German writer in 1945 (I, p. 20). There had been three traditions he could adopt, none of which was suitable.

One was Nazi literature, 'blood and soil literature', glorifying war, the Germanic race, and the life of the peasant, hostile to the cities and modern technology. Böll had taken part unwillingly in the war, he had seen it as anything but heroic; the city was his home, the countryside much less so and the ideology was repulsive to him. Of specific Nazi authors he had very little to say. In common with all other schoolchildren in Cologne he was forced to watch a performance of Hanns Johst's *Schlageter*, whose eponymous hero was one of the early Nazi martyrs. Set in 1923, it is a drama based on the illegal resistance of German nationalists to the occupying French army, the forces of international banking, and other bogeymen. The play is today best known for the words 'When I hear the word culture . . . I release the safety-catch of my Browning!' ('Wenn ich Kultur höre . . .

entsichere ich meinen Browning!'). Böll found it a weak play (J, pp. 51f.); but the word 'culture' was one he too later viewed with mistrust. Baldur von Schirach, the *Reichsjugendführer*, is another writer for whom Böll expressed his contempt: he and his school-friends used to quote to each other the quintessentially fascist lines on the total subordination of the individual to the Führer: 'I was a leaf in space and looking for my tree' ('Ich war ein Blatt im Raum und suchte meinen Baum') (ibid., p. 39). He had evidently also read Werner Beumelburg's heroic novel of the first World War *Gruppe Bosemüller* (E 1, pp. 460, 626).

A second was the literature of the *émigrés*. When Hitler came to power in 1933 there was an immediate exodus from Germany of all those writers who had any reason to fear the new regime. They included liberal conservatives like Thomas Mann, pacifists like Erich Maria Remarque and socialists like Bertolt Brecht. Very few writers of any stature remained. Böll described the tensions and mistrust between his generation and that of the *émigrés* on a number of occasions. Their works were published quite soon after the end of the war, but he was unable to make anything of them (I, p. 592). There was mistrust on both sides. The older writers looked on the younger ones at best condescendingly (Lenz, p. 49), claiming to have done it all already thirty years previously (I, p. 596). Worse still, they tended to regard anyone who had remained in Germany in the Third Reich as of necessity tarred with Nazism. Conversely those who had remained behind believed the *émigrés* had no auth-ority to describe the situation in the Germany from which they had fled. Thomas Mann's masterpiece on the relationship between German history and the modernist movement, *Doktor Faustus*, ap-peared in 1947. It was not well received in the Western zones (Schäfermeyer, 1984, p. 13). Böll criticised Remarque's novel *Zeit zu leben und Zeit zu sterben*, which purports to describe the situation in Germany during the war but gets details wrong which nobody who had actually lived there would have overlooked (Lenz, p. 48). The divergence of experience and outlook poisoned relations between those who had left and those who had stayed (I, p. 374). There was also in Böll's case the component of mistrust towards the literature of the 1920s which stemmed from the Rhinelander's resentment against Prussian Berlin (J, p. 79).

A third possibility was the literature of the so-called 'inner emi-gration', authors who had opposed the Nazis but not so overtly as to have been banned. Views on the significance of these writers, Werner Bergengruen, Hans Carossa, Gertrud von Le Fort, Reinhold Schneider and Ernst Wiechert, diverge widely. In a polemic of 1961

Franz Schonauer condemned their writings as largely escapist and a source of comfort, even propaganda for the ruling Nazis. They were tolerated because they did not in any way endanger the regime, and since they had some literary standing while not directly supporting Hitler, the outside world could be reassured that the Nazis were not as totalitarian as they were made out to be. Like the Nazi writers themselves, they were in no sense modernist; rather they continued the tradition of nineteenth-century German writing, non-urban and concerned less with social than with personal values; and since it was a literature of edification and consolation to its readers, who might find refuge in it from the hard realities of their own lives, it actually had a stabilising influence on Nazi society (Schonauer, 1961, pp. 125–53). An echo of Schonauer's analysis is to be found in Böll's novel *Haus ohne Hüter*, where the poet Rai Bach discovers that his poetry is being exploited by the Nazis for just those ends and at once ceases to write. In 1975, however, Böll was less scathing at least about some of these authors. Hans Carossa he regarded as having been an opportunist, who made concessions to the authorities by including Hitler Youth scenes in his novels. Bergengruen and Schneider on the other hand were 'very important' for him at the time because they wrote about the fascist tyranny in a disguised form — the former's *Der Großtyrann und das Gericht* was unambiguously anti-fascist; and samizdat poems of theirs used to circulate which strengthened people's moral resistance by demonstrating that there were still writers in Germany who cared (I, p. 533).

There were two more complex cases. Of the authors who remained behind in 1933 among the most prominent were Gottfried Benn and Ernst Jünger, both of whom briefly flirted with the Nazis, although ultimately they had little in common with the new rulers and in due course were prevented from publishing. After the war Benn became the guru of young German poets: his hermetic, monological poetry epitomised the modernism from which Nazi cultural policies had excluded them for twelve years; his heroic nihilism suited the intellectual climate of the early post-war years until a more socially oriented generation discovered Brecht. At Benn's last public appearance in 1955 when the poet took part in a discussion with Reinhold Schneider in Cologne on the topic 'Should poetry reform life?' ('Soll die Dichtung das Leben bessern?') Böll was introduced to the poet; Benn's account of the occasion to his friend F. W. Oelze is characteristically sneering and further evidence of the gap between the generations referred to by Böll (Benn, 1980, p. 256). Although in character diametrically opposed to the cold intellectual, Böll had considerable respect for him. In an

unpublished response to a questionnaire in 1954 he took up with
approval the distinction Benn had made between the 'Kunstträger',
the artist, and the 'Kulturträger', the guardian of culture (Benn,
1934, pp. 1916ff.; E 1, pp. 121f.); he returned to the theme in 1960 in
Wuppertal, when he spoke of the diametrically opposed interests of
the artist and those who honoured him (E 1, pp. 340ff.); and in his
speech on receiving the Georg Büchner Prize in 1967 he suggested that
Büchner as scientist and socialist united the two great German poets of
the twentieth century, Benn and Brecht, who seemed otherwise to
cancel each other out (E 2, p. 277).

Ernst Jünger was reputedly Adenauer's favourite writer and
enjoyed considerable popularity in the 1950s among conservative
readers (Kröll, 1982, p. 153). The first work of his which Böll read
was the novel *Auf den Marmorklippen* in 1939. Like *Der Großtyrann und
das Gericht* this book was regarded by all as a novel in code, *the* book
of the resistance; it was passionately discussed in Böll's family, but
for Böll himself it was too 'solemn', too 'elitist'. He found *Das
abenteuerliche Herz*, which he read during the war, more accessible,
but it was not until he encountered Jünger's account of his experiences in the First World War, his enormously successful *In Stahlgewittern*, that he began to understand, if not to sympathise with,
Jünger's admiration for the heroism of the soldier (E 3, p. 227).
Later Böll read Jünger's diary of the Second World War, *Strahlungen*,
which appeared in 1949 (I, p. 596). Jünger remained a writer whom
Böll could respect — he was never an opportunist (I, p. 533) — , but
his works were for the most part 'alien' to him (E 3, p. 229). They
seem to have been the subject of long arguments during the war. In
the semi-autobiographical 'Als der Krieg ausbrach' the narrator
reports with evident repugnance how two fellow conscripts hold
endless conversations on Jünger, while two others hold equally
endless conversations on the female anatomy (R 4, pp. 12, 24); in the
companion piece, 'Als der Krieg zu Ende war', he mockingly asks a
companion who has just been released from captivity but is trying to
sew his rank insignia back on to his uniform whether this is due to
the influence of Ernst Jünger and receives an embarrassed reply
(R 4, p. 28). Jünger had been a professional soldier from his earliest
youth; it was rumoured that he had helped to draw up the military
regulations. As a convinced civilian Böll could hardly sympathise
with him (E 3, p. 228). The contrast is instructive. In *Der Kampf als
inneres Erlebnis* (1922) Jünger, quoting Heraclitus, describes war as
'the father of all things', 'as little a human institution as the sexual
drive; it is a law of nature' ('ebensowenig eine menschliche Einrich-
tung wie der Geschlechtstrieb; er ist ein Naturgesetz') (Jünger,

47

1922, pp. 13, 43) and he has similar things to say in the 1949 *Strahlungen* (Jünger, 1949, p. 224). For Böll 'war as an inner experience' meant 'absolutely nothing' (I, p. 626; Lenz, p. 32). On the contrary, like Saint-Exupéry he retorts that if war is a law of nature it is so in the sense that typhus is (R 1, p. 308). *In Stahlgewittern* contains a number of motifs that recur in Böll's war fiction. Jünger too writes of 'the boredom which is more unnerving for a soldier than the proximity of death' ('die Langeweile, die für den Soldaten entnervender als die Nähe des Todes ist') and affirms: 'Above all the soldier must not get bored' ('Der Soldat darf sich vor allem nicht langweilen') (Jünger, 1920, p. 95). But in fact one does not have the impression of lack of incident or interest in Jünger's wartime experiences — he evidently had many opportunities for discussions and nature study. Elsewhere, he, like the characters in Böll's works, finds war too complex to understand: 'the utterances of the will to fight appeared strange and disconnected like processes taking place on another planet' ('die Äußerungen des Kampfwillens erschienen mir seltsam und unzusammenhängend wie Vorgänge auf einem anderen Gestirn') (pp. 24–5), but shortly afterwards he is reassured by the sight of a colonel giving instructions: 'Aha, there is meaning and reason behind it after all' ('Aha, die Sache hat doch wohl Sinn und Verstand') (p. 27). This insight is never vouchsafed to Böll's heroes.

In place of those writers to whom Böll found no access there came the many foreign authors whose books flooded into Germany under the auspices of the cultural policies of the occupying administrations: Camus, Greene, Mailer, Steinbeck, McCullers, Capote and others (E 1, p. 86) — even the Soviet writer Victor Nekrassov (Vormweg, p. 54). In his liberation from cultural captivity Böll devoured everything he could put his hands on (Lenz p. 50). The French existentialists were especially influential; he had already read some Kierkegaard in the 1930s and carried a selection from his diaries with him in the last months of the war (Lenz, pp. 42f.; FT, p. 108). Franz Kafka, 'the greatest' (E 2, p. 41), whose works were almost invariably interpreted in existentialist terms in these years, was a kindred spirit whom he first encountered at this time (Lenz, p. 52). Albert Camus's *L'Etranger*, 'one of the most marvellous books that reached us after 1945' ('eines der großartigsten Bücher, die uns nach 1945 erreichten') (I, p. 404), appeared in German in 1948 as *Der Fremde*. Sartre's combination of political commitment and literature was a source of continual inspiration (I, pp. 517f., 402f.). Some aspects of the existentialist outlook may in retrospect be regarded less as emancipatory than as exculpatory. This was suggested by Nicolas Born in 1977 and Böll did not disagree. The central concept of the absurdity of human existence, man's 'Geworfensein' — the term is actually Martin Heidegger's and Heidegger lived comfortably enough under the Nazis — implied that the war into which one had been 'thrown' was absurd rather than morally evil; moral decisions were thereby excluded (Lenz, pp. 51f.). Böll's presentation of war in the early works has a strong component of existentialism about it. By contrast an East German writer like Anna Seghers, admittedly an *émigrée*, whose *Die Toten bleiben jung* appeared in 1949, explained the rise of fascism not in terms of the senselessness of human endeavour but in terms of capitalist exploitation and class conflict on a national and on an international scale. This element is almost wholly lacking in Böll's early works and in this he is not untypical of the time and the place. Alfred Andersch too, both in his autobiographical 'report' *Die Kirschen der Freiheit* (1952) and in the novel *Sansibar oder der letzte Grund* (1957), adopted an existentialist position. It was not until the following decade that Böll found his way to a more political stance.

Of the American authors whom Böll read in these early post-war years the most important was Ernest Hemingway. In a 1956 review Böll mentioned Hemingway's 'marvellous novel' *A Farewell to Arms* (E 1, p. 185), which appeared in German in 1946 as *In einem anderen Land*. Böll, however, found the machismo of Hemingway's novels, their 'cult of manliness' ('Männlichkeitskult'), the 'myth of maleness' ('Mythos der Männlichkeit'), repellent and saddening (I, p. 542). Hemingway's influence was rather in the field of the short story and in his style: the short, clipped sentences, the use of repetition, the avoidance of 'because' clauses in order to stress the facticity of what was happening; it was 'the impression of reporting and objectivity' ('das scheinbar Reporterhafte und Sachliche') that Böll found fascinating. Some of the short stories were quite 'unbeatable' both in their beginnings and in their development (Lenz, pp. 50, 52).

He repeatedly declared that the short story was his favourite form. In 1961 he described it as 'for me the most attractive form of prose writing' ('für mich die reizvollste Prosaform') (I, p. 13); in 1967 it was 'still the best of all forms of prose writing' ('immer noch die schönste aller Prosaformen') (I, p. 67); and ten years later he still regarded himself as 'by nature a writer of short stories' ('von Natur ein Kurzgeschichtenschreiber') (Lenz, p. 50). Nevertheless the majority of his short stories were written before the mid-1950s and his most important collection, *Wanderer, kommst du nach Spa . . .* appeared in 1950. In this respect Böll was of his time, for the dominant literary form of the new German literature in the immedi-

ate post-war years was the *Kurzgeschichte*, with important contributions from Wolfgang Borchert, Ilse Aichinger, Ernst Schnabel,
Wolfdietrich Schnurre and many others. In retrospect Böll saw it as

> not only a current of the time, but it was a form of expression which
> corresponded to the age, which also corresponded to the experimental
> character which post-'45 literature in the Federal Republic necessarily
> had. It was a form you could experiment with to a considerable extent,
> one which also gave you scope from the point of view of length, that was
> very important.

> (nicht nur eine Zeitströmung, sondern es war eine Ausdrucksform, die
> der Zeit entsprach, die auch dem experimentellen Charakter der Litera-
> tur entsprach, den sie nach 45 in der Bundesrepublik notwendigerweise
> hatte. Das war eine Form, mit der man sehr viel experimentieren konnte,
> die auch quantitativ Spielraum ließ, das war sehr wichtig.)

(I, p. 642)

By the end of the 1950s the tide had turned — to his regret the short
story appeared no longer to convey the times (Lenz, p. 73). There
were material reasons for the blossoming of the short story: the
paper shortage made longer novels too expensive and there was a
proliferation of little journals, *Karussell*, *Das goldene Tor*, etc. in the
years prior to the Currency Reform — as money was not worth
saving, people were prepared to spend it on what they could get and
this included anything that appeared in print; once the currency had
been stabilised, however, most of these journals disappeared (Grosser,
1974, p. 87). Nevertheless, the very impermanence of this publishing
medium undoubtedly corresponded to the *Zeitgeist*. It has even been
suggested that the conditions of flux, impermanence and new beginning in post-war Germany corresponded to those which pertained in
nineteenth-century America at the time of the rise of the short story
there (Motekat, 1957, pp. 23ff.).

There *was* a German short-story tradition prior to 1945. Böll
mentions Heinrich von Kleist as an important influence (I, p. 641).
Kleist's most famous narratives, *Michael Kohlhaas*, *Die Marquise von
O.* (E 1, p. 135), *Das Erdbeben in Chili*, are usually regarded as
novellas rather than short stories, but Böll may have been thinking
of the shorter pieces written for the *Berliner Abendblätter*. Johann Peter
Hebel was another influence — one of the first books he possessed
was by Hebel (I, p. 19), who was 'godfather' to the contemporary
hybrid of anecdote, novella and story (E 1, p. 93). Hebel's 'Unver-
hofftes Wiedersehen' invites comparison. It is the story of a mining
accident in Sweden: a man is buried in an earth fall; years later his

body is found completely preserved by the salts in the soil, and the story ends with the confrontation of his now aged fiancée with the still young features of her beloved. This juxtaposition of past and present is an important motif in Böll's works, not only, but not least, in his short stories. It is the governing principle of stories like 'Über die Brücke', 'Die Botschaft' and 'Geschäft ist Geschäft'.

Elsewhere he contrasted the short story and the novella. Wolfgang Borchert's 'Das Brot' was 'a paradigm of the short-story genre, which does not narrate by means of novellesque climaxes and the explanation of moral truths but narrates by presenting' ('ein Musterbeispiel für die Gattung Kurzgeschichte, die nicht mit novellistischen Höhepunkten und der Erläuterung moralischer Wahrheiten erzählt, sondern erzählt, indem sie darstellt') (E 1, p. 163). Before 1945 the novella had been the canonical German form of shorter fiction, a linear, dramatic narrative much favoured in the nineteenth century by writers and critics alike, who developed complex theories on its form and nature. The dominance of this form may well have prevented the short story from taking on the importance that it was gaining elsewhere in the world (Doderer, 1953, pp. 77ff.). The 'liberation' of 1945 was also a liberation from the dominance of cultural pressures of the past and permitted the explosion of the short story which took place in those years, until Siegfried Unseld could declare in 1955 that the novella was totally outmoded. The novella was a 'closed' form, the short story an 'open' form and 'closed' forms were inappropriate to the post-war situation of flux and uncertainty (Unseld, 1955). Frank O' Connor entitled his study of the genre *The Lonely Voice*, regarding 'an intense awareness of human loneliness' as the keynote of the short story in contrast to the sense of community conveyed by the novel (O'Connor, 1963, pp. 19, 21). There is a strong element of loneliness in Böll's contributions to the genre, whether it be the solitude of the eccentric narrator of 'Uber die Brücke' and 'An der Brücke', that of the non-conformist narrator of 'Geschäft ist Geschäft', or that of the private soldier in the war stories for whom comradeship appears but an empty word. One formal aspect which applies to many of Böll's stories is suggested by Robert Ulshöfer: where the novella is linear, the form of the short story is more akin to the pattern created when a stone falls in a pond (Ulshöfer, 1958). The short story is concerned with the moment of impact, the moment which refers both backwards and forwards in time; it frequently portrays an encounter through which contemporary reality is illuminated. Borchert's 'Das Brot' is paradigmatic: the relationship between an elderly couple, the poverty and hunger of the post-war years are illuminated as the wife catches her husband during the night stealing down to the kitchen to eat a slice of bread. Böll's short stories are dominated by the motif of the encounter or its converse, the leave-taking: 'Kumpel mit dem langen Haar', 'Die Botschaft', 'Abschied', 'Trunk in Petöcki', 'Auch Kinder sind Zivilisten,' 'Aufenthalt in X' and many others. The experience of the war was one of such brief, transient encounters. They occurred frequently in the railway waiting-rooms in which even in the post-war years so much time was spent as people waited for the irregular train service to take them back to the place where provisions were still obtainable. 'The whole of Germany is one great waiting-room' ('Ganz Deutschland ist ein großer Wartesaal'), it was reported in 1946 (Scherpe, 1982, p. 41), and even in 1975 Böll described the 'waiting-room pattern' as an important component of his life (I, pp. 372, 26).

He was also a keen observer of indigenous literary developments — he left no book out that appeared in these years (Lenz, p. 50). Apart from the authors of short stories already mentioned, Ernst Kreuder and Günter Eich are names he particularly singles out. In an essay on Kreuder's fiftieth birthday in 1953 Böll placed him beside Borchert as the first German post-war writer of European stature (E 1, p. 100). His *Die Gesellschaft vom Dachboden* (1946), which was almost immediately translated into English as *The Attic Pretenders*, and *Die Unauffindbaren* (1948) were regarded at the time as 'Kafkaesque'; in fact they are closer to the literature of German Romanticism in their mixture of fantasy and realism. Fantasy and realism play a part in many of Böll's early stories; but whereas *Die Gesellschaft vom Dachboden* is completely lacking in concrete historical references this is almost never the case with Böll.

In 1967 Böll described Günter Eich's collection of poetry *Abgelegene Gehöfte* (1948) as the post-war German-language work which was closest to him (I, p. 65). Although some of the poems in the collection were actually composed in the 1930s, two stand out as documents of the POW experience, 'Inventur' and 'Latrine'. The latter with its famous rhyme of 'Hölderlin' and 'Urin' can be read as a statement of the questionable status of traditional cultural values in an age which had seen Auschwitz — this was to be an important preoccupation of Böll's. 'Inventur' has been regarded as even more symptomatic of the post-war situation. It consists of a series of statements, in which the poet takes stock of the few worldly possessions left to the prisoner of war, expressed in short lines, paratactical sentences, simple language. Language had been debased by the Nazis with their pompous neologisms; their extreme nationalism laid claim to all that was good in German culture and life. Those who began writing after 1945 had to begin from scratch, taking nothing for granted, creating their own traditions anew. Post-war German literature, Böll later said, was a 'literature of finding a language' ('eine Literatur der Sprachfindung') (E 2, p. 61). The political 'zero hour' of 1945 demanded a corresponding literary 'Kahlschlag' (clearing), a term coined by Wolfgang Weyrauch in 1949: the forest had to be cleared completely in order that new planting could take place. Eich's poem is the 'Kahlschlag' poem *par excellence*. However, just as there was no genuine political 'zero hour' in 1945 when the field was taken over by the sexagenarians and older, so too the concept of a literary 'clearing' has been shown to be misleading. Even 'Inventur' bears the hallmarks of traditional rhetoric (Endres, 1980, pp. 126ff.). Urs Widmer found much bombast and even residual Nazi vocabulary in the language of post-1945 texts (Widmer, 1966). Others have pointed out the continued influence of the conservative cultural functionaries in the media and in publishing, who did not suddenly change policies in April 1945 (Schonauer, 1977), while Hans Dieter Schäfer has argued that there was no caesura at all between 1930 and 1965 (Schäfer, 1981, pp. 55–71).

In this connection the founding of the 'Gruppe 47' in 1947 is significant. Following the banning of their journal *Der Ruf* Alfred Andersch and Hans Werner Richter planned a further journal *Der Skorpion*, which, however, the American authorities proscribed for its 'nihilistic tendency' before even a single issue had appeared. From politics Richter turned to literature. In September 1947 he invited his colleagues to a reunion at Bannwaldsee near Füssen. There they read to one another from the manuscripts they had brought with them, discussed and criticised them and agreed to meet the following year. And so for twenty years the 'Gruppe 47' met once or twice a year, from 1950 onwards awarding a prize for the best contribution. Günter Eich was the first prize-winner, Böll was successful at his first appearance in 1951. The format remained the same. Invitations always came from Hans Werner Richter and there were readings and discussions. As time went on the group became very influential, and although there were always those outside it who were successful, the best-known post-war West German authors have been members — Grass, Walser, Siegfried Lenz, Enzensberger, and even, briefly, Peter Handke. Most commentators on the group's development have suggested that turning to literature from political journalism was a form of resignation in keeping with the restoration of bourgeois values which was the keynote of the Adenauer era (Kröll, 1977). Others have more recently pointed out the continued political involvement of Richter, Andersch and their colleagues after the founding of the literary group (Peitsch/Reith, 1983). Since they originated in left-wing politics they tended to remain politically oriented and to oppose the ruling conservative government at least in their extra-literary activities, which included the drawing up of resolutions and protest letters. But the fact that they had been thwarted in their political ambitions almost from the beginning and had been forced to turn to literature in its place meant that in one sense literature was taking the place of politics. And so the direction that much of post-war German literature was to take was set: ersatz politics from a 'left without a home' ('heimatlose Linke').

Three weeks after his return to Cologne Böll began to write, and in the following years he produced a stream of works, mostly short stories, but also longer works. Much of his output remained unpublished — he described it as 'experimental' in the sense that he was testing his own abilities (I, p. 642). One unpublished novel written in 1946 is known to have the title 'Kreuz ohne Liebe' (anon., 1961, p. 80); this may be the novel which Böll wrote as an entry in a competition, the physical circumstances of whose writing he described in the essay 'Am Anfang' (E 3, pp. 51f.). In 1982 a short novel of 1948, *Das Vermächtnis*, was published for the first time, and a year later twenty-two unpublished stories from the years 1946 to 1952 appeared under the title *Die Verwundung und andere Erzählungen*. According to the blurb they were discovered in the archives which Böll had donated to the city of Cologne; why they had not been published he could no longer remember. Unfortunately they are not individually dated and it is impossible to say which is the earliest. In 1973 Böll estimated that between 1945 and 1947 he had published some sixty 'novellas' in ten different journals (I, p. 245). The term *Novellen* may be a mistranslation, as the original interview was in French and the word used there was 'nouvelles', but it is true that in the early post-war years a proper terminology had not yet been established and, for example, Böll's 'Wiedersehen in der Allee' was called a 'Novelle' by the editors of *Die literarische Revue* when they first published it in 1948 (vol. 3, 1948, p. 448). For this period only four publications by Böll have been traced so far, however, all from the year 1947, and he later declared that he had received his first author's payment in 1947 from the *Rheinischer Merkur* (FT, p. 56), presumably for the story 'Aus der "Vorzeit"'. The latter gives the lie to the notion of a 'clearing' in the jungle of literary style. It describes the monotony and stupidity of military discipline in a pre-war barracks, but is filled with conventional rhetoric, exclamations, metaphors, similes, even classical allusions: the commanding officers are 'merciless gods in the temple of mindlessness' ('die unbarmherzigen Götter im Tempel des Stumpfsinns') and 'not even the suffering of the many who had sweated and bled and groaned here beneath the burden of "duty" had been able to create a kind of *genius loci*' ('nicht einmal der Schmerz der Vielen, die hier geschwitzt und geblutet und gestöhnt hatten unter der Last des "Dienstes", hatte eine Art genius loci zu schaffen vermocht') (R 1, pp. 7f.). Böll's classical education was still uppermost, the education which the later story 'Wanderer, Kommst du nach Spa . . .', which uses some of the motifs of the earlier one, was to castigate.

In 1949 *Die literarische Revue* devoted much of its fourth number to works by 'young' German authors. They included Wolfdietrich Schnurre, Erich Fried and the 31-year-old Heinrich Böll and were introduced by Rudolf Hartung, who analysed their replies to a questionnaire on their views on literature. A selection of their replies was included at the end of the volume. As they have not to my knowledge been published since — Walter Ziltener was evidently unaware of them (Ziltener, 1980; but cf. Peitsch, 1982, p. 193), Böll's responses are worth reproducing in full. Asked 'What in your opinion is the task and meaning of artistic creation today?' Böll replied: 'Giving things their name. Relating reality to a symbolism which is immanent in the world' ('Worin besteht ihrer Meinung nach heute die Aufgabe und Bedeutung des künstlerischen Schaffens? — Den Dingen ihren Namen zu geben. Die Wirklichkeit einzuordnen in eine Symbolik, die der Welt innewohnt'). On the question 'To what extent does an analysis of the times determine your literary creativity?' his answer was that he attempted 'to make all "temporal phenomena" transparent, so that what is valid becomes visible' (In welchem Umfang ist die Auseinandersetzung mit der Zeit bestimmend für Ihr literarisches Schaffen? — . . . Alle "Zeiterscheinungen" transparent machen, so daß das Gültige sichtbar wird'). And in reply to the question of literary models he listed Bernanos, Hemingway, Kafka, Greene and Koestler (*Die literarische Revue* 4, 1949, pp. 245–7). The latter response was predictable; only Dostoevsky is missing from the names we might have expected. His reply to the second question puts in a rather grander manner what his later essay 'Der Zeitgenosse und die Wirklichkeit' was to say on the difference between what is topical and what is real, here the 'temporal phenomenon' and the 'valid'; it does, however, devalue the former to an even greater extent than was to be the case later. It is in his answer to the first question that Böll placed himself in the tradition of late nineteenth- and early twentieth-century symbolism — Rilke too had spoken of the poet's task to 'name' things and it would seem therefore that in 1949 Böll was more concerned with eternal verities than with a socially committed literature. In fact his practice did not always conform to this aesthetic credo.

His first independent publication, *Der Zug war pünktlich*, was written in the winter of 1946/7 although in the chaotic economic circumstances of the time it did not appear until 1949, having been accepted by a number of publishers who subsequently went bankrupt (E 3, pp. 52ff.). It is a fascinating work, whose weaknesses and strengths give interesting insights into the stage that its author had reached in his development. It takes place at the end of September 1943. Stalingrad has fallen, the Red Army is advancing, but the second front in the West has not yet been set up; the Americans and the British are still hesitating and it may take two years more before the Russians reach the Atlantic. Andreas, a young soldier, is returning from leave in the Rhineland to the Eastern front. He is struck by a premonition that he is going to die, a premonition so clear that he is even able to work out exactly where it will occur. On the train he meets two other soldiers, Willi and Siebental. The former is returning early having discovered that his wife is being unfaithful to him, and is determined to spend their savings on drink and prostitutes; Siebental has been seduced by a homosexual sergeant-major. Willi persuades the others to alter their prescribed route. After a number of unforeseeable changes of train they arrive in Lemberg, where Willi takes the two to a high-class bordello at his expense. There Andreas meets Olina, a prostitute who turns out to be working for the Polish Resistance. Andreas reveals to her his premonition. She promises to save him and his comrades, fleeing in the car which has been sent to take her to another client, a German general. But their vehicle is ambushed by Polish partisans and they all die, exactly where Andreas had foreseen it would happen.

This brief summary of the plot already indicates some of the unique features of the story. There is hardly another Böll story which is dominated by such a clear plot-based structure. It is a dramatic structure which reflects many of the fate dramas of the German classical theatre, or indeed the Oedipus Trilogy of Sophocles — all attempts to escape lead inexorably to one's predetermined fate. Numerous allusions to the partisans throughout the story appear as leitmotivs and premonitions of the end. It is a traditional novella, precisely what Böll was later to reject as a 'very aristocratic form of short prose fiction' ('eine sehr aristokratische Form der kurzen Prosa') (Q, p. 66). The closed structure implies the futility of all attempts at resistance. Life appears predetermined in a Jansenist way. Only prayer can help, prayer not to persuade God to intervene, but to enable man to endure to his end. In his demonising of homosexuality Böll was no better and no worse than most of his contemporaries. It is more disconcerting to find that he presents the Polish partisans as on a level with the German army; Olina realises that there are only 'victims' and 'executioners', that 'we too only murder the innocent' ('daß auch wir nur die Unschuldigen morden') (R 1, p. 147).

The traditional qualities are underlined by other features of the narrative. The language is often contrived, metaphorical, even bombastic. Again there is no evidence of a 'Kahlschlag' in this story. 'An invisible hand' prevents Andreas from drowning his sorrows in alcohol (p. 73); the second-hand of time revolves invisibly behind the horizon (p. 75). When he enters the brothel he hears a snatch of Schubert and it is as if somebody has pierced his heart and opened a secret sluice. References to traditional cultural values are numerous. Andreas's ambitions for life after the war are for a room of his own with music, poetry, flowers. Olina has a 'Fragonard nose . . . Fragonard mouth' (p. 133). The scenes of squalor in the trains and on the railway station are convincingly portrayed. It is in the scene between Andreas and Olina that Böll really indulges himself. Olina has been prevented from becoming a pianist by the outbreak of war. Andreas persuades her to play for him. At first she improvises some variations on a hit song of the time; the theme rises 'like a stony cliff' ('wie eine steinerne Klippe') (p. 142). Andreas finds himself transported into the seventeenth century in France. Later he plays a sonatina of Beethoven and Olina has never seen such a beautiful face. She plays him some Schubert and the tears run down his face: 'these tears are life, a wild torrent formed from countless streams' ('diese Tränen sind das Leben, ein wilder Strom, der sich aus unzähligen Bächen gebildet hat') (p. 159). Then she plays Bach, although she has never been able to play Bach before. Culture in this context is not emancipatory but escapist: in the half-darkness Andreas feels 'the whole world belongs to me' ('die ganze Welt gehört mir') (p. 142), words which embarrasingly echo the Nazi song with the refrain: 'For today Germany belongs to us / and tomorrow the whole world' ('Denn heute gehört uns Deutschland / Und morgen die ganze Welt'), which we heard only a few pages earlier (p. 116). The combination of tears, music, autumn and death is pure romanticism, an 'inwardness' which Böll had not yet overcome (cf. Q, p. 69). It is revealing that in the mid-1950s, when Böll had produced much more socially critical work, conservative reviewers should regard this story as Böll's most convincing work (Kalow, 1955; Hohoff, 1957).

Das Vermächtnis was written in 1948 but not published until 1982. The reason for the delay is not obvious. In view of the paper shortage it was easier to find outlets for shorter works; *Das Vermächtnis* has a less exciting plot than *Der Zug war pünktlich*; it also contains a number of unsatisfactory loose ends and inconsistencies, such as the mines which the narrator refers to although he is only told about them later (VM, pp. 21, 24). The narrator Fischer tells how in the summer of 1943 he was posted to a country area on the northern coast of France, where he met Lieutenant Schelling, his commanding officer, and Captain Schnecker, Schelling's rival and opposite in every respect. Where Schelling is courteous, Schnecker is a bully; where Schelling makes no secret of his scorn for the Nazis, Schnecker is an ardent fascist; where Schelling is civilised and cultured, Schnecker is a drunkard and a boaster. The suspense of the story depends on the opening revelation that Schnecker 'murdered' Schelling and escaped scot-free. Only at the close does Fischer reveal how it happened: they were sent later that year to the Russian front where Schelling distinguished himself by repulsing a Soviet attack; in the celebrations which followed Schnecker got drunk and shot Schelling dead in a rage. However, there is much less conventional 'action' in *Das Vermächtnis* than in *Der Zug war pünktlich*; instead we find long meditations on the utter absurdity and boredom of the soldier's life, motifs which recur in Böll's autobiographical writings, notably the 'Brief an einen jungen Katholiken' of 1958, which likewise describes the experience of a posting in northern France.

One significant feature of *Das Vermächtnis* which points forward to Böll's later career is the narrative technique employed. From his earliest beginnings Böll was a self-conscious writer. *Der Zug war pünktlich* has an external narrator, but events are largely 'focalised' (Rimmon-Kenan, 1983) by one of the characters. For most of the time the internal focaliser is Andreas; later focalisation alternates between Andreas and Olina. However, there are also numerous interventions by an external, commenting narrator of a kind that the later Böll was to eschew. The metaphors already noted are one indication of his presence; at the opening of the story he openly comments on the 'cabbalistic' effect of certain words, on the 'cosmic force of life' which sometimes fills with an 'illumination' those who are destined to die (R 1, pp. 66f.). Most of the narrative is told in the 'historic' present tense, no doubt to try to increase the tension, but ultimately creating an atmosphere of artificiality. *Das Vermächtnis* has a more unusual technique. It is a first person narrative, but alone of Böll's works it has an overt, personalised narratee. Fischer is directing his report at a specific person, the murdered Schelling's younger brother, whom he has found after the war. Böll's purpose may have been to draw the real reader into the narrative in order to stimulate him to action against the war criminals still at large. However, since the narratee is evidently of a higher social class than the narrator, the implication is one of a touching faith in authority, one which was to be dashed by developments in the Adenauer years. It is an 'experimental' work in the sense referred to. Some difficulties Böll had not completely mastered. The constant returning to Schelling's brother, the convention of a 'report', becomes gradually more artificial as the story, which begins in the post-war present, becomes more and more embedded in the past, while at one stage in order to maintain the fiction that Fischer did indeed witness all that he is reporting, Böll had to have him steal round the house and eavesdrop at the window on an argument between Schelling and Schnecker.

Böll had a specific reason for employing this narrative technique. Like many of his later novels *Das Vermächtnis* has a dual timescale. The main events take place in 1943, but they are related from the vantage-point of five years later. Böll's portrayal of the war in *Das Vermächtnis* contrasts with that given in most of the works he published in the immediate post-war years; the fact that it resembles quite closely the description he gave to René Wintzen in 1975 raises interesting questions of realism. To be sure, there is no explicit justification of war. The life of the soldier at the front is one of privation, and especially of tedium — it is a war primarily 'against boredom' (VM, p. 39). There is little solidarity among the men, who, while not prepared to betray a comrade who has overslept, will not attempt to cover for him either. Drunkenness, larceny, plundering are all accepted aspects of army life and the absence of women makes it still less civilised. Nevertheless, the presence in the story of a Schelling represents a rehabilitation of the Wehrmacht in 1948 which corresponds to the words of, for example, Alfred Andersch in his comment on the Nuremberg trials in 1946: 'The fighters of Stalingrad, El Alamein and Cassino, who were highly respected even by their opponents, are innocent of the crimes of Dachau and Buchenwald' ('Die Kämpfer von Stalingrad, El Alamein und Cassino, denen auch von ihren Gegnern jede Achtung entgegengebracht wurde, sind unschuldig an den Verbrechen von Dachau und Buchenwald') (Schwab-Felisch, 1962, p. 27). This is remarkable only in the context of Böll's better-known works, in which the officers are almost invariably portrayed in a negative way, but it is paralleled in other war novels of the time, for example in Theodor Plievier's *Stalingrad* (1948), in which the humane General Vilshofen similarly represents the acceptable face of the officer ethos. Schelling is not only chivalrous, cultured and contemptuous of the Nazis, he is even allowed to be good at warfare, beating off a Soviet attack through his courage and initiative. By contrast, the relatively sympathetic general of *Wo warst du, Adam?* experiences only lost battles. On the question of resistance to fascism, however, *Das Vermächtnis* is perhaps even more confused than *Der Zug war pünktlich.* Schelling makes no secret of his opposition to Hitler, openly speaking to the narrator of the disgusting way in which some parents greet their children in the morning with a 'Heil Hitler' (VM, p. 51) and turning the portrait of Hitler to the wall when he is having a private conversation with Fischer. According to Böll in 1975 even in the army one quickly knew who could be trusted, with whom one could be frank (I, pp. 523f.). Schelling describes Hitler as a 'vain genius'; he and Fischer discuss how he could be murdered (VM, pp. 66f.) — one year before 20 July 1944 — and shortly before the posting to the Russian front he speaks of action rather than words. However, he, like Andreas, is deeply religious, believes that man is born to suffer, not to be happy, and that we are subject to a divine plan, all of which appears to contradict the possibility of his intervening in order to dethrone the tyrant. This may well be the Jansenist component in Böll's upbringing.

If Böll is ambiguous in his presentation of the fascist past, his attack on conservative society is very direct. The narrative present is the late summer of 1948, a few months after the Currency Reform. A year previously there were still shortages, individuals could 'make their fortunes in American cigarettes and vague political hopes' (pp. 37f.). Today the tense faces are of those fighting not for their potato ration but in the end-of-summer sales; former officers now boast of their wartime exploits and are preparing for careers as lawyers or teachers, professions in which they can bully people who are even more defenceless than soldiers. The classlessness of the immediate post-war years has gone. The continuity between the Third Reich and post-Currency-Reform Germany is implied when Fischer resigns himself to the fact that he can cope with the new ruling class as little as with the war itself. Fischer is the witness to a past which is being forgotten, Schnecker the embodiment of this past and one who is as integrated now as then, having just received his doctorate. Fischer himself points forward to the Fred Bogner of *Und sagte kein einziges Wort*, nihilistic, indifferent to everything, spending his time lying on his bed smoking, living off his war pension and what he gets from selling off his books. While this is a convincing enough port-rayal of a mood widespread at the time, it is less plausible that such a man should take the trouble to write this report.

If we are to look for masterpieces from Böll in this early period it is among the short stories that we shall find them. The collection *Wanderer, kommst du nach Spa . . .* (1950) must be considered Böll's first major publication, and although its date of publication places it just outside the period under review, at least seventeen of its twenty-five items had already appeared before the founding of the Federal Republic and it may conveniently be discussed here. Taken as a whole it is a work which stands comparison with anything that appeared in the German language in these early years. It has its weaknesses as well as its strengths.The hysteria of 'Steh auf, steh doch auf', the pathos of 'Die Essenholer' are hard to take. But the satire on military heroism in the title story, and on the post-war restoration mentality in 'Über die Brücke' and 'Geschäft ist Geschäft' remain masterpieces of their kind.

In these stories we can see particularly clearly Böll 'experiment-ing', as he put it, with narrative techniques, styles, language regis-ters and point of view. All but three of them are first person narratives. Of these three, 'Trunk in Petöcki' is told from the limited perspective of an anonymous 'soldier' in a Hungarian inn, observing people and behaviour which he does not understand; 'In der Fin-sternis' is largely in dialogue and points forward to Böll's later plays for radio; and 'Lohengrins Tod' uses multiple points of view and includes a passage in stream of consciousness technique. Of the first person narratives two, 'Über die Brücke' and 'Die Botschaft', invoke a reader; the others are more or less immediate, existential state-ments, often so divorced from any 'real' narrative situation that they end with the death of the narrator. There is a strong Romantic or neo-Romantic component in some of these stories, where the reality of this world of misery and decay is transcended and the narrator enters into a world of light, order and fulfilment. 'Steh auf, steh doch auf' reads in places like an echo of the third of Novalis's *Hymnen an die Nacht*; 'Lohengrins Tod' is at times reminiscent of Gerhart Hauptmann's *Hanneles Himmelfahrt*. At the close of 'Die Essenholer' we even hear the voice of God. Böll's works were to continue to have a strong religious dimension, but it is only in these early stories that there is a direct transcendence of the material world. Böll also experiments with language and style in these early stories. As in *Der Zug war pünktlich* there is often a quite un-'Kahlschlag'-like striving for effect, with metaphor following metaphor, simile following personi-fication. Elsewhere, however, there is a conscious simplicity of style.

The paratactical sentences and repetitions of, for example, 'Damals in Odessa' correspond to the naïvety of the young soldier telling the tale, the understatements and repetitions of significant phrases in 'Geschäft ist Geschäft' are what make the story such a devastating critique of restoration society. We find colloquial language in 'An der Brücke', the parody of officialese in 'Mein trauriges Gesicht' and self-deprecating irony in the elevated, educated register of 'Über die Brücke'. Indeed it is the element of humour in the latter story and others which is new and one that was to become most important in the future.

Eleven of the stories are set in the last years of the war, on the Russian front, in Hungary, in France and in Germany. Thirteen are set in the post-war period, five of these after the Currency Reform. The remaining story 'Mein trauriges Gesicht' is more complex and will be discussed later. Of pre-war times there is hardly a mention. 'Wiedersehen in der Allee' refers rather disconcertingly to the last years of Weimar Germany as the 'cadaver of the republic' (R 1, p. 38). 'Peace', 'yearning', 'life' are qualities which, in a three-fold repetition, their 'fathers' knew, but which the protagonists can only momentarily sense during a lull in the hostilities. This is the story which comes closest in tone to *Das Vermächtnis*, elegiac and aphoristic. Pre-war Nazi society is presented mainly as school life, as the central figures, like their author, usually found themselves plunged into the war as soon as they left school. The bullying teachers of 'Wir Besenbinder', 'Wiedersehen mit Drüng' and 'Wanderer, kommst du nach Spa' may be taken to represent the Nazi establishment. Drüng, for example, had been admired at school for the wrong reasons, as the narrator now realises: not because he was a good pupil who helped the weaker ones, but because his father had been killed in the First World War.

'Wanderer, kommst du nach Spa' and 'Lohengrins Tod' satirise Nazi ideology most directly. The title of the former would have been immediately transparent to its contemporary readers (Watt, 1985). It is taken from Friedrich Schiller's translation of the inscription to the Spartan heroes of Thermopylae: 'Traveller, com'st thou to Sparta, announce to them there that thou didst / See us lying here, just as the law did command' ('Wanderer, kommst du nach Sparta, verkündige dorten du habest / Uns hier liegen gesehn, wie das Gesetz es befahl') (Schiller, 'Der Spaziergang'). From the destruction of the German armies at Stalingrad onwards there had been a concerted attempt by Goebbels and his ministry to parallel the heroic stand of Leonidas against the Persians at Thermopylae with the efforts of the Germans to hold back the 'barbaric' Russians.

Plievier's *Stalingrad* describes the incredulity and despair of those still hoping to be flown out when they hear Goebbels's speech and realise that they have been sacrificed:

> My soldiers, millenia have passed, and prior to these millennia there stood in a little narrow pass in Greece an infinitely brave and bold man with three hundred of his men, Leonidas with three hundred Spartans. The sky was darkened with the number of arrows and the three hundred did not waver, did not retreat, and then the last of them fell . . . and now there stands the inscription: Traveller, if you come to Sparta, report that you saw us lying here as the law commanded. . . . And similarly in times to come they will read: If you come to Germany, report that you saw us lying in Stalingrad, as the law commanded.

> (Meine Soldaten, Jahrtausende sind vergangen, und vor diesen Jahrtausenden stand in einem kleinen Engpaß in Griechenland ein unendlich tapferer und kühner Mann mit dreihundert seiner Männer, stand Leonidas mit dreihundert Spartanern. Der Himmel verdunkelte sich von der Zahl der Pfeile, und die dreihundert wankten und wichen nicht, und dann fiel der letzte . . . und da steht nun der Satz: Wandrer, kommst du nach Sparta, berichte, du habest uns hier liegen sehen, wie das Gesetz es befahl . . . So wird es auch einmal heißen: Kommst du nach Deutschland, so berichte, du habest uns in Stalingrad liegen sehen, wie das Gesetz es befohlen hat.)

> (Plievier, 1948, p. 335)

Unlike Plievier, who has his characters reflect on the quotation and its incongruity with their present misery (pp. 346, 351), Böll allows the situation to speak for itself. Sparta has become Spa, the Belgian health resort, because when the narrator wrote the words on the school blackboard in a handwriting exercise he ran out of space. But there is nothing of the health resort about the place of the action, a German city in flames during a bombing raid, nor is there anything of the Leonidas about the narrator, who knows that his name will shortly adorn the war memorial under the words 'passed out from school to the front and fell for . . .' but in place of the 'Führer, Volk und Vaterland' which would normally complete the sentence he cannot think of any cause for which he might be dying (R 1, p. 199). The classical heritage, of which Schiller's words are one example, has been abused in the Nazi education system, which juxtaposed a replica of the Parthenon frieze with pictures celebrating German militarism and propagating racialism. The mutilated quotation of the title relates both to the physical state of the narrator, who has lost both legs and an arm in the service of this ideology, and to the mutilation of the classical heritage itself. The final phrase of the quotation, 'as the law commanded' ('wie das Gesetz es befahl'), does not occur in the story itself, but Böll could assume that his readers would insert it and thereby pose the question of resistance to unjust laws. It is a phrase to which Böll was to return on a number of occasions. In the same collection the narrator of 'Mein trauriges Gesicht' is beaten 'as the law commanded' by the police who arrest him (R 1, p. 275), and the phrase forms the title of Böll's review of H.G. Adler's study of the deportation of the Jews from Germany, *Der verwaltete Mensch* (E 3, pp. 120ff.). On the trial of Adolf Eichmann Böll commented that the word 'command' could not be permitted to absolve people from responsibility; more Germans than were suspected had refused to carry out unjust commands (E 1, pp. 450ff.). And the question of civil disobedience was to become acute once more in the 1980s when Böll joined in the peace movement's blockade of the US army base at Mutlangen.

'Lohengrins Tod' turns to the other side of the German cultural heritage, the Romantic Wagnerian one, again as abused by the Nazi leaders. The Lohengrin of this story is a thirteen-year-old boy, who has been fatally injured when he fell from a moving train in the attempt to steal coal for his family. He was born in 1933, 'when the first pictures of Hitler at the Bayreuth Festival were shown on all the newsreels' ('als die ersten Bilder Hitlers auf den Bayreuther Festspielen durch alle Wochenschauen liefen') (R 1, p. 249), and inflicted with his Wagnerian name by evidently pro-Nazi parents (one of his brothers is called Adolf). He has never been baptised — the Nazis were eclectic in their choice of motifs from Wagner. Like his mythological counterpart he refuses to divulge his name — 'never shalt thou question me' ('Nie sollst du mich befragen') (Wagner, 1848, p. 276) — but only because it embarrasses him. The parents who gave him the name have disappeared. His mother is probably dead; she appears to have been the less fanatical of the two, calling him 'Grini' and inveighing against the Nazis at times. His father is off on some dubious unspecified business — no Parsifal he. Nevertheless, there is something of the Lohengrin about this child. In the absence of his parents he has to look after his younger brothers, defending them from hunger and the neighbours. 'Lohengrins Tod' is rather more about the immediate post-war years, a time when armed soldiers shoot at young children and when doctors are engaged in illicit drug-trafficking, when ambulancemen are more concerned about making a profit out of the blanket given by a sympathetic woman to cover the injured boy than with humanitarianism. In this context the child-thief Lohengrin paradoxically becomes an epiphany of love and selflessness in a hostile, ugly world. This story, set before the Currency Reform, does not present an image of a 'class-less society', more one of a jungle in which only the strongest will survive.

The war itself is depicted in these stories not as action but as situation. There are no heroes; in contrast to *Das Vermächtnis*, nobody is given the opportunity to be heroic. The characters are invariably ordinary soldiers waiting to be sent off to their deaths ('Damals in Odessa', 'Wir Besenbinder'), sitting in pubs getting drunk ('Trunk in Petöcki', 'Aufenthalt in X', 'Unsere gute, alte Renée'), in dugouts under fire ('Wiedersehen in der Allee', 'Die Essenholer', 'In der Finsternis'), in a military hospital recovering from injury ('Auch Kinder sind Zivilisten') or, more usually, wounded on a stretcher waiting to be examined by a doctor ('Wanderer, kommst du nach Spa', 'Wiedersehen mit Drüng'). Keywords are indolence, boredom ('Faul-heit', 'Langeweile'), 'dirt, lice, hopelessness', ('Dreck', 'Läuse', 'Hoff-nungslosigkeit'), 'tired, desperate' ('müde', 'verzweifelt'), 'fear' ('Angst') and 'indifference' ('Gleichgültigkeit'). The war is lost, at best one can hope to survive. Nowhere is there any attempt to analyse the causes of the war or to attribute responsibility. Of the atrocities listed in the Nuremberg trials we find very little. 'In der Finsternis' relates an incident in which a German soldier is found stealing gold fillings from the corpses of Russian soldiers; but he appears as terrified as anyone and is at once dispatched by one of his comrades. An atmosphere of fatalism prevails, similar to that of the longer works of this time. In 'Aufenthalt in X' we encounter a soldier who runs amok, has to be restrained from shooting an officer and proclaims his intention of deserting and going into hiding. But the narrator himself reflects that '[there] is no escape', the 'thugs' of the Wehrmacht will catch up with one sooner or later. Böll has no alternative ideology to offer other than the conviction that when the vale of tears has been crossed the next world will be one of fulfilment and light. Human happiness is merely transitory ('Wiedersehen in der Allee'). That Böll distrusts German patriotism goes without saying, that he finds French patriotism equally pernicious is in this context revealing ('Unsere gute, alte Renée'). The narrator of 'Wiedersehen in der Allee' dismisses as 'empty words' the propa-ganda on *both* sides of the conflict.

With the stories set in the post-war period, more or less contem-poraneous with the time of writing, Böll began the documentation of the progress of West German society which was to be a hallmark of his future work. The Currency Reform is not referred to directly but for this group of stories it is a clear watershed. The narrator of 'Kumpel mit dem langen Haar' has just avoided arrest when the

65

police raided the premises of a gang of black-marketeers; that of 'An der Angel' has to sell his watch to a black-marketeer for the price of a railway platform ticket. The narrator of 'So ein Rummel', however, has been forced to seek legal employment now that the disorder has come to an end, and that of 'Kerzen für Maria' finds that with the end of power cuts the stock of candles which represent his sole assets have become almost worthless. 'Lohengrins Tod' showed the unacceptable face of the black-market economy; 'Geschäft ist Geschäft' suggests another side to it. The former black-marketeer has 'gone straight', is evidently well-nourished, looks self-assured and — the Hemingway conjunction is cleverly chosen — the narrator observes him scolding a little girl who does not have the money for a lollipop. The implications are Brechtian: the immediate post-war years were chaotic, but this disorder afforded the disadvantaged an opportunity to slip through the net, to make a living; the new order will be pitiless.

Just how pitiless it will be is suggested as early as 1948 in the story 'Der Mann mit den Messern', which can be read as an analysis of the psychology of post-war German society. Jupp has been left only with a canteen of cutlery out of the ruins of the war. With utter determination he has trained himself to become an expert knife-thrower, performing perilous acts in which, for example, one of his knives comes hurtling towards his head only to be intercepted at the last moment by a block of wood. He depends for his livelihood on giving people a thrill, the audience has to know 'that blood *might* flow' ('daß Blut fließen *könnte*') (R 1, p. 25). Coming so shortly after a war in which blood flowed copiously, this is cynical, but Jupp explains and excuses: they are all 'exhausted' ('erloschen') after the past upheavals and need to be stimulated; moreover they are frightened, 'dragging their fear behind them like a heavy shadow' ('schleppen die Angst hinter sich wie einen schweren Schatten') (p. 27), and by showing that he is not afraid he is giving them courage and the ability to forget. It is not too implausible to project this analysis into the future and explain the Economic Miracle in terms of the Germans' *Angst* and their willingness to forget the past. For the narrator, however, who allows himself to become Jupp's assistant, the man to be ringed with knives, the audience is a 'lustful, thousand-headed monster sitting expectantly in the darkness waiting to pounce' ('lüsternes, vieltausendköpfiges, gespanntes Ungeheuer, das im Finstern wie zum Sprung dasaß') (p. 32). Similarly monstrous behaviour is to be found in 'So ein Rummel', where the circus milieu as a symbol of post-war society is repeated; here a level-headed, business-like 'woman without an abdomen' negotiates with the narrator over a job, while encouraging her children to play games of 'war-wounded' and 'refugee' — the war and its consequences have already become a game. In 'Über die Brücke' there seems indeed to have been no break between pre-war and post-war society at all: the German housewife carries out her window-cleaning schedule regardless of whether the bridges have been blown up or not — to read this as the demonstration of a heroic will to survive (Schwarz, 1967, p. 15) is as much to miss the point as it would be to regard Brecht's Mother Courage as the epitome of positive bourgeois virtues. As the narrator of the earliest of the stories in the collection, 'Die Botschaft', realises when delivering the belongings of a dead comrade to his unfaithful widow: 'Then I knew that the war would never be over, never, as long as somewhere a wound was bleeding that it had inflicted' ('Da wußte ich, daß der Krieg niemals zu Ende sein würde, niemals, solange noch irgendwo eine Wunde blutete, die er geschlagen hat') (R 1, p. 11). It is this insistence by Böll that the war was not over, one which contrasted with the attitude of so many of his fellow-countrymen, that was to become the central theme of his work.

In a way it is artificial to distinguish between the war stories and those set in the post-war years. Böll implies an embarrassing continuity. In peacetime the individual is as helpless and as exposed to forces beyond his control as he was in war. The 'thugs' of 'Aufenthalt in X' have become the bureaucrats of 'An der Brücke' and 'Mein teures Bein'. A central image common to both groups of stories is the railway system with its waiting-rooms and station platforms where people are addressed by an anonymous, disembodied voice in a loudspeaker, have to obey instructions and depend on external authority. In *Der Zug war pünktlich* Andreas blamed the 'sonorous voices' of the railways for Germany's ills, voices which equally send the soldier to the front and the Jew to the gas chamber (R 1, pp. 72, 78). In 'Abschied', set in 1947, the 'sonorous voice' has become an 'official whip' (R 1, p. 220); the main enemy of the narrator of 'An der Angel' is the railway administration which he is convinced is preventing him from being united with his beloved. And although after the war the individual is not in immediate danger of losing his life, the solutions which Böll proposes are not very different. Both wartime 'Wiedersehen mit Drüng' and post-war 'Steh auf, steh doch auf' propose a transcendence of human suffering in the hereafter. The narrator of 'Aufenthalt in X' momentarily escapes by deliberately missing his train (as Böll himself did from time to time), and the narrator of 'An der Brücke' deliberately omits his girlfriend from the statistics of those whom he is supposed to be counting crossing the bridge; but the former knows he will be caught in the end, while the latter is told by his superiors that they always allow for errors of that kind. There remains only the purely individualistic satisfaction of having asserted one's independence for one moment, or, like Jupp's assistant in 'Der Mann mit den Messern', having found a niche, a job in which he needs only to stand still and dream for a while.

Those who interpret 'Mein trauriges Gesicht' as simply an attack on Communism therefore miss the point. For Böll bureaucracy is totalitarianism, depriving man of the choice even of smiling when he feels like it; 'Mein trauriges Gesicht' merely extends the image to its extreme. As it is the only story of the collection to have no 'real' setting in time or place one is tempted to assign it to the large group of utopian or dystopian stories which appeared in these years, partly under the influence of George Orwell's *Nineteen Eighty-Four* (Hermand, 1982). The story appeared in 1950, five years after Hitler's suicide. It cannot be coincidence that the narrator has just been released from prison after serving a five-year sentence for smiling on the day the 'boss' died and general mourning had been ordained (R 1, p. 274). Today he is given a ten-year sentence for looking melancholy when everyone has been ordered to be happy — the slogan of the present leader is 'Happiness and Soap' ('Glück und Seife'). Sadness, melancholy and mourning were states of mind for which the swift reconstruction of Germany left no time or place. Almost twenty years later Alexander and Margarete Mitscherlich were to publish their psycho-sociological study of the post-war West Germans, *Die Unfähigkeit zu trauern* (Mitscherlichs, 1967). In it they diagnose a narcissistic failure to confront the crimes of the past, to remember them and to work out an adequate response, a failure to carry through the 'work of mourning' ('Trauerarbeit'). Jochen Vogt has pointed out isolated similarities between Böll's and the Mitscherlichs' diagnosis (Vogt, 1978, pp. 73, 86, 136), without, I believe, seeing the full import. In places the Mitscherlichs' study reads like a commentary on the works of Böll. They give as an especially crass example of the mentality they are describing the decision to allow former soldiers to wear the decorations they received in the Third Reich — but without the swastika, thereby isolating the decoration from the actual circumstances under which it was received (Mitscherlichs, 1967, pp. 67f.; Vogt, 1978, p. 136). But Böll castigated the decision as early as 1956:

> In this connection the decision to allow the old war decorations *without* swastika becomes a mendacious trivialisation without historical parallel.

They were awarded *with* swastika, with the same swastika under which the murders took place in the concentration camps. Let those who want to bear their decorations bear them *with* swastika, then we shall know where to find those who are not our brothers.

(In diesem Zusammenhang wird der Entschluß, die alten Kriegsauszeichnungen *ohne* Hakenkreuz zuzulassen, zu einer lügnerischen Verniedlichung, die in der Geschichte noch ihresgleichen sucht. Sie wurden *mit* Hakenkreuz verliehen, mit jenem Hakenkreuz, unter dem in den Konzentrationslagern die Morde geschehen sind. Sollen die, die ihre Auszeichnungen tragen wollen, sie *mit* Hakenkreuz tragen: wir werden dann wissen, wo wir die zu suchen haben, die nicht unsere Brüder sind.)
(E 1, pp. 172f.)

A few years later he complained 'pain has not turned into wisdom, mourning has not become strength' ('Schmerz ist nicht Weisheit, Trauer nicht Kraft geworden') (E 1, p. 373). 'Mein trauriges Gesicht' contains the earliest example of the motif in Böll's works. The narrator watches the seagulls: 'But I too was hungry like them, tired too, but happy in spite of my mourning, for it was lovely to stand there with my hands in my pockets, watching the gulls and drinking my mourning' ('Aber auch ich war hungrig wie sie, auch müde, doch glücklich trotz meiner Trauer, denn es war schön, dort zu stehen, die Hände in den Taschen, den Möwen zuzusehen und Trauer zu trinken') (R 1, p. 269).

Böll does not choose to leave his readers in despair. It is not with 'Mein trauriges Gesicht' not yet with the 'monsters' of 'Der Mann mit den Messern' that he concludes his collection, but rather with the ostensibly more conciliatory 'Kerzen für Maria'. Inspired by an encounter with two innocent young people the narrator repents his sins and donates all his unsellable candles to the Virgin Mary. But there is a social aspect to the ending even of this story. For he also resolves to have nothing to do with the business world again. This implied indictment of 'Wirtschaftswunderdeutschland' is one which is to be repeated in Böll's later works.

4

Years of Hope (1949–1955)

The Federal Republic of Germany was founded in 1949 out of the three Western zones of occupation. A few weeks later the Soviet zone became the German Democratic Republic and the division of Germany was sealed. A constitution, the *Grundgesetz*, had been drawn up in May; elections for the new Federal Parliament, the first free general elections for over sixteen years, took place in August; Parliament met for the first time on 7 September. Theodor Heuss, a liberal, was elected President, while the real political power was in the hands of the Chancellor, Konrad Adenauer. Adenauer was the leader of the Christian Democratic Union (CDU), which with its Bavarian allies the Christian Social Union (CSU) had obtained the highest number of votes; however, his party was able to form the first government of the Federal Republic only with the support of the liberal Free Democratic Party (FDP) and the right-wing German Party, and Adenauer came to office with a majority of one. The CDU/CSU was to remain in power until 1969, and continued to be headed by Adenauer until 1963, when he retired, most reluctantly, at the age of eighty-seven.

It was in the years 1949 to 1955 that Böll established himself as a writer. Books by him appeared in each of these years. From 1953 his novels were serialised in national newspapers, usually the *Frankfurter Allgemeine Zeitung*, whose literary editor, Karl Korn, had become one of Böll's most enthusiastic patrons. In May 1951 Böll was invited to his first meeting of the 'Gruppe 47' in Bad Dürkheim, read 'Die schwarzen Schafe' to his assembled colleagues and was awarded the prize of 1,000 marks — only one vote ahead of Milo Dor. Hans Werner Richter has described the occasion. Böll was completely unknown; Richter had never suspected that there could be literary talent in Cologne. He was given the money in banknotes and at once went to the post office to send it off to his family: 'My children are starving and are sleeping in the coal box' ('Meine Kinder hungern und schlafen im Kohlenkasten') he told Richter (Richter, 1986, pp. 63–79). He continued to attend meetings of the group throughout the 1950s, reading from 'Nicht nur zur Weihnachtszeit' in 1952, *Irisches Tagebuch* in 1955 and 'Hauptstädtisches Journal' in 1957.

Recognition by the 'Gruppe 47' was important. Nevertheless, at the end of 1951 his contract with the Friedrich Middelhauve Verlag was terminated by mutual agreement; his books had not sold well. Richter encountered him again in Munich looking for a publisher who would give him an advance of 300 marks a month, but in vain. Middelhauve was a right-wing member of the FDP (EZ, p. 67); Böll eventually obtained a contract with the Cologne publishers Kiepen-heuer und Witsch, whose publishing profile tended more to the left, and it was with them that *Und sagte kein einziges Wort* marked Böll's first financial success, going into a second printing within the year. He did occasional work as a reader for them (E 3, p. 274), and from 1952 onwards he was also writing reviews and other contributions for such disparate newspapers and periodicals as the *Frankfurter Hefte*, then the voice of left-wing Catholicism (Limberg, p. 10), the conser-vative *Frankfurter Allgemeine Zeitung*, the more liberal *Süddeutsche Zeitung*, the Hamburg *Sonntagsblatt*, literary journals like *Das literari-sche Deutschland*, *Die Literatur* and *Akzente*, and a number of others. He had also found an outlet for his writings in the radio, then one of the most important patrons of young writers (E 1, pp. 91f.). 'Nicht nur zur Weihnachtszeit' was first broadcast in 1951, a radio play 'Die Brücke von Berczaba', based on a chapter of *Wo warst du, Adam?*, in June 1952, and Böll gave his first radio talk, 'Jünger Merkurs' in November of the same year. Besides the prize of the Gruppe 47 he received the René Schickele Prize in 1952, the Süddeutscher Erzählerpreis and the Kritikerpreis für Literatur in 1953, and the prize of the *Tribune de Paris* in 1954. In 1953 the success of *Und sagte kein einziges Wort* enabled him to move with his wife and three sons into a house of his own in the suburbs of Cologne. In the same year he was one of a group of West German writers who visited Paris to meet French colleagues, and France was the first foreign country to publish his works and further his reputation — *Documents* and *Allemagne d'Aujourd'hui* published translations of his shorter works from 1951 onwards, and in 1953 the latter journal even printed Böll's first autobiographical statement (E 1, pp. 113ff.).

Looking back in 1985 Böll had no clear memory of the founding of the Federal Republic. A more important caesura had been the Currency Reform of the previous year. Nevertheless he voted for the Christian Democrats in 1949, and 'probably' again in 1953, al-though by 1957 he was no longer willing to support them (Limberg, p. 10). As we have seen, Böll was initially inspired by an ideal of Christian socialism, one which the CDU's Ahlen programme of 1947 seemed ready to realise. Although the programme on which the CDU eventually fought the election was far removed from its initial manifesto, Böll could, it seems, still believe that the Christian Democrats were his best hope for Germany's future. It was the successor to the Catholic Centre Party of the Weimar Republic, which his father had always supported, although it had widened its appeal to include Protestants as well. In view of the attacks he later made on the Centre politicians Kaas and von Papen, it might seem surprising that Böll should support such a post-war grouping. His vote for the CDU may well have been a vote against the alternative. The Social Democratic Party (SPD), unlike the Christian Democrats, was not a new party. Alone of the Weimar parties it had stood up to Hitler and voted against his Enabling Legislation in 1933. Its leaders had had to emigrate or had been put in concentration camps, tortured and murdered. Because of this the SPD had the moral standing to adopt a more overtly nationalistic line than the other parties — and did so. In a famous debate in November 1949 when it was announced that the Federal Government had made concessions over German sovereignty in the Saar and the Ruhr in exchange for a partial ending of the Allies' dismantling of German industrial plant, Adenauer was accused by Kurt Schumacher, the leader of the SPD, of being the 'Chancellor of the Allies'. The SPD was the party most concerned to bring about the reunification of Germany, whereas Adenauer was much more interested in integrating the Federal Republic into the political and economic system of Western Europe and the United States. Böll's whole upbringing had made him distrust 'Prussia' and its capital Berlin, and the reunification of Germany was not a priority for him; in this he resembled Adenauer himself, who in the early 1920s had even supported the creation of a quasi-autonomous Rhineland state. The SPD was in a situation not unlike that of the *émigré* writers whom Böll and his contemporaries equally unfairly distrusted. Later, however, when Böll reviewed the first volume of Adenauer's memoirs in 1965 one of the reproaches he made of his fellow-Rhinelander was the Social Democratic one that he had sealed the division of Germany and locked its two halves into the military complexes of the two Great Powers (E 2, p. 180).

In 1967 Böll described the years 1945 to 1955 as 'a time full of hope' ('eine hoffnungsvolle Zeit'); this hope had, however, been progressively dashed as the Germans found re-militarisation on the one hand and capitalism on the other forced upon them (Q, p. 141). In the first half dozen years of Christian Democracy the occupying powers gave up their rights one by one, until in 1955, when the Paris agreements took effect, the Federal Republic had obtained virtual autonomy (to this day the occupying powers retain certain residual rights). This was paid for, however, by a simultaneous integration into the Western Alliance. Re-militarisation was a product of the cold war and especially of the Korean War, which broke out in June 1950. A few months later the three Western powers had resolved that the Federal Republic should be rearmed; Gustav Heinemann, later to become the first Social Democratic President of the Federal Republic, resigned his post as Minister of the Interior and left the CDU in protest against Adenauer's encouragement of the discussions. In due course and as one of the provisions of the Paris agreements, the Federal Republic became a member of NATO, and at the beginning of January 1956 the first units of the Bundeswehr were formed. It was, according to Böll, the realisation that the powers which had liberated Germany were going to betray them in this matter of rearmament that activated his political interest: 'That was very obvious, round about '50, '51, that we were to be re-militarised again, that they were treating the old Nazis and real war criminals very, very tenderly, letting them out of prison and hiding them somewhere, old generals, politicians too' ('Das war sehr deutlich zu spüren so 50, 51, daß wir wieder aufgerüstet werden sollten, daß man sehr, sehr gnädig mit alten Nazis und regelrechten Kriegsverbrechern umging, die alle entlassen wurden und so irgendwo versteckt, alte Generäle, auch Politiker') (Q, p. 138). One of Böll's earliest non-literary publications was a review of the film *The Desert Fox*, in which James Mason plays Rommel. The film was popular among West Germans, wrote Böll, because the self-sacrifice of Rommel cleansed them of their guilt, and he observed: 'No doubt about it: the time of the Allied stain remover has begun. . . . The visit to collective guilt is now being succeeded by the detour of forgiveness' ('Kein Zweifel: die alliierte Fleckwasserperiode hat begonnen. . . . Dem Besuch der Kollektivschuld folgt nun der Bogen der Verzeihung') (E 1, p. 45). While there are obvious differences between Böll's Lieutenant Schelling in *Das Vermächtnis* and the historical Erwin Rommel — the latter, as Böll points out, was still convinced of Hitler's uprightness in 1944 — it is nonetheless indicative of a harder line taken by Böll in these years.

A strong anti-militarist theme runs through these early essays. In a review of Alfred Andersch's autobiography *Die Kirschen der Freiheit* (1952), in which the author traces the steps which led to his desertion from the German army in Italy in 1944, Böll noted the silence which had fallen over the anti-war books of the immediate post-war years and the preference for the 'gentle war literature of the Romantics and the memoirs of the generals' ('milde Kriegsliteratur der Romantiker, die Memoiren der Generale'), which he found sinister in the face of threatening re-militarisation (E 1, p. 66). In the same year he wrote enthusiastically on Jaroslav Hasek's *Schwejk* (ibid., pp. 68–70), but a year later less so on James Jones's *From Here to Eternity*, which he found more ready to compromise on the military life (ibid., pp. 82–5). He preferred William Saroyan's *The Adventures of Wesley Jackson*, which he reviewed in 1954 and related directly to the current developments: 'We know one thing only: by re-militarisation they are applying the one means we know for sure has always had disastrous consequences' ('Wir wissen nur eins: Sie wenden — indem sie remilitarisieren — das einzige Mittel an, von dem wir genau wissen, daß es immer unheilvolle Folgen gehabt hat') (ibid., p. 139).

His attack on the decision to allow former soldiers to wear their decorations but without the swastika (E 1, pp. 172f.) implied that re-militarisation was directly related to the West Germans' failure to face up to the crimes of the National Socialists, their speedy forget-ting of the past as soon as it was convenient. In his review of Adenauer's memoirs Böll draw attention to the cynicism with which Adenauer had suggested to the Americans in 1950 that any of those who had been imprisoned for their part in the Nazi crimes could be released under the pretext that they were ill (E 2, p. 184). The two most notorious cases in which highly suspect former Nazis were rehabilitated were those of Hans Globke and Theodor Oberländer. The latter had been a professor in Danzig, Königsberg and Prague and had demanded the expulsion of the Polish population from the areas annexed by the Germans in 1939. As leader of the Expellees Party he was included in Adenauer's coalition government of 1953 and again in 1957, by which time he had joined the CDU. Globke was an even more sinister case. He had been a top civil servant in the Ministry of the Interior under Goebbels and had in 1936 written a commentary to Hitler's anti-Semitic laws; he became one of Adenauer's closest colleagues, first heading a government depart-ment, in 1953 becoming permanent secretary in the Chancellor's office, and accompanying Adenauer on all his travels. In 1982 Böll suggested that the presence of Globke was one reason that so few *émigrés* returned to West Germany after the war (EZ, p. 61). The process of information and enlightenment was a very slow one. In 1952 only 32 per cent of West Germans regarded Germany as having been responsible for the Second World War (Grosser, 1974, p. 307), and although reconciliation with Israel and reparations for the crimes that had been committed against the Jewish people were cornerstones of Adenauer's foreign policy, sealed in the Reparations Treaty of 1952, Böll registered with dismay in 1954 that in a school class of forty it had turned out that not one pupil had heard of the

Holocaust (E 1, p. 133).

While West Germany was normalising relations with the Western world, at home the 'Economic Miracle' was getting under way. The CDU had abandoned its Ahlen programme of extensive nationalisation. Instead, under the guidance of Economics Minister Ludwig Erhard, it pursued the goal of the 'social market economy', designed to remove as many bureaucratic restrictions on industry and commerce as possible while allowing state intervention where necessary to stimulate the economy and to look after the needs of the poorer and weaker members of the community. At the same time financial aid was pouring in from the United States under the terms of the Marshall Plan. Food rationing ended on 1 March 1950. In the same month a bill to encourage house building with the help of public money was passed. Thereafter the building industry flourished: between 1950 and 1955 almost 3 million homes were completed and unemployment dropped accordingly. Production limitations for West German industry were abolished; the founding of the European Coal and Steel Community in 1952 with the Federal Republic as a member was a further stimulus to the economy. The Volkswagen 'Beetle' began to triumph in the car markets both at home and abroad. In 1954 the Federal Republic's football team even won the World Cup. Ten years after the end of the war it could seem as if everything was forgiven and forgotten. In a Calvinist kind of way the West Germans seemed justified by faith, faith in their own efforts; their material success demonstrated to the world that they were indeed of the elect.

Böll was not convinced. In an essay of 1952 he described the office blocks which were rising out of the ruins in the German cities as 'unreal', 'a theatre set'; he feared that they were buildings from which people were going to be 'administered', not only by state organisations but by private ones, insurance companies, banks and the like. As we have seen, anti-individualist bureaucracy was already a theme of the early stories. Böll continued with a statement of his artistic credo, one which was to remain valid for the rest of his career: 'It is our task to point out that man does not exist merely to be administered — and that the ravages done to our world are neither merely external nor so trivial that we can presume to heal them in a few short years' ('Es ist unsere Aufgabe, daran zu erinnern, daß der Mensch nicht nur existiert, um verwaltet zu werden — und daß die Zerstörungen in unserer Welt nicht nur äußerer Art sind und nicht so geringfügiger Natur, daß man sich anmaßen kann, sie in wenigen Jahren zu heilen') (E 1, p. 35). This was some distance from the notion of 'ordering reality into the immanent symbolism of the world' that he had been propagating in 1949. His stance was thus pro-individual and anti-materialist, and his voice was to remind his compatriots that the Nazis had not merely damaged Germany in a material sense. The term 'Economic Miracle' itself he denounced as 'blasphemous' — miracles were worked by God (E 1, p. 134). In 1953, in an unpublished review of Francis Stuart's *The Pillar of Cloud*, which describes the Germany of the years 1945 to 1948, he wrote scathingly of the 'whipped-cream Germans' ('Schlagsahne-Deutsche'); here too for the first time he used the term 'restoration' to describe post-Currency-Reform society (E 1, pp. 119f.).

By 'restoring' the old 'middle-class' values of 'family egoism' and a 'striving for possessions' the 'Restaurationszeit', Böll believed, had destroyed the unprecedented degree of equality created in the immediate post-war years. From 1949 onwards this equality gave way to competitiveness and a hierarchy based on wealth, justified by Adenauer in the name of 'Christian values' which had to be protected against any however mild form of 'socialism'. Reviewing Adenauer's memoirs, Böll remarked how frequently the term 'Christian ideals' recurred and how it turned out to mean no more than private property and the importance of a strong army with which to defend it (E 2, p. 178). The apparent success of West German capitalism placed most dreams of socialism out of the question. What was taking place simultaneously in the 'socialist' part of post-war Germany, the German Democratic Republic, was no encouragement. The uprising of 17 June 1953 and its suppression by Soviet troops helped Adenauer to win his second term of office; the brutally enforced collectivisation of East German farms was a nationalisation which the Ahlen programme 'had not foreseen' (Limberg, p. 10). Nevertheless Böll refused to allow the deficiencies of the East to blind him to the weaknesses of the West: slogans such as 'fatherland, honour, nation' were just as abstract and empty as 'socialist realism' (E 1, p. 103).

What Böll meant by 'middle-class values' ('Bürgerlichkeit') is not immediately clear; it is not in the first place the self-confident patrician 'middle-classness' of a Thomas Mann, but rather a petty-bourgeois mentality which places greater weight on outer respectability than on inner rectitude, prefers the status quo to experiment, stasis to dynamic change (see Amery, 1963; Schröter, 1982, p. 32). Two short satirical pieces of the early 1950s, 'Die schwarzen Schafe' and 'Nicht nur zur Weihnachtszeit' may clarify Böll's attitude.

One of the king-pins of bourgeois respectability is the steady job. In 'Die schwarzen Schafe' Uncle Otto, the 'black sheep' of the family, has no profession. He has plenty of plans, each of which will make his fortune, but none of which he carries out; instead he terrorises his relatives by borrowing money from them at the end of every visit. Yet Uncle Otto is charming, an excellent conversational-ist, well-informed on every subject under the sun, particularly good with children, and to the utter shame of his family, when he dies in a traffic accident having just collected a large sum of money which he had won in a lottery, they find that he has made a note of every little sum of money he had borrowed from each of them over the years. His nephew and godson, the narrator of the story, becomes the 'black sheep' of the new generation. He too has plans, but never fulfils them: within a single afternoon he decides to be in turn a painter, a gardener, a mechanic and a sailor, falls asleep believing he is a born teacher only to awake in the conviction that he is pre-destined to become a customs officer. His one 'lapse' comes when he is persuaded to take a job in a joinery; the trashy furniture which is turned out there further convinces him of the overriding importance of his own 'freedom'. He too will repay his debts to conventional society and he hopes that his black sheep successor will do so too: the closing words of the story are nicely ambiguous: 'The main thing is that he owes them nothing' ('Hauptsache, daß er ihnen nichts schuldig bleibt') (R 1, p. 307). The conflict between individual liberty and the middle-class profession is a theme to which Böll returns again and again in the works of these years. Fred Bogner, in the novel *Und sagte kein einziges Wort*, changes his job every three years because he cannot take any paid occupation seriously. Con-versely, a whole series of stories involve a bizarre profession of one kind or another: 'Der Lacher' (1952) is about a professional cla-queur whose laughter is used for radio-effects and to encourage people to laugh at third-rate comedians' jokes. 'Bekenntnis eines Hundefängers' (1953) is about a man who chases up unregistered dogs. The narrator of 'Hier ist Tibten' (1953) holds two doctorates but has the profession of railway station announcer. A little later 'Der Wegwerfer' (1956) describes the profession of the man who saves people's time for them by sorting out their mail and throwing away unwanted 'bumph' — he is also planning to become an 'unpacker' in a large store, where he will save customers the trouble of unpacking the goods they buy. The satire in 'Der Wegwerfer' is clearly at the expense of industrial, consumerist society. In the others the bizarre profession is a parody of the respectable middle-class one. This becomes clear when we read 'Es wird etwas gesche-hen' (1956), where the narrator describes the hectic atmosphere in Wunsiedel's factory: Wunsiedel's deputy had while still a student supported seven children and a paralysed wife, been a sales representative for four different firms and still managed to pass his examinations with distinction; while doing a doctorate in psychology and local history his secretary had supported a paralysed husband and four children by knitting, breeding alsatians and singing in nightclubs under the stage-name of 'Vamp 7'. When Wunsiedel dies of a heart attack the narrator joins a funeral undertaking as a professional mourner, a job which offers him the satisfaction of doing nothing and having time to meditate. Böll distinguishes between conveyor-belt work in a factory and the work of the craftsman. In 'Die schwarzen Schafe' the narrator notes that in their spare time the workmen in the factory make very serviceable furniture, simple footstools or boxes which will last for generations. Similarly at the end of *Wo warst du, Adam?* Feinhals, the architect, realises how important it is to know one's trade and build 'simple, good houses' (R 1, p. 444) — and not to take oneself too seriously. As a writer Böll was himself in the privileged position of the independent craftsman — and it is the craftsmanship of the writer that he emphasised when describing his profession (I, p. 355). His critique of the work ethos, what he later called 'Leistungsverweigerung', is grounded in the belief that other values are more important. After the war the Germans earned the often awestruck respect of their European neighbours by their industriousness, their dedication to productivity and efficiency. Böll implies that this industriousness was a desperate attempt to forget the past, the unwillingness to 'meditate', or, in the Mitscherlichs' terms, to 'mourn'.

The other central motif of Böll's critique of middle-class values is the family. If Böll's autobiography takes the latent form of the Buddenbrooks' 'Decline of a family', the satire 'Nicht nur zur Weihnachtszeit' does so even more obviously. Its opening words could hardly be more direct: 'Among our relations symptoms of decline are becoming apparent' ('In unserer Verwandtschaft machen sich Verfallserscheinungen bemerkbar') (R 2, p. 11). The self-consciously pompous style of the narrator is a further echo of Thomas Mann, albeit of the later Mann of for example, *Doktor Faustus*. Respectability, that quintessentially bourgeois virtue, has, the narrator goes on to inform us, become no more than a 'crust' beneath which the moral fibre of this family is being eaten away. The problem began with the war — not that this family suffered anything more serious than the loss of their annual ceremony of decorating the Christmas tree, for the reverberations of the falling bombs disturbed the delicate mechanism of the mechanical dwarfs and of the angel which whispered 'Peace'. Uncle Franz made the same kind of profits with his greengrocer's business in the war as he had done in peacetime, they had a secure air-raid shelter and the two sons escaped active service. But the Christmas tree had been the centre of Aunt Milla's life, decorating it had been her special weakness, a weakness which, the narrator admits, is 'fairly wide-spread in our fatherland' (R 2, p. 13). When war comes to an end the ceremony is reinstated at the first opportunity, but when it is time for the decorations to be dismantled and the tree to be taken down, Aunt Milla has a hysterical fit from which she recovers only when the tree is hastily set up again. From this point on the family experiences the nightmare of keeping Christmas going all the year around. They adjust to circumstances, Uncle Franz signs a contract with a firm which will provide a regular supply of trees, a retired priest is persuaded to come every evening to converse with Aunt Milla, the children and other members of the family are gradually replaced with actors and wax models. 'The festival continues' ('die Feier wird fortgesetzt'), the narrator concludes (R 2, p. 34). But while outward appearances are kept up, Uncle Franz has taken a mistress, cousin Franz has become a boxer — a most 'unbourgeois' profession — , his brother Johannes has joined the Communist Party and their sister Lucie has begun to patronise dubious night-clubs.

The story is a satire on post-war West German restorative society: a society which is unwilling to remember the disagreeable events of the war — the narrator even feels obliged to apologise for men-tioning them. The Christmas celebrations have lost contact with their original cause: the peace-whispering angel was silenced not because of the military aims of the Nazis but for purely mechanical reasons. Their restoration is the exemplar for the political restora-tion, and Christmas is the traditional family festival *par excellence*. The importance of the family institution for German life is suggested by the fact that alone among the major European countries, from 1953 to 1969 the Federal Republic had a separate Ministry for Families. Helmut Schelsky saw the German family as a bulwark against industrialisation and collectivism, a place where the individ-ual could retain his identity, the one part of German society which even Hitler was unable to penetrate. Böll's own experience in the 1930s might seem to confirm this view. On the other hand Rolf Dahrendorf has suggested that the family is a pre-industrial, back-ward-looking phenomenon, fostering private rather than social virtues, respectability, tidiness, rather than good citizenship, apolitical and therefore potentially undemocratic and unwilling to resist a Hitler so long as he left it alone (Dahrendorf, 1965). The story 'Nicht nur zur Weihnachtszeit' is a good touchstone for these opposing attitudes, for it was the first work by Böll to provoke public controversy over these precise issues. When North-West German Radio in Hamburg repeated the broadcast of the story on 30 December 1952 the director of the Protestant Church's office for broadcasting affairs, Hans-Werner von Meyenn, objected in an open letter to Böll: while accepting that the commercialisation of Christmas was widespread and unfortunate, he claimed that it could become so only in a world in which rationality and abstract intellectualism was predominant. Man needed his 'Gemüt', that untranslatable German word which relates to the emotions, sentiment, the life of the soul, and which is associated with such family occasions as Christmas and other religious festivals; Böll was with his story contributing to the stunting of the 'Gemüt' in our age. Von Meyenn pointed to developments on the other side of the Iron Curtain, where the 'tree of German Christmases' was under attack from atheist Communism and where the 'Gemüt' was in especial danger. In this polemic we are reminded of Schelsky's diagnosis of the family with its rites and festivals as a haven of anti-totalitarianism in the Third Reich. Böll's reply was uncompromising. The values of the 'Gëmut' had *not* prevented the German family man with his love of children and animals from doing his duty even when that duty had consisted in murdering people in a concentration camp. Brutality and 'Gemüt' were, said Böll, closely related (E 1, p. 77); Eugen Kogon had made a similar point a few years earlier (Kogon, 1947, p. 50). Their relationship had been one of the themes of *Wo warst du, Adam?*, which appeared a few weeks before the first broadcast of 'Nicht nur zur Weihnachtszeit' in 1951. One of the scenes of this novel begins with the description of the driver of a green furniture van and his mate on a night journey. When they stop for a break the one proudly shows the other a photograph of his three-year-old daughter with her pet rabbit; he is on the point of bringing out a photograph of his wife when there is a tumult in the van which he quells by banging on the doors with his submachine-gun before returning to their conversation. It emerges that they are taking a consignment of Jews to an extermination camp. Later we hear that the victims could not imagine that the person who had banged on the doors like that could be human at all. Having 'Gemüt', being a family man, was for Böll no guarantee of humanity.

Böll concluded his defence of 'Nicht nur zur Weihnachtszeit' by declaring that he did not believe that it did any harm 'to give our West German restorative self-regard a shock'. Von Meyenns's letter may be viewed also as documenting the new conservatism in cultural as well as in social attitudes. Böll's report on the meeting with

French colleagues in Paris in 1953 is interesting for his refusal to take sides in the arguments which he says broke out over, for example, Ernst Jünger, or to identify with any of the post-war groupings he mentions — 'left, right, conservative and Jacobin' (E 1, pp. 90ff.). Nevertheless, he had already, in two important manifestos, 'Bekenntnis zur Trümmerliteratur' (1952) and 'Der Zeitgenosse und die Wirklichkeit' (1953) made his own position clear. In the latter, as we have seen, Böll stated his belief that the 'key' to reality was what was topical and everyday. 'Bekenntnis zur Trümmerliteratur', however, is the more famous. Appropriately enough he was invited to read it to an audience in the waiting-room of the main railway station in Cologne as part of a series of 'Wednesday conversations' (Weninger, 1952). He later described the context in which it was written: critics were attacking the literature of these years for concentrating on the unedifying aspects of life, the ruins and the black market, and for failing to provide a vision of wholeness, a 'whole world' ('heile Welt') (Lenz, p. 73). Some conservative critics, among them Friedrich Sieburg, had retained their position of authority through the Third Reich into the 1950s (Hinderer, 1971; Schonauer, 1977). A typical statement is Sieburg's:

> Public life has become sensibly conservative, sensibly inasmuch as it no longer permits deficiencies to become institutions. To be sure, there are still those who have lost their rights, who are humiliated, insulted, but in so far as they are a social phenomenon their condition is altered by the State or by the various power groups. The Federal Republic has succeeded in gaining a good conscience and will not allow intellectuals, artists and writers to disturb it.

> (Das öffentliche Leben ist einsichtsvoll konservativ geworden, einsichtsvoll insofern, als es nicht mehr duldet, daß Mißstände zu Institutionen werden. Wohl gibt es noch Entrechtete, Erniedrigte und Beleidigte, aber wo sie sozial faßbar sind, da wird ihr Zustand vom Staat oder von den Machtgruppen geändert. Es ist der Bundesrepublik gelungen, sich ein gutes Gewissen zu verschaffen, und sie wird sich von den Intellektuellen, den Künstlern und Schriftstellern darin nicht stören lassen.)
> (cit. Schonauer, 1977, p. 247)

These words were to be echoed by Schelsky twenty years later. Against it Böll declared in his essay that it was precisely the task of the writer to remind his readers that not everyone had survived the war intact, that there was suffering and injustice and exploitation in the world. He suggested that the Revolution of 1789 might have come as less of a surprise to the French nobility had their reading included more descriptions of the real world than games of blind

81

man's buff and shepherds and shepherdesses and he pointed to Charles Dickens as a model for the responsible writer. In conclusion he cleverly turned the tables on the conservative critics with their classicist leanings by pointing out that Homer, the father of European literature, told of war, of the destruction of Troy, of the return of the soldier Odysseus; his literature too was 'the literature of war, ruins and homecoming soldiers' ('Kriegs-, Trümmer- und Heimkehrerliteratur') (E 1, p. 35).

The first half of the 1950s was not an especially fruitful one for German literature. Böll never tired of pointing out how his generation had been decimated in the war and that it was not surprising if there was a dearth of new writers — Wolfgang Borchert, one obvious talent, had died in 1947 a belated victim of the war. H. M. Waidson's 'mid-twentieth-century survey' of post-war literature, which appeared in 1959, contains a large number of names which are almost forgotten today (Waidson, p. 1959). Ironically it was in 1959, with Günter Grass's novel *Die Blechtrommel*, that West German literature first become widely noticed outside the German borders. Its 'provinciality' has been diagnosed (Drews, 1980, p. 6). Heinrich Vormweg suggests that what was 'new' was the turning away from the early political reportage, a 'return to the ivory tower' (ibid., p. 12), and in his introduction to a 1962 anthology of fifteen years of the 'Gruppe 47' Fritz J. Raddatz was astonished to discover that the words 'Hitler, concentration camp, atomic bomb, SS, Nazi, Siberia' were wholly absent from the collection (Richter, 1962, p. 55). Böll's writings form an honourable contrast. Otherwise the strengths of German literature lay in the field of lyric poetry, where Paul Celan, Ingeborg Bachmann and Günter Eich made their distinctive contributions in what was on the whole a hermetic, modernist mode in the European post-Baudelaire tradition, although even this was a critical distortion of the time, not least in the case of Ingeborg Bachmann (Witte, 1983). Significantly enough, in his words on the death of Ingeborg Bachmann it was her political commitment that Böll stressed, quoting the lines from the poem 'Früher Mittag' (1952): 'Seven years later / in a house of the dead, / yesterday's executioners / drink dry the golden goblet' ('Sieben Jahre später / in einem Totenhaus, / trinken die Henker von gestern / den goldenen Becher aus') (E 3, p. 63); lines which he adapted later for his own poem on the newspapers *Bild* and *Welt*, 'sieben Jahre und zwanzig später' (H, pp. 39f.).

Böll's sympathetic review of Alfred Andersch's autobiography *Die Kirschen der Freiheit* in 1952 has been mentioned; he regarded it as a 'clarion call' in the sultry cultural climate of West Germany in which generals' memoirs viewed the war through rosy spectacles

(E1, pp. 66f.). Two other major writers of prose fiction were Arno Schmidt and Wolfgang Koeppen. The former was 'a revelation': *Brand's Haide* (1951) was 'unforgotten' (Lenz, p. 50). The novel is a fine example of the 'literature of returning soldiers' ('Heimkehrer-literatur'); its evocations of the shortages — of food, of clothes, of electricity, of lodgings — are indeed memorable, and unlike Borchert's *Draußen vor der Tür* it describes them without pathos, in a tone rather of self-deprecating irony. In three important respects Schmidt's writing differs from Böll's. The one is the historical dimension which it contains — the church archives which the narrator is researching contain accounts of earlier refugees — and related to this is the literary dimension, the direct allusions to Fouqué, Wieland and others; Böll's early writings on the whole lack any sense of history, whether literary or political, where there are literary allusions they serve rather to debunk a misused tradition, as in 'Lohengrins Tod', than to make it serve contemporary needs. Another is Schmidt's idiosyncratic style, its mixture of the colloquial, even slangy, with powerful, highly poetic language, English phrases, quotations from eighteenth-century authors, and various typographical devices, what Böll calls the 'gimmicks' ('Spielereien') which Schmidt became famous for. By contrast the style of Böll's early prose is relatively conventional; his attempts at the grand style using metaphor, simile and personification are usually unfortunate. And finally there is Schmidt's militant atheism, which prompted Böll to remark in a review of the later *Das steinerne Herz* that the atheists can be just as determinedly dogmatic as the Christians (E 1, p. 207).

Wolfgang Koeppen had published novels already in the 1930s and is in some ways closer to the older generation of the Jüngers and the Bergengruens. But the three novels he published between 1951 and 1955, *Tauben im Gras*, *Das Treibhaus* and *Der Tod in Rom*, are very clearly works of the post-war years in their setting, themes and styles and ones which link with Böll's preoccupations of that time. Koeppen is not even mentioned by Waidson, although today he appears a major figure. In many ways his novels have greater political bite to them than Böll's; *Der Tod in Rom* concerns the rehabilitation of former Nazis; *Das Treibhaus* was regarded at the time as a *roman à clef* on the political scene in Bonn, and was rejected because events in East Germany at the time of its appearance made it appear inopportune. Linder suggests that Koeppen's political commitment came too early for the Federal Republic; Böll's came later and for this reason he was successful both in the 1950s and later (Linder, 1986, pp. 114ff.). Böll was one of those who elected Koeppen to the office of 'town writer' (*Stadtschreiber*) in Bergen-Enkheim in 1974 (*Frankfurter Allgemeine Zeitung* 31.8.1974, p. 21).

Both Schmidt and Koeppen are more obviously 'modernist' writers than Böll, who has usually been regarded as a realist in the nineteenth-century tradition. That this is at best a half-truth is clear from the number of occasions in the early short stories when everyday reality is transcended in a mystical experience of the hereafter, usually when the narrator dies and his death is merely an incident on the road to fulfilment. In fact Böll's novels of the 1950s bear many of the marks of modernism as the latter was perceived in West Germany at the time, when it was widely felt by critics and scholars that German literature had to catch up with international developments from which National Socialist policies had excluded it. The 'modernist' novel, for example, distrusted the external 'omniscient', commenting narrator–focaliser. In 1954 Theodor W. Adorno declared that anyone who wrote like the nineteenth-century novelist Stifter was 'lying'; the excision of the omniscient narrator was the only possible response to the situation of the individual in an absurd, bureaucratised world (Adorno, 1954). Plot was to be reduced to a minimum. At the 1955 meeting with French colleagues, among them Robbe-Grillet, all, Böll reported, including presumably himself, had rejected both the plot novel and the psychological novel (E 1, p. 148). Narrated time was similarly reduced; in its place came 'spatialisation' techniques, using montage and leitmotivs (Frank, 1958; Reid, 1967). Montage is especially interesting. Brecht regarded it as central to his concept of 'epic', i.e. narrative theatre, contrasting with traditional 'dramatic' theatre's adherence to the concept of organic growth (Brecht, 1930, p. 20). Georg Lukács, on the other hand, rejected montage as a mere 'gimmick' (Lukács, 1938), and in the 1950s Lukács was the chief protagonist of socialist realism, which Böll in these years categorically rejected (E 1, pp. 103, 160) — not until the late 1960s under the impact of his reading of Solzhenitsyn did he admit that it had its virtues (E 2, p. 329). *Wo warst du, Adam?*, which Böll published in 1951, is significant in this context. One of Böll's own favourite works (I, p. 25), it takes as its subject matter the war but succeeds in developing forms which much more satisfactorily describe it than in the earlier longer stories. In 1961, in the first major interview he gave for publication, when he had published the more complex *Billard um halbzehn*, he denied there was any real difference of technique between the novels he had written from *Wo warst du, Adam?* onwards, and stated that it was with this work that he had first devised a system of colours as an aid to composition. He used a kind of diagram with three layers, the one

representing the present, the second the level of time remembered in
the reflections of the characters, the third consisting of the leitmotivs; each leitmotiv and each character was allotted a different colour
(I, p. 17). He continued to employ this technique for his later novels;
reproductions of the graphs have been published for *Haus ohne Hüter*
(anon., 1961, p. 71) and *Ende einer Dienstfahrt* (Schröter, 1982, pp.
74f.), and Böll had his own personal greetings card printed with a
coloured reproduction of that for *Gruppenbild mit Dame*. It is a device
which has more to do with montage than with organic growth.

The montage technique in *Wo warst du, Adam?* is most evident in
the relative autonomy of the nine chapters of the novel. Each
chapter is centred on a separate incident, and in few cases does this
incident lead on to the chapter which follows. From earliest times
critics suggested that *Wo warst du, Adam?* was not a novel at all,
merely a collection of short stories (Andersch, 1951; Kalow, 1955;
Stresau, 1964). However, Böll always insisted that it was a 'Roman',
and the critics' reservations are perhaps indicative of their own
expectations based on nineteenth-century forms rather than of what
Böll actually wrote.

The 'plot' — Böll himself described it as 'very economical' (I,
p. 19) — relates to the fortunes of a group of soldiers in the closing
months of the war on the Eastern front. In a review Böll drew
attention to the pattern of the 'group hero' which is to be found in
many war novels, whether Werner Beumelburg's heroic *Gruppe
Bosemüller* or Remarque's pacifist *Im Westen nichts Neues* (E 1, p. 460).
Wo warst du, Adam? begins by leading the reader to expect a similar
pattern. In Chapter 1 we are introduced briefly in turn to a general,
a colonel, a lieutenant, a captain and finally to the private soldier
Feinhals, as the thousand-man-strong battalion is divided into smaller
and smaller units. But none of these figures turns out to be aware of the
others, there is no group solidarity in this novel. The colonel,
Bressen, becomes the central figure of Chapter 2, the lieutenant is
the Greck of Chapter 4, the captain is Bauer, whose history is
recounted in Chapter 3, while Feinhals is the major figure of
Chapters 5 and 9, and to a lesser extent also of Chapters 6 and 8. In
the concluding chapter the general and the colonel of the opening
are observed being taken for interrogation by the Americans; Feinhals, alone of the others, has survived, but at the end he too dies,
shot by a fanatic of his own side. The technique is not unlike that of
Die Toten bleiben jung by Anna Seghers, which had appeared two
years earlier. Although Böll's novel is on a much smaller scale, he
still manages to introduce the stories of a number of other characters: Dr Schmitz and Sergeant Schneider, who remain behind with

the wounded while the Red Army advances; Finck, who has been sent on an absurd mission to buy a case of Tokay wine for his superior officer and finds himself dragging it across the enemy line of fire; Filskeit, the fanatical commandant of an extermination camp; Frau Susan, an innkeeper; and Ilona, the Jewish teacher with whom Feinhals falls in love and who is transported to the extermination camp administered by Filskeit. With the exception of Feinhals, none of these characters is allowed to develop; each has his scene and departs, usually in a violent death. Feinhals's development is schematic; at the close of the novel he has learned that in his profession of architect he should not take himself too seriously but should be content to be a conscientious craftsman — important insights, which are to remain significant in Böll's work, but not entirely motivated by the events which we have seen him experience.

But the chief aspect of *Wo warst du, Adam?* which contributes to the montage effect is the variety of focalisers which it employs, usually introducing a new focaliser with each chapter. Its beginning is an open one, just as the beginnings of Böll's novels from now on are to be: 'First a large, yellow, tragic face went past them, that was the general' ('Zuerst ging ein großes, gelbes, tragisches Gesicht an ihnen vorbei, das war der General') (R 1, p. 308). The 'they' referred to turns out to be the ordinary soldiers of the German army, sceptical where heroics are expected of them, sympathetic where they feel sympathy is being offered. There is no external, commenting narrator here, such as we find in Plievier's *Stalingrad*, or indeed at the beginning of Böll's own *Der Zug war pünktlich*, and on the whole this remains the case throughout the novel. In the course of the first chapter this collective point of view is gradually reduced to that of one man, Feinhals. It comes therefore as a surprise when we read the opening words of Chapter 2: 'He heard a voice say "Bressen"' ('Er hörte, daß eine Stimme "Bressen" sagte') (p. 318), and gradually realise that the 'he' is not the Feinhals of Chapter 1 but Bressen himself. At the end of the chapter Bressen notices a soldier with his arm in a sling, who is then addressed by the doctor as 'Feinhals'. In the course of Chapter 3 we encounter a chest labelled 'Oblt. Dr. Greck' and in the following chapter its owner becomes the central figure, turning out to be the lieutenant with the preoccupation with other people's medals whom we met at the beginning; similarly the Schniewind of the final chapter is introduced by name at the end of the preceding one. Not all of the chapters play hide-and-seek with the reader in this way. Chapter 3, for example, begins with an ironic comment from an external narrator on the number of sergeants in the German army with the name of Schneider and there are other places where an external narrator communicates information to the reader on what has been happening elsewhere. Nevertheless, the overall effect of the narrative technique is one of internal focalisers. Its function is threefold. In the first place it enables Böll to present the war from a variety of angles, ranging from the convinced fascists Filskeit and Bressen through the inhibited, self-centred Greck and the helpless Feinhals and Ilona to the outsider Frau Susan. Secondly, it reduces the status of the individual hero. Feinhals is the most important single figure, although he is 'on stage' for less than half the novel. But somebody who can be relegated to being a mere figure in the background has permanently lost his claim to be a hero in the nineteenth-century meaning of the term. This is a statement about the relative insignificance of individual man in modern warfare. And thirdly, the technique emphasises the monadic nature of the war. These are people who have little in common, little to say to one another, people who are not bound together in comradeship, as ideology would have it. *Das Vermächtnis* contained long dialogues between Fischer and Schelling. In *Wo warst du, Adam?* there is nobody with whom Feinhals can speak freely at all. At one point he encounters a Lieutenant Brecht, who tries to draw him out, suggesting it is a 'shitty war' ('ein Scheißkrieg'), then, evidently fearing that Feinhals may be a Nazi, modifying his statement to mean that it is a war they are losing; but Feinhals remains silent (p. 386). And even when the war appears over Feinhals cannot bring himself to tell Finck's father how his son was killed.

Montage is one modernist aspect of *Wo warst du, Adam?*; another is the use of leitmotivs of various kinds. These can be thematic, as with the somewhat overdone insistence that moral stature goes in inverse proportion to the number of medals one has been awarded, or with the epigraph's quotation from Saint-Exupéry that war is a disease — the General has malaria and Greck suffers from dyspepsia and colic. They can also be used for characterisation: the 'narrow face' of Bressen, the preoccupation with other people's medals in the case of Greck. Colours are important as linking devices. The red stars on the Russian tanks at the end of Chapter 3 become the patches of colour perceived by Greck at the beginning of Chapter 4; these resolve themselves as piles of reddish-yellow apricots and green cucumbers which become in Chapters 6 and 7 the red and green furniture vans which respectively bear Feinhals to the front and Ilona to the gas chambers. One other important aspect of Böll's narrative technique is the way in which from time to time a striking image is underlined: the sun setting between two rows of houses; the pot of geraniums which an enraged caretaker throws after the departing German troops and which forms a symmetrical pattern of fragments in the midst of which the roots of the plant become visible; the Stifter-like scenes which Feinhals perceives through his telescope as he sits on watch in a remote country area; and finally the coffin in the coffin-maker's window which Feinhals finds coming closer and closer. Each of these images slows down the narrative and with its symbolic implications — the 'immanent symbolism of the world' — breaks through the realist convention. An aesthetic pattern in the modernist mode is created which tends to isolate the novel from the socio-political reality which it is ostensibly describing.

This is unfortunate as by comparison with Böll's earlier war stories *Wo warst du, Adam?* contains a much greater degree of sharpness. The artillery necessary to hold the lines at the front is lacking because it is being used to defend the staff quarters. The fate of the Jews hinted at in *Der Zug war pünktlich* is presented here in all its starkness. Filskeit is a mixture of the historical Rudolf Höss, the pedantically correct governor at Auschwitz, and Heinrich Himmler, the passionate amateur violinist; he is an ardent music-lover, whose early artistic ambitions, were, like Hitler's (Durzak, 1971, p. 34), thwarted, as he saw it, by the Jewish establishment. The conventional cultural references which spoiled the earlier work are missing; instead Böll confronts head-on the paradox that cultured men could be capable of inconceivable brutality. Like Andreas and Olina Filskeit had once wished to study music, but he lacked the professional distance to his subject; now he has a choir in his camp; the new arrivals are first required to sing, those who pass the test are spared for a few months, the others go straight to the gas chambers. Here and there Böll hints at reasons for the war. He points at parallels between civilian and military life in the career of Bressen: in peacetime he had worked in a restaurant where it was important to be able to understand the social hierarchy; in the army the hierarchy is simply more explicit. War thus appears a continuation of the class struggle. Frau Susan is not unlike Brecht's Mother Courage. She too perceives the absurdity of war in which men are paid to do nothing; but she is also happy to make her profits out of the war when she finds the situation of her inn to be strategically important. The partisans who were discounted in *Der Zug war pünktlich* are presented in a more ambiguous light here: Frau Susan regards their activities as ridiculous, blowing up a bridge which nobody uses apart from her customers; but if we step outside Frau Susan's limited perspective we become aware that because of this action a German unit has been stationed there unproductively for several months.

Nevertheless, as in the early works we find a basic pessimism with regard to the possibility of the individual's influencing his situation. From the outset the attitude of the soldiers is one of 'Melancholy, compassion, fear and a secret rage' ('Trauer, Mitleid, Angst und eine geheime Wut') (p. 308). The first three of these emotions are passive ones. The fourth is more active. In a key scene of *Mother Courage and her Children*, produced by Brecht in Berlin in 1949, Courage addresses a young soldier who has come in a rage to complain about his ill-treatment by his commanding officer. She dissuades him, his rage is 'not long enough', and she goes on to sing the 'Song of the Grand Capitulation'. Anger was for Brecht a productive, potentially revolutionary emotion, but it needed to be properly directed and motivated. None of the men in the novel is prepared to bring his revolutionary potential into the open. They have all capitulated. There is a reference to 20 July 1944, but only to the trial of the conspirators — it began on 7 September — after the attempt had failed. Schmitz reads the newspaper headline: 'Trial of traitors begins' ('Prozeß gegen Hochverräter hat begonnen'), but he at once puts the paper down (p. 332). Resistance of this kind seems futile, not even worth thinking about. A few pages later he, the one quasi-hero of the novel, who refuses to leave the sick and the wounded while the Red Army advances on his hospital post, remarks that the fleeing civilians are misguided: 'It's absurd to flee; at that rate they won't escape the war' ('Es ist sinnlos zu fliehen; in diesem Tempo werden sie dem Krieg nicht entgehen') (p. 339). It is not the Russians, nor even the Nazis who are inescapable, but war itself, mythologised in the Saint-Exupéry quotation of the epigraph as a 'disease', a natural disaster. Nowhere is this despair clearer than in the scene in which Feinhals waits for Ilona in the inn where they had agreed to meet. 'He knew it was absurd to wait and at the same time he knew that he had to wait. He had to give God this opportunity to turn things in a way that would have been nice, although he was certain that things had long since turned out differently: she would not return' ('Er wußte, daß es sinnlos war, zu warten, und wußte zugleich, daß er warten mußte. Er mußte Gott diese Chance geben, alles so zu wenden, wie es schön gewesen wäre, obwohl es für ihn sicher war, daß es sich längst anders gewendet hatte: sie würde nicht zurückkommen') (p. 374). And sure enough, Ilona is now on the way to the extermination camp and Feinhals is picked up by the military police. God does not intervene. The existentialist metaphysics of the novel are expressed by Ilona, who, rightly, as Feinhals realises, declares that the purpose of prayer is 'to console God' ('um Gott zu trösten') (p. 444), 'that it was better not to grow too old and not to build one's life on a love which was real only for moments, while there was another, eternal love' ('daß es besser war, nicht sehr alt zu werden und sein Leben nicht auf eine Liebe zu bauen, die nur für Augenblicke wirklich war, während es eine andere, ewige Liebe gab') (p. 293). In this respect *Wo warst du, Adam?* reproduces some of the Jansenistic inwardness of Böll's earlier works.

Wo warst du, Adam?, like its predecessors, was almost completely ignored by the public; the publishers needed six or seven years to sell 3,000 copies (I, p. 139). Böll's next novel, *Und sagte kein einziges Wort*, published in 1953, marked the true beginning of his reputation. Karl Korn in the *Frankfurter Allgemeine Zeitung* called it a sensation and declared: 'When in future anyone asks me what the Germans have to show that is truly powerful and authentic, I shall name Böll' ('Wenn mich künftig einer fragt, was denn die Deutschen heute an Büchern von wirklicher Kraft und Wahrhaftigkeit vorzuweisen hätten, werde ich den Böll nennen') (Korn, 1953). To the publishers' surprise a second printing was necessary within the year (I, p. 140), although it seems that they had energetically advertised it to ensure its success (Conard, 1981, p. 26). A play for radio, 'Ein Tag wie sonst', based on the novel's last chapter was broadcast just as the novel was appearing, and is referred to in Christine Brückner's first novel, *Ehe die Spuren verwehen*: 'The author, one Böll, has been mentioned frequently in the last few years' ('Der Verfasser, ein gewisser Böll, wird in den letzten Jahren häufig genannt') (Brückner, 1954, p. 90). Robert Neumann even found it worth parodying under the title 'Und piepste nicht' ('And didn't give a peep') (Neumann, 1955, pp. 321–2).

It is the first of Böll's published novels to deal with the immediate, contemporary present — in this case September 1952. The Economic Miracle is under way, the shops are full of goods which public address systems encourage people to buy. Leisure-time is catered for too: in September the dummy in the shop window is no longer reading the novel with the suitably escapist title *Ferien vom Ich* ('A holiday from yourself') in a deckchair but instead is advertising winter sports. No fewer than seven radio programmes compete for listeners' attention on a Sunday morning. Commercial groups hold large-scale congresses, which are an occasion to advertise their services. In the novel it is the druggists, who have invaded the city in large numbers, filling the hotels and bombarding the population metaphorically with the slogan 'Confide in your druggist' ('Vertrau dich deinem Drogisten an') and literally with advertising material and free samples — the climax comes when they drop from aeroplanes a shower of red balloons in the shape of storks with broken necks, advertising contraceptives. Prompted by Nicolas Born in 1977, who saw this aspect of the novel as one which anticipated the 'consumer fetishism' ('Konsumfetischismus') of later years, Böll described advertising, totally lacking in the years before the Currency Reform, as a primary example of the restoration (Lenz, p. 59). It is a motif which recurs in his work: in the short story 'Krippenfeier' (1952) Benz notes that a set of figures for a Christmas crib costs 256 DM and reflects that if Joseph had had that amount of money at his disposal he would not have had to make do with a stable. In the novel itself the sounds of the aeroplanes and of the cannons used by the druggists in another advertising stunt are associated with the war: 'The noises contained the whole of the war: droning of aeroplanes, barking of explosions' ('Die Geräusche enthielten den ganzen Krieg: Brummen von Flugzeugen, Gebell von Explosionen') (R 2, p. 170). Implicitly the war is not over, the war which looms large in the memories of the protagonists.

Not everyone shares in the new prosperity. Since the Currency Reform the lights have been permanently at 'green for the strong, red for the weak', in a 'jungle' of economic competitiveness where those with 'vitality' prosper (E 1, p. 177). The contrast is explicit in *Und sagte kein einziges Wort*. The first chapter describes the pressures to which people are subjected from an early age, as Fred Bogner gives private tuition in Latin and mathematics to a succession of schoolchildren, not all of whose parents can afford to pay him and for most of whom the effort seems hardly worth while. Those who fail to make the grade live in substandard housing in districts like the one behind the railway station, where the air is filled with the sickly sweet smell of a chocolate factory and the few hotels are cheap because the poverty here deters tourists. *Und sagte kein einziges Wort* is the novel of a marriage which is on the point of breaking down partly because of the lack of the material circumstances which would enable it to be a success. Fred and Käte Bogner lost their home in a bombing raid and now have to bring up their three children in a single room which is part of their landlords' own flat, separated from their neighbours by a thin partition which fails to muffle even the most intimate sounds. Their landlords, the Frankes, live in spacious splendour, they too have preserved their Christmas tree decorations through the war and their living room has not changed in thirty years, but Frau Franke watches severely over the Bogners' children, lest they are too noisy or make splashes in the toilet. Fred is one who lacks 'vitality'. He has left home, unable to bear the pressures of their material surroundings, which have led him to lose his temper with his children and beat them. Occasionally he sleeps in the basement of a mansion whose caretaker is a friend of his; the indignation with which he describes the luxurious splendour of this house, with its gardens, its library, its bathrooms, a house which is empty for nine months of the year, contains genuine hatred of the affluent. More frequently he sleeps rough. Käte and he meet to consummate their marriage in cheap hotels, sometimes in parks. The children have been told that their father is ill. In the course of the novel affairs reach crisis point; the children learn that Fred is not ill, Käte discovers she is pregnant again and declares to Fred that she is no longer prepared to put up with the compromise, either he returns home or the break will be permanent. *Und sagte kein einziges Wort* has a much stronger story line than *Wo warst du, Adam?*.

There are obvious implications of class conflict in the novel, which contrasts the fates of the wealthy and the poor, the strong and the weak. This conflict reaches into the domain of the Roman Catholic Church itself. Frau Franke is a pillar of the Church and Käte suspects that she intervened to prevent them from being allotted a council flat in order to be seen selflessly to have to do without one of her own rooms. The Bishop himself is a friend of the owner of the mansion so envied by Fred and appears to see nothing unchristian in the existence of so much unused living space in the midst of a housing shortage — one of Böll's observations on the behaviour of the Church after the war was on the empty space in vicarages which was never used to house the homeless (I, p. 147). Like Frau Franke the Bishop likes to be seen to have a 'social conscience' and insists that working-class people take part in the religious procession; but as they have to borrow ill-fitting dinner-jackets for the occasion this draws attention to class differences all the more (cf. E 2, p. 538). Even within the Church there are differences of class. The Church of the Seven Sorrows of Mary is situated in the poorest quarter of the city, its fabric, damaged in the war, has been repaired as cheaply as possible and it is draughty, dirty and ugly. Its priest is anything but brilliant: his sermons lack rhetorical fervour, his war-record is poor and he is evidently infatuated with one of the women in his congregation. When Käte confesses her hatred of the priests who live in big houses he is not even sure whether he can grant her absolution, although he goes on to admit to her his own hatred of his superiors, of the priests who travel from one conference to another, living in first-class hotels and complaining of the dirt they encounter in his church. He is incompetent, but sympathetic to Käte and her plight.

Und sagte kein einziges Wort is the first major work of Böll's to attack the Church in the name of Christianity. It is perhaps the first example of the influence of the Catholic Renewal in France on

German literature, the movement in the earlier part of the century which criticised the Church's preoccupation with externals and propagated a new spirituality. The novels of the Catholic Renewal in France had made a strong impression on him and his family when they read them in the 1930s. In contrast to the novels of German Catholics like Gertrud von Le Fort and Reinhold Schneider those of François Mauriac, Georges Bernanos and the older Léon Bloy had a 'liberating' effect. The highly critical depiction of the clergy in the works of Bernanos, for example, had been startling (I, p. 530). Bloy was probably the most important of the three for Böll. For years *Le sang des pauvres* was 'like the Bible' for him and his family (I, p. 529), and although he turned away from Bloy in revulsion when in 1942 he read his diaries and came across the wish Bloy had expressed in 1916 that the whole of Germany might starve to death (E 1, pp. 266f.), Böll remained sufficiently impressed to write a survey of Bloy's works in German translation in 1952, a survey which remained unpublished (E 1, 49–55), although on it was based his review of *Das Heil und die Armut* which appeared a few months later in 1953 in *Welt der Arbeit*. Bloy's anticlericalism, wrote Böll, made that of the non-believers appear 'limp' (E 1, p. 54). The survey, when dealing with Bloy's central theme of poverty (ibid., pp. 52, 89), reads like a commentary on *Und sagte kein einziges Wort*, as when Böll writes: 'To be poor is frightful, because in our society there is no room for the poor, because they no longer have any status, they who are entitled to the first rank. If it is awful to be poor and a Christian in our society, then one thing is worse: to be rich and to call oneself a Christian' ('Arm sein ist fürchterlich, weil es in dieser Gesellschaft keinen Platz mehr für die Armen gibt, sie keinen Rang mehr genießen, sie, denen der erste Rang zukommt. Wenn arm sein und Christ sein in dieser Gesellschaft schrecklich ist, so gibt es noch etwas schrecklicheres: reich sein und sich Christ zu nennen') (ibid., p. 53). A more contemporary kindred spirit from abroad was Graham Greene, whom Böll had named in 1949 as an influence together with Bernanos, and a translation of whose *The End of the Affair* with its epigraph from Bloy he reviewed in 1952 (E 1, pp. 35–40). More relevantly for *Und sagte kein einziges Wort*, Greene's *The Power and the Glory* with its 'whisky priest' had appeared in West Germany in 1948, in paperback in 1953.

Because of the critical aspects of the novel, *Und sagte kein einziges Wort* had a stormy reception in some Catholic circles. Böll reported that he had received 'nasty letters . . . , even threats' ('böse Briefe . . . , auch Drohungen' (I, p. 140); the novel was a 'frightful shock' (I, p. 151). For the Bogners are both devout, practising

Catholics. The episode with the druggists juxtaposed with Käte's unwanted pregnancy confronts the Church's teaching on contraception directly. A central aspect of the controversy was the novel's presentation of marriage. As the ending implies that Fred is going to return home, some of the early reviewers claimed that it was a novel which upheld the indissolubility of marriage (Wiegenstein, 1953; Coupe, 1964). Böll himself regarded it as a novel which criticises the institution of marriage (I, p. 394). Käte dreams of a life without marriage, something which is promised in the world beyond the grave, a world where she can listen to liturgical chants and be with men who do not wish to have sex with her, and Fred seems to agree, when he tells her: 'It would be nice to see you again in a life in which I could love you . . . without marrying you' ('Es wäre schön, dich wiederzusehen in einem Leben, in dem ich dich lieben könnte . . . ohne dich zu heiraten') (R 2, p. 190). From Käte's point of view marriage is a convenience for men; she is the one who has marital duties, has to submit to the indignity of appearing to the hotel proprietors as a prostitute, while Fred can do as he likes, knowing that she will come when he calls her. When Böll discussed the novel in Catholic circles this was a topic which created especial controversy, particularly when he declared that he could not imagine a marriage succeeding without irony; not only was he touching on theological questions, he was also undermining male authority (I, pp. 551f.).

This reaction suggests that in *Und sagte kein einziges Wort* Böll was also challenging conventional bourgeois gender roles. At first sight the novel does not bear this out: Käte is the archetypal German *Hausfrau*, devoted to her *Kinder*, her *Küche* and her *Kirche*, and our initial impression is of her cleaning the floor and walls of her living quarters, while Fred is the breadwinner and errant male, travelling all over town to give tuition, looking for a hotel room and for somebody who will lend him money. Böll had shortly before referred to Homer as the father of European literature, to the *Odyssey* as the earliest example of 'the literature of returning soldiers' (E 1, p. 35). Wolfgang Koeppen's *Tauben im Gras* included the peregrinations of Odysseus Cotton, a black GI in occupied Germany. Böll also knew Joyce's *Ulysses*, to which he alluded frequently in his essays of the time. Fred too has returned from the war. His wanderings through the city and his final decision to return home — the novel ends with the words 'nach Hause' ('home') — suggest that in *Und sagte kein einziges Wort* there is the submerged pattern of the *Odyssey*. Käte would be the Penelope of the novel. Her apparent domesticity is perhaps overdone: it is not plausible that in the middle of her scrubbing she should suddenly realise that it is Sunday, a day of rest. Dirt and cleanliness are motifs which preoccupied Böll throughout his life: 'Über die Brücke' satirises the window-cleaning programme which survives the war; the narrator of *Entfernung von der Truppe* had to clean out latrines in the war; in *Gruppenbild mit Dame* Lev Gruyten is a dustman. In 1966 Böll pointed out the ideological connotations of 'cleanliness': the Poles, Jews and Russians whom the Nazis were resolved to exterminate were presented to the German people as 'dirty' (E 2, p. 216). Later in the novel Käte almost compulsively starts to rub the dirt from the statue of an angel, until she finds that it looked much better dirty. This suggests that the motif of house-cleaning has more of a symbolic significance — Käte calls it the 'struggle against the dirt mobilised by the war' ('Kampf gegen den Schmutz, den der Krieg in Bewegung gesetzt hat') (R 2, p. 106). Böll deliberately exaggerates her efforts in order to stress the drudgery. She is a militant Penelope. The housewife is traditionally isolated; Käte is inspired with a vision of international sisterhood, of women of all races washing, digging, cooking while their menfolk sit around the fire, of the bitter faces of her sisters in London, New York, Berlin and Paris waiting for the call of their drunken husbands. Later in the novel she sees the girl in the café as a younger version of herself, she too at the mercy of a man who will leave in her the traces of what *he* calls love. In passages like these Böll is unusually direct in his presentation of resentment to male domination. Käte is by far the more dynamic of the two partners, she is the one who takes decisions. In this way the tension between the mythical pattern and its realisation in the novel must activate the reader's consciousness.

Böll later spoke of the generation moulded by the war and what preceded it; the soldier's experience of existential uncertainty resulted in nihilism and indifference to success (I, p. 544). Fred Bogner is one such character. He appears to Käte as typical of his age when she calls him 'this bored, indifferent contemporary' ('dieser gelangweilte, gleichgültige Zeitgenosse') (R 2, p. 188). He is almost forty-four at the time the novel takes place, and would therefore have experienced even more consciously than his author the 'disintegration of bourgeois society' in the inter-war years. He is a man who, according to Käte, was 'too early filled with indifference towards everything that other men have resolved to take seriously' ('der zu früh von Gleichgültigkeit erfaßt wurde gegen alles, was ernstzunehmen andere Männer sich entschlossen haben') (p. 106). He despises authority and regulations of all kinds. In the first chapter we see him ride tram-cars without paying; later we hear that he went absent without leave when Käte was expecting their first child. He has no wish to make a career, having worked in turn as drugs-salesman, photographer, library assistant, in a carpet factory, as removal man, and he is now a telephone operator in the Church's central office. He spends his free time drinking, visiting cemeteries and playing on fruit-machines with money he has borrowed from friends. He is one of the 'undeserving poor', painfully irritating to all do-gooders.

One ambiguity of the novel is the extent to which the Bogners' difficulties are created by external circumstance or by their own fecklessness. Fred states: 'For a bigger flat you need money, you need what they call energy, but we've got neither money nor energy. Not even my wife has any energy' ('Für eine größere Wohnung braucht man Geld, braucht man das, was sie Energie nennen, aber wir haben weder Geld noch Energie. Auch meine Frau hat keine Energie') (R 2, p. 127). His last sentence is contradicted by the reader's own experience of Käte. She has the energy; it is her subordinate position which prevents her from putting it to good effect. The war destroyed the home which might have enabled them to lead a 'normal' marriage, but 'normality' in marriage is being questioned all the time. When Fred beats his children he blames it on their poverty: 'our poverty has made me sick' ('die Armut hat mich krank gemacht') (p. 158). But later Käte challenges him: it is not because of their living accommodation that he has left them, and Fred has no answer. Possibly the war is to blame in another way, by destroying Fred's will to live, and he admits that since the war he has been thinking almost constantly of death. But he goes on to say that it was not the war that destroyed him, he would have been just the same had the war never happened. Fred's preoccupation with death goes back to his childhood and the death of his mother, when, not understanding what it meant, he had gone on his own to the cemetery to visit her. Death is the 'only truth he never doubts' ('die einzige Wahrheit, an der mir nie Zweifel kommt') (p. 146). Today he regularly visits cemeteries, and at funerals sometimes is mistaken for one of the mourners — again the theme of mourning is struck in Böll's fiction.

The social criticism of the novel is in fact tempered by the strong existentialist undercurrent of the novel (I, p. 519). Camus was very important for Böll (I, p. 137). His Meursault is perhaps the first example of the post-war anti-hero, a category to which Fred Bogner also belongs. In the reader which Böll brought out in 1978, he included Meursault's account of his trial, a strangely distanced account, in which the heat of the courtroom is more important than the verdict (ML, pp. 83ff.). Fred is 'l'étranger' of *Und sagte kein einziges Wort.* If death is the one truth of life then life itself is absurd, especially all the formal devices used by men to try to give it meaning. Both Fred and Käte see their children repeating the routine gestures they themselves performed as children. The random movements of the balls in the fruit machines on which Fred spends so much time symbolise the arbitrary, absurd 'rhythms' of everyday life to which Fred and Käte's encounters are subject. The Church and society are criticised in the name of authenticity and spontaneity. Advertising is singled out less as an aspect of capitalism than as the attempt to persuade people to buy what they do not wish or need, to persuade them to behave inauthentically. The Bishop is 'photogenic', a popular subject for the covers of Church magazines; the exterior is more important than the interior self. And marriage itself is like the formal dress which the Bishop insists the working-class men wear in the procession, the legal strait-jacket to authentic, spontaneous love (I, pp. 560f.). The implied 'happy ending' is entirely existentialist. Fred does not reply to Käte's ultimatum. When she falls asleep in their hotel bedroom he is even tempted to go to the dance in the hotel downstairs without her. The following morning is 'a day like any other day', as the title of the radio play put it; the bus is more punctual than time itself, the advertising industry is hard at work, in the office Fred's employers are as preoccupied with trivial pursuits as ever. Fred is sent to the bank to pay in some money. And suddenly he catches sight of Käte, without at first recognising her, realises the uniqueness of their relationship, is completely bowled over and resolves to return to her. The authenticity of the decision is guaranteed by the spontaneity of the action.

It is a Christian existentialism — the uniqueness of their relationship consists in the fact that they have prayed together. As in *Wo warst du, Adam?* there is a strong element of inwardness in Böll's depiction of the human condition. This element is emphasised by the novel's title. It is taken from a Negro spiritual which Käte hears on the radio: 'they nailed him to the cross, nailed him to the cross . . . and he never said a mumbaling word' (R 2, p. 107). By implication life on earth is a calvary and no tinkering with social institutions will alter that. The external reality of *Und sagte kein einziges Wort* is full of words, the advertising slogans of the druggists, the blandishments of the fairground attendants, the clichés of the Bishop. Fred's angelic mother, who could never turn a beggar away from her door, used to suffer in silence. The talkative dragon Frau Franke contrasts with her kind-hearted taciturn husband. The mongol child Fred and Käte encounter cannot speak a word, but appears to be in contact with some higher reality.

As in *Wo warst du, Adam?* Böll makes effective use of shifting narrative perspectives. In this case he restricts himself to two, those of Fred and Käte, who relate the novel in the first person in alternate chapters. What is 'modernist' about this technique is that there is no indication of why, when or for whom they are writing. There is no suggestion anywhere that they are collaborating, as Jim Hawkins and Dr Livesey do in Stevenson's *Treasure Island*. People whom they meet independently, the girl in the café, for example, are described anew as if the reader had not already met them. There is no community of narrative, just as there is no community in their marriage. They are not looking back at past events in traditional autobiographical manner. There are no 'prolepses' (Rimmon-Kenan, 1983), no anticipation of a future beyond the events narrated, implying, for example, that their marriage is by now completely restored. By contrast, *Das Brot der frühen Jahre* is told from a vantage-point which enables Fendrich to look back and wonder what might have happened had he not met Hedwig. *Und sagte kein einziges Wort* consists of two interlocking interior monologues. Because of this mirrors are important throughout. The outer appearance of each narrator is established when they catch sight of themselves in a mirror. This feature emphasises their isolation. Some early commentators were puzzled by the technique and suggested that they were each keeping a diary (Grenzmann, 1953, p. 442). A contemporary English novel, *Turtle Diary* (1975) uses a similar technique, and Russell Hoban felt the need to justify it through the title. But there is no internal or external evidence of diary form in Böll's novel. Rudolf Majut lists a number of earlier examples of the technique, most of them questionable (Majut, 1960, col. 1695). Gerd Gaiser's novel *Schlußball* (1958) on the other hand was to break the narrative into ten 'voices'.

What is especially memorable about the novel is the sense of the locations it conveys, locations which, almost literally, smell of a specific moment in history. Smells are a prominent aspect: the smells of damp clothes in the tram, of vinegar in a kitchen, sugar-beet syrup in the priest's house, fresh bread in the café. At times the characters seem almost monomaniacally preoccupied with details; everything is given its colour, the design of the banknotes is described exactly, with the result that the realism has an almost magical quality. Fred and Käte are apart for most of the novel, but community is established through the places they visit — mostly independently of one another: the Church of the Seven Sorrows, the shack containing a café, the Hotel Holländischer Hof and the fairground. The last of these was a very common motif of these years: one year later Fellini's film *La Strada* was first shown, and one of the most powerful scenes of Werner Bräunig's unfinished novel on the development of post-war Germany is set on a fairground in late 1949 (Bräunig, 1965).

Böll's next novel, *Haus ohne Hüter*, appeared just over a year later, in the autumn of 1954. While it was being serialised in the *Frankfurter Allgemeine Zeitung* Böll published an article in *Die Zeit* complaining of the pressures that publishers were putting on their authors to write the 'big novel', the novel with the format of *Gone with the Wind* (E 1, pp. 135f.). *Haus ohne Hüter* may have been influenced by these pressures. Almost as long as *Wo warst du, Adam?* and *Und sagte kein einziges Wort* put together, it concerns five major characters: the eleven-year-old Martin Bach and his widowed mother Nella, Martin's friend Heinrich Brielach and his widowed mother Wilma, and a friend of Martin's father, Albert Muchow. But in addition there are several Dickensian minor characters who live in the Bach household: Glum, a 'displaced person' from Siberia who spends his spare time studying theology and laboriously drawing an enormous map of Europe; Bolda, their housekeeper; and Nella's mother, Frau Holstege, a terrifying old lady who at any moment is liable to drag Martin off to an expensive restaurant or to parade her chamberpot in a roomful of guests, proclaiming that her urine has blood in it. In this portrayal of three generations of a declining middle-class family there are again echoes of Thomas Mann's *Buddenbrooks*. Heinrich too associates with several colourful personalities: 'uncle' Leo, the tram-conductor who lives with his mother, and Frau Borussiak, the kindly neighbour whose songs of consolation which she sings as she works ring through the block of flats where they live. But to a much greater extent than in the previous novel Böll introduces the personalities of the dead: Nella's husband, the poet Rai Bach, Wilma's husband Heinrich, and, possibly the most 'alive' character of the novel, Albert's Irish wife Leen, who died of peritonitis in pre-war London after they had been married only a year.

The narrative technique reverts to that of *Wo warst du, Adam?* The story is narrated extra-diegetically, i.e. in the third person, but the narrator is only rarely also the focaliser. Instead we have a complex montage of five separate internal points of view, those of the five major characters of the novel. Again the openings to the individual chapters are important indicators of the technique and frequently leave the reader momentarily in the dark as to the identity of the focaliser, when the narrator temporarily witholds the name of the character involved and refers only to 'he' or 'she'. The technique underlines one of the themes of the novel , the lack of communication between the characters, especially between the adults and the children. It also creates difficulties of interpretation, as much of the overt criticism in the novel is levelled by characters whose 'reliability' is doubtful. This is especially true of Nella but to some extent it applies to all the adults.

For the first time Böll was trying to convey the perspective of an adolescent, someone for whom almost by definition the world appears as a strange, inexplicable place. Martin sees the diners at Vohwinkels Weinstuben as monsters; he is baffled by what Grebhake and Wolters, two older boys, were up to in the bushes with open flies and red faces. His slightly more mature friend Heinrich is learning to come to terms with the difference between those who have money and those who lack it; he sees the world as a frozen pond whose ice is liable to break at any moment. In spite of the uncertainties of the adolescent focalisers, it is paradoxically their view on society that appears to the reader more reliable than that of the adults, since in many cases what they cannot understand, the hypocrisy of adult behaviour and values, is *not* to be understood but criticised and changed. In this respect Böll is operating within a time-honoured tradition which in German literature goes back at least to Grimmelshausen's *Simplicissimus*. Only occasionally does the narrator become more overt. In Chapter 2 Heinrich is contrasted with Albert's uncle Will, who had been pampered all his life, something which could not be said of Heinrich; the circumstances of Heinrich's birth are then narrated, and gradually the focus moves to that of Heinrich himself as the succession of 'uncles' whom he can remember begins. Very occasionally the focaliser is a minor character: a travelling salesman (R 2, p. 392) and Albert's employer Bresgote (p. 417).

The past plays an important role in *Haus ohne Hüter*. In April 1954 in the *Kölnische Rundschau* Böll described a recent incident in which a school-teacher had discovered that not one of the forty children in her class had heard about the systematic extermination of the Jews in the Third Reich. They had been taught about outmodedly patriotic places like Leuthen, Waterloo and Austerlitz, but places like Auschwitz, Treblinka and Majdanek were unknown to them (E 1, pp. 133f.). In a key scene of the novel Albert takes Martin for the first time to an old fort in the woods and explains that here he and Martin's father had been tortured by Nazis and their schoolmate Absalom Billig, a Jew, murdered. Martin is confused and frightened. The word 'Nazis' does not mean much to him; at school he has been taught to believe that the Nazis were 'not so bad'; worse than the Nazis were the 'Russians', or the 'immoral' behaviour of

Heinrich's mother, living with a man to whom she is not married R 2, p. 469). The fort itself is now being used commercially to grow mushrooms and its owner knows nothing of its past history. Although the proprietor, curiously enough, is French, Böll is implying that contemporary West German society has repressed its guilty past by means of business and anti-Communism. 'Don't forget', Albert insists, 'Your father was kicked and beaten here, and I was too' ('hier . . . wurde dein Vater getreten, geschlagen — wie ich — vergiß es nicht') (p. 470). And yet Martin has been brought up by a mother who *cannot* forget that a Nazi officer Gäseler sent her husband senselessly to his death, and by a grandmother who has the habit of hearing him recite the catechism and includes questions relating to the death of his father, making him repeat three times the name of the man responsible. Martin's ignorance is as much the fault of his family as of his teachers. Both Nella and her mother have a personal feud with an individual Nazi rather than with the political phenomenon of Nazism. In the Mitscherlichs' terms, Nella is 'narcissistic', preoccupied with the personal wrong that has been done to her (Mitscherlichs, 1967, pp. 57ff.). Böll contrasts the romantic and unpolitical notions of revenge harboured by Nella and Frau Holstege with the beginning of the more important task of enlightenment which Albert is now undertaking, and which is one of the purposes of the book itself. The really sinister feature of Gäseler when he turns up is that he is a perfectly ordinary citizen who has on his own admission 'systematically wiped out [his] memory' ('systematisch meine Erinnerung geschlachtet'), and declares that 'one must forget the war' ('man muß den Krieg vergessen'), while at the same time being able to refer nostalgically to 'Erwin's' (i.e. Rommel's) army (R 2, pp. 435f.). Gäseler is not one to 'mourn' the past.

As in *Wo warst du, Adam?* Böll furnishes the reader with little analysis of the causes of the Nazi catastrophe — the limited point of view adopted makes this inappropriate. In the earlier novel there was the association of economic structures with military ones in the career of Bressen; in *Haus ohne Hüter* capitalism is similarly related to militarism in the description of the fortunes of Holstege's jam factory. It is one of the few places in the novel where the external narrator is more overt. Frau Holstege loves to show Martin the archives of her late husband's business, and it does not escape the eleven-year-old's attention that the graphs show a rapid rise in production from 1933 onwards, one which his grandmother is happy to explain with enthusiastic descriptions 'of camps, mass assemblies, meetings, party congresses' ('von Zeltlagern, Massenversammlungen, Veranstaltungen, Parteitagen'), concluding with the triumphant and naïvely revealing declaration that '[wherever] wars have been fought by Germans they have been associated with rising production figures in the jam industry' ('Wo immer Kriege von Deutschen geführt werden, sind sie mit steigenden Produktionsziffern in der Marmeladeindustrie verbunden') (p. 332). Otherwise Böll is content to present the Nazis as brutal, their war as unheroic and mindless, and, a new theme in his fiction, he points to the responsibility of the Church, whose priest Pater Willibrord prayed for 'Führer, Volk und Vaterland' (p. 387).

The Third Reich is reflected only in the memories of the adults who lived through it. In this way the past is shown to be not over, nor will it be over until it has been properly digested. The narrative present of the story is the autumn of 1953. In comparison to the setting of *Und sagte kein einziges Wort* that of *Haus ohne Hüter* is much less obviously the aftermath of war. One of the Rhine bridges is still a bombed ruin, but otherwise the impression is largely one of prosperity — the ruined bridge is juxtaposed with tennis courts and white-clad people. The previous year Böll had suggested it was time that someone wrote the novel of the 'whipped-cream German' (E 1, p. 120). *Haus ohne Hüter* is to a certain extent just that. The hunger years are over, at least for some, and the most grotesque scene of the novel takes place in Vohwinkels Weinstuben, a high-class restaurant to which Martin's grandmother regularly insists on taking him and where he is equally regularly sick. However, one of the central themes of the novel is that not all West Germans are able to partake in this prosperity, and that contrary to the declarations of conservatives like Sieburg, the society of the Federal Republic is class-based. The Bachs are wealthy; Martin's grandmother owns a factory and his mother has no need to earn a living. The Brielachs are poor: Wilma works in a small bakery, her dead husband was a car mechanic, the man she is now living with is a tram-conductor. Nella leads a life of parties and frequent absences from home; she has a succession of male admirers, although she appears to be sexually celibate, and she has no desire or need to remarry. Wilma has had a succession of 'husbands'; she is now faced with an unpayable dentist's bill for 1,200 marks for treatment without which she will lose the attractiveness to men which has enabled her to survive so far; neither can she afford to remarry even if she wished to as she would then lose her widow's pension. When in the end she moves out their utter poverty is revealed: Heinrich's bed still consists of an old door nailed on to blocks of wood. But the difference between the Bach and Brielach households is not merely one of money, as Heinrich is well aware. It is a difference also of values, even of

102

language: Martin is shocked by the obscenity which Wilma hurled at the baker and which Heinrich had earlier heard in the mouth of Leo; it is not a word which he can imagine in Martin's family. And Martin realises that there is a system of values used by his school-teachers whereby the children of wealthy or prominent parents are given preferential treatment. It is true that Heinrich and Martin are good friends; indeed Martin prefers the margarine of the Brielach household to the butter he is compelled to eat at home. But it is becoming clear that there are barriers between the two which are going to be increasingly difficult to cross.

The most obvious indication in *Haus ohne Hüter* that the 'wounds inflicted by the war' are still 'bleeding' in post-war German society is the theme of the war widows and orphans. In 1975 Böll spoke of the theme of 'widowhood' as a difficult and complex one, one which was more of more general import than the specific historical prob-lem in post-war Germany, and one which could easily be reduced to the merely sexual (I, p. 568). Albert lost his wife even before the war. As in *Und sagte kein einziges Wort* the institution of marriage appears problematical. Neither Nella nor Wilma was married long enough for a conventional marriage relationship to be established. Wilma, however, remembers how her father used to bully her mother, while Nella's refusal to remarry is due at least partly to her recollection of an incident at the beginning of the war when 5,000 wives came to visit their husbands and 5,000 couples had to be accommodated in barracks, stables, wherever there was room, so that, as Nella sees it, the school-beginners of seven years later, the cannon-fodder of twenty years later could be conceived — the similarity with the position of Käte in *Und sagte kein einziges Wort*, compelled to meet Fred in a hotel room in order to fulfil her 'marital duties' is startling. What Böll described as the 'legal strait-jacket' of marriage here takes on its most perverted expression. Marriage is a social institution upheld by the Church and the conservative school-teachers who treat children differently according to whether their mothers are legally married or not. On the other hand Albert refuses to contemplate a sexual relationship with Nella unless she marries him, partly because he fears the effect this would have on both Martin and Heinrich. It is here that one of the main difficulties of interpreting the novel arises. On the face of it Albert represents stability, decisiveness, someone whom the children can look up to and respect — qualities which none of the other adult characters possesses. He is the one who is to take charge of Martin at the end, tell him about the Nazis; he may even be a future — real — husband for Wilma, as the ending of the novel implies. There are two questionable aspects to this role. One is his relationship to the notion of 'order', the other concerns the status of the female characters in the novel.

Both Nella and Wilma are living in 'disordered' circumstances as a result of the war: Nella finds no meaning in life any more and Wilma has drifted from one man to another. Frau Borussiak tells Wilma it is time she 'brought order' into her life (p. 283). Marriage would be a form of order in social terms. But elsewhere in the novel 'order' is associated with disagreeable characteristics. The man Frau Borussiak would like Wilma to have married was Karl, the man Wilma liked least. He was a local government employee, unlike Heinrich's other 'uncles' he wore a suit, and he refused to allow Heinrich to patronise the black market. Heinrich thinks of him as 'Neues-Leben-Karl' because he was always speaking of the need to begin a 'new life'. He is now a respected member of the community and refuses even to greet Heinrich or Wilma in the street. His successor, Leo, is related to 'order' of a different kind, the pedantic concern for his own appearance, his immaculately manicured fingernails and his perfect teeth — but cleanliness of this kind is a negative attribute in Böll's system of values. In this context the behaviour of Albert becomes more dubious. He is the one who takes it upon himself to create 'order' in the Bach household, cleaning out the rats from the cellar and seeing to the repairs to the roof. He even seems determined at the close of the novel to take Martin away from Nella and see that he is brought up in the more ordered circumstances of his own mother's household at Bietenhahn. 'Everything's going to change' ('Es wird alles anders werden'), he tells Martin, unconsciously echoing the very words used by the baker to Wilma when he has persuaded her to leave Leo and come to live with him (pp. 465, 460). The reader may well wonder how much credence to give to either Albert or the baker.

Similar doubts arise when we examine the respective roles given to the men and the women in the novel. Wilma is a woman who is always dominated by men. As a result she is bitter about them: 'All men are cowards' ('Alle Männer sind Feiglinge'), she says (p. 250). But she is not only their victim, she cannot cope without their help, even if it is only that of her son Heinrich, who has charge of the household accounts. In the Bach household Albert again appears the authoritative personality in a household of helpless, even hysterical women. Frau Holstege is independent but grotesque. Nella is the *femme fatale*, able to seduce any male with her smile, but unable to organise her own life. She was a conventional member of the Hitler Youth until Rai met her; his first act was to remove her brown jacket and throw it in the corner without even asking her permission. In a novel in which the men are so strong and the women so weak Albert's suggestion to Nella that she ought not to think of getting a job, as she does not need the money and it would be more important for her to look after her son Martin, is ominously patriarchal.

We are therefore justified in questioning the status of Albert in the novel. The narrative technique gives him no greater status than that of any other of the major characters. His enlightenment of Martin on the nature of National Socialism does not go very far, and leaves Martin with many unanswered questions. Much the same could be said of his helpless and evasive replies to Martin's earlier questions on sex. He is not quite the tower of strength he might have been. But it is in his own brief marriage to Leen that we find clearer evidence of attitudes we are being invited to adopt. It was a blissfully happy one, much more obviously so than that of any of the other couples. It was one in which both partners were equal, indeed if anything Leen was the dominant partner, a teacher at a school run by nuns who invariably referred to Albert as 'Miss Cunigan's husband' (p. 346) — the cross on her grave even bore the name 'Cunigan'. Leen rejected conventional conceptions of tidiness — even her bed was littered with objects which she simply swept on to the floor at night. Leen is an epiphany of sexually and professionally fulfilled, emancipated woman; their marriage is a utopian one — looking back Albert can scarcely believe it happened. In the reality of the novel nothing of this kind is present. The wife of the baker to whom Wilma eventually moves implies further interesting questions. Initially she appears to Wilma as a monster of frigidity, who hates all men, refuses to perform her 'nightly duties', has her hand firmly on the till and was even in the past an active Nazi. But when Wilma moves into the spare room in the baker's household she appears friendly and sympathetic, evidently quite content to let Wilma take over the sexual side of marriage while she looks after the shop. Here is a further anarchic motif in the novel, the *ménage à trois* which the unpublished novel of the 1930s may have described (J, p. 65).

Two further aspects of contemporary West German society are significant in *Haus ohne Hüter*. The one is the presentation of school as a symbol of repressive, restorative society. Martin's school is failing in its duty to enlighten the children on the true nature of National Socialism and instead is presenting the Russians as bogeymen; the hypocritical moral values of the teachers are also apparent. School is the place where individual strength of character is 'broken' (p. 399). A parallel is implied between those arriving late for school and those whom Albert sees arriving late for work. The term 'ABC-Schützen' (literally 'ABC marksmen') for school-beginners, although perfectly normal, in Nella's mouth implies a parallel between school and the army (p. 265). School here stands for West German society as a whole. The other aspect is the cultural establishment, dominated by former Nazis like Schurbigel, whose 1934 dissertation bore the title 'Unser Führer in der modernen Lyrik' ('Our Führer in modern lyric poetry') (p. 257), who became a committed Christian after the war, and who in 1953 is still the country's leading expert on modern lyric poetry, painting and music. In Nella's resentment at the way in which every detail of Rai's private life is being scrutinised in the then fashionable biographical approach to literature — she sees these literary scholars as 'haruspices' rummaging in dustbins — we may see something of Böll's private resentment against the pressures to which he himself as a successful author was being subjected. More general, however, is the attack on the misappropriation of art by a conservative elite. Even after his death Rai is being manipulated for reactionary political purposes. On the one hand he can be seen as a victim and opponent of the Nazis, thus justifying those who, themselves Nazis, had encouraged him at the time; on the other he can be seen as a victim of the Russians, and in the cold war climate his death can take on a different colour, one which is equally favourable to those same ex-Nazis. Böll's critique concerns the Sieburgs of his day; it also relates to the way in which his own works were being 'assimilated' by the conservative establishment which preferred to ignore the concrete criticisms contained in *Und sagte kein einziges Wort* in favour of those aspects which suggested an inner transcendence of social reality (Nägele, 1976 a).

Und sagte kein einziges Wort contained a strong element of French existentialism, especially in the character of Fred. In *Haus ohne Hüter* it has become self-conscious to the point of parody. Sartre and Claudel are the favourite reading of the 'intellectual skirt-chasers' whom Nella despises (p. 256). When he discovers that the cellar has been taken over by rats Albert suggests that the place would make an excellent setting for an existentialist film. Nella is a more dynamic existentialist than Fred Bogner, more of a *rive gauche* type perhaps, unable to take seriously the people she meets, whom she sees as behaving inauthentically, like bad actors in a third-rate film. Böll introduces an incongruous scene in which Bresgote, who has fallen in love with Nella without having exchanged even a word with her, offers to kill Gäseler and tries to rape her: 'Did desperadoes have to be unshaven?' ('Mußten Desperados unrasiert sein?') she thinks, as he advances (p. 475). Much more clearly than in the case of Fred Bogner, Nella is *not* the novel's mouthpiece.

The novel ends in the quasi-utopian setting of Bietenhahn, out in the countryside, where Albert's mother keeps an inn and where the Bachs celebrate a family reunion to which even Heinrich is invited. Nella has resolved to turn over a new leaf, having discovered that Gäseler is not worth the emotional energy she has invested in hating him; a ritual cleansing takes place when she goes for a swim in an open-air pool. Heinrich's mother has moved to another 'uncle'; but when Albert was helping in the removal Heinrich noticed a momentary glance of understanding between him and his mother and it is the memory of this glance and the hope that it may turn into something more permanent that closes the novel. What *Der Spiegel* maliciously called Böll's 'consolation effect' ('Trost-Effekt') is very strong at the end of *Haus ohne Hüter* (anon., 1961, p. 77). It is a hope for a better life purely in the private sphere. For it is juxtaposed with an uncompromisingly pessimistic picture of society. The Brielachs' move to their new home is a calvary, accompanied by whistles and catcalls from the surrounding spectators. The guests at the inn in Bietenhahn sing the same old songs they sang in the 1930s. When Frau Holstege learns that Gäseler is in the vicinity she insists on confronting him personally. It comes to blows, but Albert reports resignedly: 'We were no match for them' ('Wir kamen nicht gegen sie auf') (p. 497). In the socio-political sphere the years of hope were at an end.

5

A Feeling of Responsibility
(1955–1963)

On 5 May 1955 the Paris Agreements came into force; the Federal
Republic had attained full sovereignty. Four days later it became a
member of NATO and on 2 January 1956 the first units of the new
Federal Army were formed in Andernach. Compulsory national
service for men was agreed by Parliament, with the support of the
SPD, in July 1956. Re-militarisation against the 'enemy abroad' was
combined with measures against the 'enemy within': a month later
the Communist Party was declared unconstitutional and banned by
the Constitutional Court, a measure more symbolic than real, in
that the Communists had been increasingly losing support and
represented by now a tiny, insignificant part of the population.
These were years of militant anti-Communism in West Germany,
when the Federal Foreign Minister Heinrich von Brentano could
compare the later poems of Bertolt Brecht to those of the Nazi poet
Horst Wessel (Wagenbach, 1979, p. 136). Böll later referred to the
'witch hunt for intellectuals and Communists' organised by the
committee 'Rettet die Freiheit' (Rescue Liberty) (E 2, pp. 577f.);
this was a committee which was constituted in Cologne in February
1959 under the chairmanship of Rainer Barzel, later to become the
CDU's candidate for the Federal chancellorship, and which was
alarmed about those intellectuals who were critical of the Federal
Republic's achievements, were in favour of a *rapprochement* with East
Germany and were opposed to the Bundeswehr's being equipped
with atomic weapons (Barzel, 1959).

In the elections of 1957 Böll for the first time did not vote for the
CDU (Limberg, p. 10). In this he was, not for the only time, out of
step with his fellow-countrymen, who returned Adenauer to power
with his first and only absolute majority. The economy had been
growing steadily by over 8 per cent per annum since 1950, by 1957
there was effectively no unemployment, and Adenauer's appeal to
voters 'not to rock the boat' ('Keine Experimente') was widely
accepted. In January 1958 the Treaty of Rome came into effect. The
European Economic Community opened up new markets for West

German firms, and by 1960 the hourly earnings of an industrial worker were the highest in the community, bar Luxemburg (Kloss, 1976, p. 85). The logic, if not the intention, of these two basics of Adenauer's policies, the economic integration of the Federal Republic into Western Europe and its military integration into the Atlantic Alliance, was to consolidate the division of Germany. Thus at each step the German Democratic Republic responded by becoming more closely integrated in the Eastern bloc, militarily in the Warsaw Pact, economically in Comecon. When in August 1961 the Berlin Wall was built to stem the outflow of refugees from East Germany to the West, Böll commented that one thing it did prove was the bankruptcy of the Federal Government's 'politics of strength'. Having for years acted on the assumption that the Soviet government might be forced to make concessions over the division of Germany — the 'Hallstein doctrine', first activated in 1957, declared that the Federal government would break off diplomatic relations with any state which recognised the German Democratic Republic — Adenauer would now be forced to negotiate under far less favourable conditions than before (E 1, p. 472). In 1959 Adenauer had suffered a loss of prestige when he attempted to manipulate the office of the Federal President, first announcing his intention to stand for that office, then, apparently when he realised that the President held less political power than he had assumed, standing down again. In the parliamentary elections of 1961 the CDU/CSU lost ground but were still able to form a government in coalition with the FDP. But Adenauer's moral standing was further reduced when in October 1962 on the orders of his Minister of Defence, Franz Josef Strauss, the offices of the weekly *Der Spiegel* were invaded by police, its editors arrested — one of them in Franco's Spain — , and Adenauer announced to the Federal Parliament that an 'abyss of high treason' had been uncovered, charges which were never substantiated. Strauss was forced to leave office, and a year later Adenauer himself stood down as chancellor.

The years 1955–6 marked a caesura in the literary scene too. 1955 was the year in which Thomas Mann died. The following year Bertolt Brecht and Gottfried Benn died. All at once the German-speaking world had lost its greatest novelist, dramatist and poet, writers as radically different from each other as could be, but each of whom represented a link with the literary past. Looking back in 1977 Böll had the impression that it was only from the mid-1950s onwards that the new German literature began to be recognised, that conservative prejudice began to be overcome (Lenz, p. 74). This coincided with the moment when the Gruppe 47 began to become a 'public institution', a media event rather than a workshop, something which Böll regretted, while recognising the paradox: up to 1955 the Group was practically invisible and therefore had no influence on the developments of post-war Germany; after 1955, as a public and therefore quasi-official institution, it had lost any chance it might have had to influence these developments (E 2, pp. 163ff.). A further factor was the emergence of a new generation of writers. In 1955 Martin Walser, ten years younger than Böll, was awarded the prize of the Group. In 1957 Alfred Andersch's *Sansibar oder der letzte Grund* was published, a novel set in the late 1930s in Germany and owing much to Böll's *Wo warst du, Adam?* and *Haus ohne Hüter* in its technique of multiple focalisation. The following year Gerd Gaiser's *Schlußball* appeared, satirising the newly affluent West Germany society through similar techniques. Both Andersch and Gaiser had experienced the Nazis and the war as adults. But in 1959, almost simultaneously with the publication of Böll's *Billard um halbzehn*, there appeared radically new literary forms from Günter Grass (born 1927) and Uwe Johnson (born 1934), *Die Blechtrommel* and *Mutmassungen über Jakob*, and 1959 was widely regarded as the year in which West German literature made a European impact.

These were the years in which Böll's popular reputation was established. Cheap paperback editions of *Wo warst du, Adam?* (1955), *Und sagte kein einziges Wort* (1957) and *Haus ohne Hüter* (1958) were published by Ullstein. The former also appeared in the GDR in 1956, the first of Böll's books to be printed in East Germany. From 1957 his short stories began to be anthologised for schoolchildren and interpretations of them to appear in *Der Deutschunterricht* and *Wirkendes Wort*, journals for teachers. The first independent publications devoted to Böll appeared in 1958: a twenty-four page pamphlet by the Luxemburger Léopold Hoffmann, and a bibliography of his works and their reception by Hanne-Christa Bertermann. By 1961 *Der Spiegel* could describe Böll as 'Germany's most successful post-war author'; translations of his works had appeared in eighteen countries; world-wide sales of his books had passed the 2 million mark; and 'for some years' already there had been initiatives to put him forward for the Nobel Prize for literature, initiatives which, *Der Spiegel* maliciously remarked, came from abroad, not from the Federal Republic (anon., 1961, pp. 71f.).

It was at this time that Böll on his own account developed a new feeling of 'responsibility' for the future course of his country's history, having hitherto been content to let others make the decisions (Lenz, p. 56). His involvement took various forms. He was associated, although not very actively, with the Grünwald Circle which Hans Werner Richter, Gerhard Scszesny and Hans Jochen Vogel founded in March 1956 to counter what they perceived as an upsurge in neo-fascist activities (Richter, 1986, p. 78). In March 1958 he signed the manifesto *Kampf dem Atomtod* ('Fight atomic death'), which appealed to the government to reject nuclear weapons and support a nuclear-free zone in Europe (Wagenbach, 1979, pp. 144f.). He had been a founder member of the Cologne branch of the Society for Christian–Jewish Cooperation at the beginning of the 1950s, and in 1959 he helped to found the Germania Judaica in Cologne, an archive which documents the history of the Jews in Germany (FT, p. 117). In November 1960 he was one of a number of West German writers who expressed their solidarity with the 121 French intellectuals who had publicly defended the right to disobey orders in the war in Algeria, and was involved in the controversy which ensued when Friedrich Sieburg argued that it was the duty of intellectuals to support the authority of the State (Wagenbach, 1979, pp. 176f.). In the same month he and numerous writers, among them Grass, Hans Magnus Enzensberger and Walser, protested against Adenauer's declared intention to set up a government-controlled television channel and threatened to boycott it (ibid., p. 178). His essays and speeches became not only more frequent, but also more biting. The address 'Wo ist dein Bruder?' which he gave in March 1956 during the 'Week of Brotherliness' organised by the Society for Christian–Jewish Cooperation has already been quoted with its attack on West German prosperity, which Böll saw as founded on dubious moral values and still more dubious economic ones (E 1, pp. 167ff.). In the same year he visited Sweden, one of the first post-war German writers to do so (E 3, p. 199), and Poland, where one of the people he met was Marcel Reich-Ranicki, for whom two years later Böll was able to stand surety when he decided to leave Poland and settle in the Federal Republic (Reich-Ranicki, 1985). The 'Polish Spring' which brought Gomulka to power had just begun and Böll's account of his journey was relatively optimistic as regards the political situation there. He was impressed by the working-class Catholicism he found — only in Ireland did one otherwise find working-class people in the churches. But he also warned his fellow-countrymen against attempting to adjust Poland's Western boundaries, as conservative politicians were urging (E 1, pp. 210ff.). The question of the Oder–Neisse frontier is touched on again in the first of his three 'Wuppertal speeches', 'Die Sprache als Hort der Freiheit' (1959), which set out one of his fundamental credos: the writer's responsibility to his own medium, language, which can so easily be abused by demagogues. A second speech

111

(1960), was more radical still. In it he denied that there could be any real understanding between society and the writer; paradoxically, in view of his own popularity, he cited the painter Van Gogh, the prototype of the artist whose recognition came only after his death. The most notorious of the essays of these years, however, was his 'Brief an einen jungen Katholiken' (1958), a bitter polemic against the role of the Catholic Church in the Third Reich, a role which the Church was continuing to play under Adenauer, preoccupied with the dangers of sexual immorality while ignoring those of political immorality, supporting — at least tacitly — both Hitler's militarism and the new Bundeswehr. This 'letter' was to have been broadcast on South-West German Radio, but the newly appointed Catholic controller banned it (anon., 1959). Böll's quarrel with his Church was to become an important aspect of his writing in the years that followed, culminating in the postcript he wrote to Carl Amery's critique of the Church's social position, *Die Kapitulation oder Deutscher Katholizismus heute*, and the novel *Ansichten eines Clowns*, both of which appeared in 1963.

Böll's active involvement in journalism at the beginning of the 1960s is a further indication of the radicalisation of his standpoint, the recognition that imaginative literature was not enough. In 1960, together with his friends Walter Warnach and H.A.P. Grieshaber, he helped to found a new quarterly journal, *Labyrinth*, edited by Werner von Trott zu Solz. Von Trott was from an old-established noble German family — his brother Adam was a member of the Kreisau Circle and was executed in 1944 for his part in the plot to assassinate Hitler; in 1931 Werner had joined the Communist Party and in 1942 he converted to Catholicism (E 2, pp. 186ff.). His book *Widerstand heute* was one which had the greatest influence on Böll (EZ, p. 10); an extract from it concludes Böll's 1978 reader *Mein Lesebuch*. The journal aimed at a renewal of German Catholicism and a somewhat mystical *rapprochement* between the two Germanies. An editorial preface to the second issue described the journal's editors as people who 'have not yet got beyond 1945. They cannot live without their fatherland. They perished with it, they have entered into its lost nature and history: into their labyrinth' ('sind noch nicht über 1945 hinausgekommen. Sie können ohne ihr Vaterland nicht leben. Sie sind mit ihm untergegangen, sie sind eingegangen in seine verlorene Natur und Geschichte: in ihr Labyrinth'). The journal was directed neither at East nor at West Germans: 'It seeks the Germans in East and West who have fallen down through the imaginary floor of post-war Germany, who do not assert themselves as Russians against the Americans nor as Americans against the

Russians, but rather open themselves up to both and try to encounter both with understanding, and who in the tragedy of world
conflicts experience their own' ('Es sucht die Deutschen in Ost und
West, die durch den imaginären Boden Nachkriegsdeutschlands
durchgebrochen sind, die sich nicht als Russen gegen die Amerikaner und nicht als Amerikaner gegen die Russen behaupten, sondern sich beiden aufschließen und ihnen gerecht werden wollen, die
in der Tragödie der Weltgegensätze ihre eigene erfahren') (*Labyrinth*
1, 1960, no. 2, p. 3). One of Böll's contributions was a long discussion with Warnach on the historical role of Germany within the
Catholic Church. Böll confessed to a dilemma: he had the feeling
that the whole of German history had been lost because of the crimes
of the Nazis, but at the same time recognised the need to take
responsibility for the past. In the Middle Ages Germany's role had
been to protect the Church; any such future role could come about
only through a position of political and military weakness, the great
opportunity which 1945 had granted and which was now being
squandered (I, pp. 26ff.). Böll was evidently at this stage trying to
break out of his isolation, but the context within which he was
operating was not a political one. Other contributions to the journal
were less mystical. In June 1961 he denounced Cardinal Frings's
appeal to Catholics to invest in stocks and shares; this crass identification of the Church with capitalism forgot that St Francis had been
'married to poverty' and implied that the poor could not be Christians (E 1, pp. 455ff.). Two major essays, 'Hierzulande' and 'Zwischen Gefängnis und Museum', appeared in the first and second
issues respectively. The former foreshadowed even more directly
than hitherto the thesis of the Mitscherlichs: Böll accused his
compatriots of having learned nothing from the war and the years of
hunger that followed it: 'How few are the faces in this country which
reveal that their owners are capable of mourning and memory. . . .
Pain has not become wisdom, mourning not strength' ('Wie wenige
Gesichter in diesem Land lassen erkennen, daß der Besitzer der
Trauer und der Erinnerung fähig ist. . . . Schmerz ist nicht Weisheit,
Trauer nicht Kraft geworden' (E 1, pp. 372, 373). In the second he
described the two Germanies as exact complements of one another:
in the West, the 'museum', one could write what one pleased,
provided it was done in an aesthetically satisfactory manner, while
in the East, the 'prison', that would be denounced as formalism, and
direct political criticism of the system was impossible. *Labyrinth*
failed to attract enough readers and folded after five issues. Böll
continued his journalism in the service of the weekly *Die Zeit*, at first
irregularly, later fortnightly with a series of nineteen 'Letters from

the Rhineland' under the pseudonym Lohengrin (1962–3), in which he satirised the behaviour of the CDU, the Catholic Church and the media from the point of view of a provincial school-teacher. The success of the series prompted a further one, 'Briefe an einen Freund jenseits der Grenzen', letters to a citizen of the GDR under the pseudonym Loki.

Many of these pieces are ephemeral, the scandals they refer to now completely forgotten. The 'Briefe an einen Freund jenseits der Grenzen' take up the theme of divided Germany, meting out ridicule at censorship on both sides, drawing attention to the activities of the 'Central Committee' both of the Catholic Church in the West and the Communist Party in the East. One piece which Böll wrote for *Die Zeit* has never been republished, 'Gesamtdeutsches Jägerlatein', the account of an occasion in a restaurant in East Berlin with two GDR colleagues, who end up talking about their hunting activities, while across the room he observes a working-class family celebrating something but obviously taken aback at the size of the bill (*Die Zeit*, 2.3.1962, p. 12). It provoked controversy at the time, when Böll was accused in the East German weekly *Sonntag* of having given in to pressure from the Bonn authorities to criticise the GDR in order to compensate for the fact that his books were being published there (Reich-Ranicki, 1962). Böll's position in these years was more that of a radical nonconformist Christian than of a political thinker. He consistently attacked the CDU, but mainly because he regarded its politicians as having misappropriated the adjective 'Christian'. His sympathetic 1961 study of Karl Marx concluded by asserting that Marx had aimed to overcome man's self-alienation; but on the one side Marx's teaching had been used to justify inhumanity and on the other, in modern capitalism, materialism had been adopted whole-heartedly (E 1, p. 413). Other writers were becoming more directly involved in party politics at this time. In 1961 Martin Walser edited a widely-distributed anthology of statements by writers and intellectuals pleading for a change of government; they included Grass, Enzensberger, Amery and Richter, but not Böll (Walser, 1961). In 1963 in an article entitled 'Was heute links sein könnte', while polemicising against both CDU and SPD, he reserved his most biting scorn for the latter, a party with a tradition, unlike its conservative opponent, but a tradition which it had betrayed. Evidently Böll himself felt betrayed by the SPD, having once already been betrayed by the CDU. In 1959 at Godesberg the SPD had undertaken a major revision of its policies, deleting for the first time all reference to nationalisation, accepting the structures of capitalism in an attempt to widen its appeal beyond the confines of the working classes.

It was at this time that Ireland began to play an important role in Böll's work. Already in *Haus ohne Hüter* we find the idealised figure of Leen, Albert's Irish wife; later, along with his wife Annemarie, Böll translated various books, especially plays, by Irish writers, Brendan Behan, J.M. Synge, Tomás O'Crohan, Bernard Shaw and Flann O'Brien, and he wrote a a number of essays on Irish affairs. He first visited Ireland with his family in 1954, returning there regularly for holidays and to write. In 1958 he bought a house in Dugort. From December 1954 he published a series of impressions of Ireland in the *Frankfurter Allgemeine Zeitung*, and these eventually came out in book form in 1957 as his *Irisches Tagebuch*.

Irisches Tagebuch today is remarkable mainly for its period charm. In a kind of epilogue which he wrote for the *Frankfurter Allgemeine Zeitung* in 1967, he admitted that he probably had experienced Ireland at a historic moment, just as it was about to make the great leap forward into the twenty-first century. The dogs no longer chased the cars, having got used to them; the newspapers were no longer filled with pictures of nuns; safety-pins were no longer the universal fasteners; the smells had gone — this he regretted, smells play a major part in the sensual spectrum of his novels. More ominous in his view was the arrival of 'The Pill', which was succeeding where no British governor had ever succeeded, in reducing the numbers of Irish children (E 2, pp. 255ff.). The existentialist component in Böll's outlook is illustrated by his respect for the Irish love of improvisation; family planning would be the reverse of this, a motif which is repeated more than twenty years later in *Fürsorgliche Belagerung*.

While recognising the changes that had taken place, Böll refused to retract anything he had written. And one may doubt whether the book was ever intended as a realistic portrait of Ireland at all. It is prefaced with the proviso: 'This Ireland exists: but anyone who goes there and does not find it has no claims on the author' ('Es gibt dieses Irland: wer aber hinfährt und es nicht findet, hat keine Ersatzansprüche an den Autor') (R 3, p. 11). Marcel Reich-Ranicki perceptively described *Irisches Tagebuch* as 'a disguised book on Germany' ('ein verstecktes Deutschland-Buch') (Reich-Ranicki, 1963, p. 135). It was not written for the Irish but for Böll's fellow-countrymen, and it betrays Böll's continued concern for contemporary Germany even when he was ostensibly writing about a distant land. Many of the motifs from Böll's novels recur here: cigarette-smoking, tea-drinking, cinema-going. But more important are the contrasts with West German life styles. The Irish love of improvisation

Heinrich Böll: A German for His Time

contrasts with the Germans' desire to build for eternity — only to find everything destroyed by the following generation. In 1962 Böll compared the relationship of the French to their national history with that of the Germans and went on:

> I should say that a revolution is only possible where tradition is very strong. These things are connected, but in our case we simply lack both an awareness of history and of tradition, tradition even in the more or less banal meaning of the word, business traditions or political ones. And that's why we have never had any revolutions, any genuine counter-movements.

> (Ich würde sagen, daß eine Revolution nur da möglich ist, wo die Tradition sehr stark ist. Das hängt miteinander zusammen, während bei uns einfach sowohl das Bewußtsein für Geschichte wie das für Tradition fehlt, Tradition auch in einem mehr oder weniger banalen Sinne, Geschäftstradition etwa oder politische. Und deshalb gibt es bei uns auch keine Revolutionen, keine echten Gegenbewegungen.)

(I, p. 28)

In Ireland he found traditions: Irish history was continuous. 'Skelett einer menschlichen Siedlung' ('Skeleton of a human settlement') contrasts the gradual decay of an abandoned house in Ireland with the violent destruction of property in Germany's wars — and Böll's children promptly proceed to raze what is left of the old settlement. 'Kleiner Beitrag zur abendländischen Mythologie' ('Small contribution to Western mythology') describes two ruins on an island, the one from the sixth, the other from the twentieth century, but whose stones are indistinguishable. In the context of Böll's portrayal of German society the most significant, forward-pointing feature of Irish society is the emphasis he places on the life of the community, something which is missing in his depictions of West German society and its lonely individuals at this time. It is a community in which even the bureaucrats, the officials, the railway personnel, the bank-managers, those representatives of an inhumane and fascistoid bureaucracy in Böll's early works, are friendly and helpful. Both *Und sagte kein einziges Wort* and *Haus ohne Hüter* portrayed the poverty of the Bogners and the Brielachs as 'disgraceful' in the eyes of West German society; on the steamer crossing to Ireland Böll felt that 'Europe's social order was already taking on a different shape: poverty was not only "no disgrace" but neither an honour nor a disgrace' ('hier schon nahm Europas soziale Ordnung andere Formen an: Armut war nicht nur "keine Schande" mehr, sondern weder Ehre noch Schande') (R 3, p. 11). *Haus ohne Hüter* showed deep class divisions in West German society; a cinema audience in

116

Ireland realised the 'classless society' (p. 48). Böll's analysis of Irish society was hardly profound, nor politically perceptive; it is meaningful only in the context of his attitude to his own country.

Hidden away in one of the episodes, however, is an even more interesting remark. In a bar in the back streets of Limerick, surrounded by impoverished men in rags drowning their troubles in Guinness, he describes his companion's fear for his own safety in such surroundings. This, says Böll, is one of the stupidest of prejudices. Much more dangerous were the prosperous drinkers in the bar of the Shelbourne Hotel in Dublin. If only these men in rags *were* more dangerous (p. 43). One reproach made of Böll by critics outside West Germany in these years was that he nowhere suggested that the victims of society had any redress or could do anything to change the situation. This passage of *Irisches Tagebuch* implies approval for more radical behaviour — and when the current 'troubles' in Northern Ireland broke out in 1969 his immediate reaction was one of understanding. In a newspaper article he outlined the injustices of British rule in the North, the discrimination against Catholics practised there, contrasting it with the absence of confessionalism in the South, and concluding with the hope that the newly discovered republican and socialist traditions would not become the common enemy for Protestants and Catholics alike (E 2, pp. 456ff.). He seemed to be envisaging a revolution based on the kind of traditions he had suggested a few years earlier were lacking in Germany.

Böll's next longer work to be published after *Haus ohne Hüter* was the story *Das Brot der frühen Jahre*, written, according to the author's note, in Keel, Achill (Ireland) between July and September 1955, and serialised in the *Frankfurter Allgemeine Zeitung* in December of the same year. Like its two predecessors, it contains no direct references to events of the time but its angry tone may be taken to imply Böll's own frustration with what was happening in the Federal Republic. It is set within one day, Monday, 14 March (R 3, p. 128), and as Böll was concerned with calendar accuracy in the case of his next novel *Billard um halbzehn* (Conard, 1981, pp. 133f.), the year must be the year of writing, 1955 (unfortunately there is an inconsistency in the text, which elsewhere refers to the 15 March (R 3, p. 115); this would place the story in 1954). As in *Haus ohne Hüter*, West Germany's increasing affluence is evident in the crowded cafés and the washing-machines which the central figure, Walter Fendrich, services; he himself, twenty-three years old, drives his own car. But almost more important than this present is the memory of the past. Fendrich has, it is true, nothing but scorn for his landlady's

117

husband, Herr Brotig, a Fred Bogner viewed from without, who is always complaining about 'his lost youth, which the war allegedly stole from him' ('seine verlorene Jugend, die ihm angeblich der Krieg gestohlen hat') (p. 113). He himself was only fourteen or fifteen when the war ended. The 'early years' referred to in the title are the immediate post-war years, the years prior to the Currency Reform, years of physical deprivation and hunger, which contrast with the later years of material well-being but spiritual deprivation, the comfortable but empty life that Fendrich was leading until the day he met Hedwig, which the story describes.

The germ of the story was Böll's observation that a whole generation of young West Germans of Fendrich's age had developed an 'almost brutal vitality . . . a kind of nihilism' ('eine fast brutale Vitalität . . . Art Nihilismus'), understandably in view of the destruction and starvation in the world in which they were growing up (Q, pp. 111f.). *Das Brot der frühen Jahre* is reminiscent of John Osborne's play *Look Back in Anger*, which came out a year later in England and was an immediate success in West Germany too. Walter Fendrich is an 'angry young man', and to some extent Hedwig shares his views, rejecting the bourgeois conventionality of Hilde Kamenz, for example. Their youth is emphasised in Hedwig's encounter with a man in the street, who was 'old, at least thirty-five' ('alt, sicher fünfunddreißig') (p. 164), or Walter's realisation how 'old' his landlady is — 'at least forty' (pp. 168f.): Böll himself was thirty-seven at the time. Like Jimmy Porter's, Fendrich's 'anger' is undirected, more a feeling of impotent rage than of revolutionary fervour. He has no political awareness whatsoever; ministers and party functionaries fill him with indifference and the exhortations his father receives to take part in demonstrations, to do something for the cause of liberty, do not interest him either. His is the 'ohne mich' ('count me out') generation. 'Hatred' is a major component of his character and a leitmotiv of the story, occuring a dozen or so times in the narrative and directed against such disparate objects as his job, doctors, his employer, washing-machines, 'decisive people', the word 'cheap' and the trees that architects draw in their plans. Its converse is the word 'indifferent' — there seems to be nothing in between. He is looking *back* in anger, as he reminds Ulla, the daughter of his employer Wickweber, at his feeling of impotence when he first began to work for him, his hunger for bread while the Wickwebers grudged every penny they had to give their employees; the only 'fun' he and his fellow-apprentices had was 'hatred'. There is a strong undercurrent of violence in his character, but it is not one directed so much against his employers or the social establishment, as against himself or the objects around him: when salvaging property from the post-war ruins he always destroys the mirrors in order not to see his face in them. Ominously, he prefers to clean his razor-blades on the papers meant for women to wipe their lipstick on and which bear the image of a woman's red lips. When he first sees Hedwig he has 'for one mad moment the wish to destroy that face, as the painter destroys the stone from which he has taken only one impression' ('für einen wahnsinnigen Augenblick lang den Wunsch, dieses Gesicht zu zerstören wie der Maler den Stein, von dem er nur einen einzigen Abdruck genommen hat') (p. 116) and as he leaves the railway station with her he thinks 'that I would possess her and that in order to possess her I would destroy anything that might prevent me from doing so' (daß ich sie besitzen würde und daß ich, um sie zu besitzen, alles zerstören würde, was mich daran hindern könnte') (p. 117). The machismo of his character is confirmed later when, only a few hours after their first meeting he thinks of her as 'territory' which he has 'discovered' and on which he has not yet 'planted his stake' ('Ich hatte das Land entdeckt und immer noch nicht mein Zeichen eingesetzt') (p. 164).

All of this makes for an interesting study of nihilistic youth. However, the story is seriously flawed both by its own standards and by external standards which Böll himself would later accept. An example of the latter is Fendrich's attitude to women. Clearly we need not view his authority as that of the text. But Hedwig herself is extraordinarily unemancipated even for 1955. She has come to town to train as a teacher, because her father believes she should be able to support herself. But she is not enthusiastic about the prospect and merely blushes when Fendrich offers to support her. The reader is left with the impression that after their night of love Walter and Hedwig got married and lived happily ever after, she as housewife and he as breadwinner.

Even in the story's own terms there are inconsistencies which cannot merely be explained according to the limited narrative perspective. *Das Brot der frühen Jahre* is a first person narrative, like *Und sagte kein einziges Wort*. It is possible to explain the confusions over whether it was 14 or 15 March, whether Hilde Kamenz is a 'relative' (p. 145) or merely an 'acquaintance' (p. 166) by reference to Fendrich's unreliable memory, although this would cast doubt on other features of the narrative. Unlike the earlier novel, it is told from a vantage-point later than the events which it describes. At the beginning Fendrich writes: 'Later I often meditated on the way things would have turned out if I had not met Hedwig at the station' ('Später dachte ich oft darüber nach, wie alles gekommen wäre,

wenn ich Hedwig nicht am Bahnhof abgeholt hätte') (pp. 95, 117).
We do not know whether Fred Bogner's return to his family will be
permanent; here we must assume that Fendrich's transformation
through love has been so. *Das Brot der frühen Jahre* is the story of a
conversion, like so many dramas of German expressionism. Conard
compares Fendrich's encounter with Hedwig to St Paul's Damascus
(Conard, 1981, p. 114), and Strindberg's *To Damascus* was a seminal
influence on expressionist playwrights. Fendrich's career has the
familiar three stages. His initial idealism is thwarted by Wickweber
and the realisation that in order to get on in life one has to cheat and
be ruthless; there follows his cynical acceptance of this life, including
his engagement to Wickweber's daughter; finally he meets his
Damascus when his eyes are opened by his encounter with love. As
in expressionist drama the Christ symbol is never far away; in the
story Fendrich is 'scourged' by the lights of the traffic (pp. 167,
170). But he does not write like one who has undergone a transformation of this kind; much of the old cynicism seems still present,
cheating the customer over his expenses (p. 96), rejecting the
inferior custard and cigarettes of the early post-war years (p. 110).

Two further aspects of Böll/Fendrich's style are significant. One is
the often obtrusive symbolism. The 'bread' of the title is a favourite
motif of Böll's; in one of his rare commentaries on his own works he
spoke of an

> aesthetics of bread in literature, the bread that in the first place is the real
> bread baked by the baker or by the housewife, the peasant. . . . A sign of
> brotherliness, not only that, also of peace, even of liberty . . . the most
> effective aphrodisiac . . . host, wafer, mazzoth, magically transformed
> into the tablet which takes its form from the host, standing for brotherli-
> ness, peace, liberty, aphrodisiac.

> (Asthetik des Brotes in der Literatur, des Brotes, das zuerst das reale, vom
> Bäcker oder von der Hausfrau, vom Bauern gebackene ist. . . . Zeichen
> der Brüderlichkeit, nicht nur, auch des Friedens, sogar der Freiheit . . .
> das wirkungsvollste Aphrodisiakum . . . Hostie, Oblate, Mazze, magisch
> verwandelt zur Pille, die ihre Form von der Hostie hat, Ersatz ist für
> Brüderlichkeit, Frieden, Freiheit, Aphrodisiakum.)

> (E 2, p. 83)

Less satisfactory is the constant presence of the colours red and
green. Red is associated with all that Fendrich rejects; Scharnhorst's
collar in the school portrait (Prussian militarism); Iphigenie's lips
(the classical heritage); the ace of hearts (love? chance?); the station-
master's cap; Ulla's coat and the ink with which she scores out the
name of a dead employee; Hilde's car; and many other objects.

A Feeling of Responsibility (1955–1963)

Green is its opposite: the colour of Hedwig's parents' house, her coat, her pullover; Fendrich even feels her hair must be green and wishes to buy her green roses. In *Wo warst du, Adam?* Böll had used similar contrasts; here it is so overdone that the reader is left pondering in the end over the significance of Hedwig's blushing, or of her red lipstick. There is also an inordinate number of similes in the text — up to ten in the space of two pages at one point; the seconds pass like coins one throws into the water; his view is perforated like a metal sheet in the factory; something like an ocean lies between him and the car; he thinks of Ulla like someone who suddenly decides to switch on the light in the room where someone has died (pp. 128ff.). Imagery related to water is especially prominent, possibly in keeping with Fendrich's profession, servicing washing-machines, but the latter itself is symbolic of society's search for cleanliness without atonement. In his *Probleme der Lyrik* (1951) Gottfried Benn denigrated similes as the mark of an inferior writer. Here the effect is undoubtedly overdone, but again it is a feature of the 'Wandlungsgeschichte' pattern, whereby the reader has to be persuaded of the genuine nature of the conversion by all possible means. West Germany is a 'desert' (p. 170); Böll's response to materialist society is to be found purely in the oasis of personal relationships and a diffuse aesthetic symbolism.

For all its weaknesses this was the text chosen by Herbert Vesely when he made the first 'new wave' West German film in 1961. The film was not a success, neither with the critics nor with the public and it has been blamed for the delay in launching the 'young German film' (Jansen, 1984, p. 17). It tried to outdo Resnais and Antonioni in its complicated system of flashback patterns and reflects more closely the narrative pattern of Uwe Johnson's *Mutmassungen über Jakob* as the people Fendrich has left in the lurch try to reconstruct what happened on the fateful day. The story too constantly moves between past and present, as Fendrich remembers the 'early years'. He is preoccupied with time itself; the seconds-hand of his watch is 'a very precise little machine which was cutting slices from something invisible, from time, and it milled and drilled in the void, and the dust which it drilled from the void settled on me like a magic spell, turning me into a motionless column' ('eine kleine, sehr präzise Maschine, die Scheiben von etwas Unsichtbarem abschnitt, von der Zeit, und sie fräste und bohrte im Nichts herum, und der Staub, den sie aus dem Nichts herausbohrte, fiel über mich wie ein Zaubermittel, das mich in eine unbewegliche Säule verwandelte') (p. 128). He shares this temporal paralysis with other characters of this period, i.e. Nella Bach and Robert Fähmel; only at the end, as

121

he makes love to Hedwig, does he regain time again, in a remarkable vision in which myth, history and personal biography fuse together and even the smiling Mozart from Hesse's *Der Steppenwolf* seems to be present. The final sentence, however, ends in a particularly unfortunate manner: 'and I realised that I did not want to get on, I wanted to go back, to what I did not know, but back' ('und ich wußte, daß ich nicht vorwärts kommen wollte, zurückkommen wollte ich, wohin, wußte ich nicht, aber zurück') (R 3, p. 172). While 'getting on' is to be taken in the sense of 'getting on in life', i. e. materially, the converse is obscure. He cannot seriously wish to return to the 'early years' of hunger and exploitation, and the final effect is that of a Fendrich just as confused as he ever was.

In the same year the collection of five short stories *So ward Abend und Morgen* appeared, all of them written earlier. It includes the story which has been most anthologised, 'Die Waage der Baleks', which is almost unique in Böll's output in being set wholly in the historical past, around 1900. In 1956 a further collection, this time of 'amusing stories' was published, *Unberechenbare Gäste*; again it contained stories written earlier. Then in 1957 Böll published a further long short story on the clash of generations with the Karl May-like title *Im Tal der donnernden Hufe*. It was the first of Böll's works to appear in the Insel-Bücherei, a series of little books noted for their exquisite layout, which frequently included large print, wide margins, gothic letters and a colourful hard cover; Rainer Maria Rilke's *Die Weise von Liebe und Tod des Cornet Rilke* had founded the success of the series in 1912 and there was frequently an aura of kitsch about these editions. Böll's story unfortunately fitted this pattern.

Paul and Griff are two fourteen-year-old boys who can find nothing in the adult world to identify with. Paul is preoccupied with sexual longings but has been taught to regard sex as sinful and is determined to shoot himself. Griff finds life simply boring and spends his spare time lying in the loft of an old outhouse, smashing jars of jam against the wall and dreaming of adventure. Katharina Mirzow is a girl of their age who is physically well-developed and whose figure provokes the local chemist and the local teacher to lust; she herself, however, takes her body so for granted that she naïvely unbuttons her blouse when she finds Paul staring at her breasts. Sexual symbolism abounds: the 'hairy tennis balls' over which Paul wants to shoot himself are explicitly related to female breasts, but must also have connotations of testicles; Paul's father's pistol, lovingly cleaned every Friday evening, is evidently phallic — that it is never used implies Paul's misunderstanding over his parent's sexuality; women's handbags are a further object of Paul's sexual curiosity. What is embarrassing about the story is the way in which Böll tries to suggest that adolescent sexuality is normal but its suppression is equally normal. Paul views Katharina's breasts and then contents himself with firing his father's pistol in the air as she leaves in the train. Günter Grass only a few years later gave a more realistic, less romanticised picture of adolescence in his *Katz und Maus* — and more than sixty years earlier Frank Wedekind in his *Frühlings Erwachen* had implied a more subversive view of puberty.

Nevertheless, Böll's depiction of adult West German society remains a critical one. Paul's father is sentimentally attached to his wartime experiences, lovingly cleaning his revolver every Friday evening before going off to drink with his friends. The history teacher is determined to rehabilitate the memory of Admiral Tirpitz, whose aggressive militarism was a main cause of the First World War. In the background is the constant noise from a rowing regatta in which Paul's older sisters are prominent — adult society is preoccupied with escapist sports. Unusually for Böll the setting is the wine-growing part of the Rhineland. In the same year Böll wrote of the difference between the 'wine-drinker's Rhine' and the 'schnapps-drinker's Rhine' — his own was the latter (R 3, p. 222) — and a few years later he disparaged the romantic Rhine of wine and song and the Lorelei: Cologne's carnival was more political than that of Basle (E 1, p. 337). But as in *Das Brot der frühen Jahre* his criticism of West German society in *Im Tal der donnernden Hufe* has an explicitly unpolitical basis. Katharina's mother is a Communist; but her Communism is presented as sterile, nostalgic, dogmatic, her slogans no more than incantations (R 3, p. 262). In November 1956 Nikita Khrushchev, whose name appears in a newspaper headline quoted three times in the story, had ordered the Soviet army to put down the uprising in Hungary. Böll was one of those who protested publicly (E 1, p. 202). But he has no alternative political solution to offer at this stage. *Im Tal der donnernden Hufe* appeared simultaneously in Frankfurt and in Leipzig, where its message must have seemed equally innocuous.

This diagnosis is confirmed by a contemporary review of *Irisches Tagebuch* and *Im Tal der donnernden Hufe* by Curt Hohoff. After the initial achievement of *Der Zug war pünktlich*, Böll had been 'threatening' to become a 'committed writer'; but these two latest works demonstrated that his talent was not allowing itself to be confined by political commitment; in them he had freed himself 'from the fug of inferior tobacco and wash-houses' (Hohoff, 1957, p. 1209). Hohoff's review prompted the essay 'Zur Verteidigung der Waschküchen', in which he accused Hohoff of petty-bourgeois prejudice which assumed that only scenes from the affluent milieu were worthy of presentation in literature. He concluded with a neat allusion to the literary cold war in divided Germany: 'in the meantime there exist theories of art which declare that anything that does *not* belong to the working classes is not worth portraying in literature. Is it that in our blessed society a counter-theory is being formulated?' ('inzwischen gibt es Kunsttheorien, die alles was *nicht* arbeitende Klasse ist, für literaturunwürdig erklären. Sollte sich in unserer gesegneten Gesellschaft eine Gegentheorie dazu bilden?') (E 1, p. 300; cf. Lenz, p. 74).

One area in which the literary cold war was particularly evident was that of satire, and it is Böll's satires of these years that represent his most convincing achievements: 'Doktor Murkes gesammeltes Schweigen' (1955), 'Es wird etwas geschehen' (1956), 'Hauptstädtisches Journal' and 'Der Wegwerfer' (1957) and 'Der Bahnhof von Zimpren' (1959). The first four of these were published together with the earlier 'Nicht nur zur Weihnachtszeit' in 1958. For the philosophers and literary theorists of German idealism from the end of the eighteenth century onwards, satire was a problematical concept, inasmuch as its *purposefulness*, its express aim to correct vices or follies, contradicted their belief that art had to do with beauty and beauty was defined by its very lack of purpose. In his *Über naive und sentimentalische Dichtung* (1796), Schiller regarded all modern literature as either elegiac or satirical, but was uneasy about the status of the latter as literature. Hegel regarded 'humour', the harmonising of opposing contradictions, as the pinnacle of the comic art, rather than satire, which is directed at removing them (Heise, 1964). This was the attitude rejected by, for example, Brecht in his *Flüchtlingsgespräche*, when Kalle reports that when his mother had no butter she used to spread humour on his bread (Brecht, 1961, p. 107). As late as 1964 Helmut Arntzen could point out the dearth of West German articles on satire, while in East Germany, where literature was given an express social function, the reverse was the case. Thus in 1959 in the GDR Georgina Baum had attacked bourgeois theories of comedy for discounting satire, while in the following year, in one of the few West German contributions on the genre, Kurt Wölfel had followed the traditional line that the satirist was aesthetically inferior to the epic writer: the former 'rejected' the world, while the latter attempted to treat it with 'understanding' (Arntzen, 1964). In this context there is considerable significance in Böll's turning to satire in order to stimulate his fellow-countrymen's self-awareness.

Some of the motifs from these stories are to be found in the longer works of the time. Doktor Murke's silences repeat on a satirical level the idea contained in the title of the novel *Und sagte kein einziges Wort*. In that novel too we find the motif of the graveyard where Fred likes to walk, occasionally being taken for one of the mourners or even on one occasion for the secret admirer of the dead girl; 'Es wird etwas geschehen' ends with the narrator leaving the hectic activity of Wunsiedel's factory and becoming a professional mourner. Where the satire is more aggressive, possibly even more emancipatory than the novel, is in its use of the grotesque to arouse the reader's laughter, to distance him from the characters and therefore to provoke him to think of alternatives. Fred Bogner is helpless, but we tend to identify with him; the narrator of 'Es wird etwas geschehen' is opportunistic, but the value of meditation he adopts is one which may be fruitful. Murke resists Bur-Malottke merely by giving him a few bad moments, making him decline the words 'that higher being which we honour' ('jenes höhere Wesen, das wir verehren') through all its cases in order that this phrase may be inserted in place of the word God; this gives Murke private satisfaction, as does his collection of silences, but neither of these activities will dislodge the Bur-Malottkes from their position of power. However, from the outset when we witness Murke's 'existential gymnastics', we are unable to take him altogether seriously and are therefore invited to find our own, more fruitful solution.

Böll's satires were more deliberately constructed than his novels: 'A satire is a plannable form of literature, one that comes into being in one's brain and then . . . has to be given material form' ('Eine Satire ist eine planbare Form der Literatur, die im Gehirn entsteht, und dann . . . versinnlicht werden muß) (I, p. 566). They all began with an 'idea': in the case of 'Doktor Murke' it was the notion of a collection of silences, and it took him a whole year, possibly even two, before he had worked out the context in which to place this idea; he then wrote it out in the space of a single day (Q, p. 112; Lengning, 1972, p. 106). With 'Nicht nur zur Weihnachtszeit' we may assume that the germ was the notion of Christmas all the year round, with 'Der Wegwerfer' the observation that so much unwanted mail drops through the letter-box that a professional bumph-destroyer might be appropriate; with the other satires the germ is less obvious. 'Doktor Murke' is appropriately set in a radio station. Between 1952 and 1962 no fewer than seventeen plays for radio by Böll were broadcast; he had ample experience of the setting, a place where a constant stream of words has to be transmitted, not all of which can be memorable. The satire is at the expense of the professional broadcasters, the infighting which goes on in broadcasting and the pretentious rubbish which goes out under the name of culture. But what gives it more bite is the character of Bur-Malottke, a confirmed Nazi up to 1945, a convinced Christian in the immediate post-war years, now, ten years later, regretting this religious enthusiasm and determined to erase from all his radio talks the word 'God'. In the character and career of Bur-Malottke Böll has summed up the opportunism which he regarded as disastrously typical of his fellow-countrymen. He has also placed in the story a reminiscence of his own school-days when one of his teachers made the class reduce four pages of Hitler's *Mein Kampf* to two (J, pp. 50f.; R 3, pp. 190). 'Es wird etwas geschehen', 'Der Wegwerfer' and 'Der Bahnhof von Zimpren' are more general satires on the absurdities of Western industrial society and its hectic, meaningless activity. Only 'Hauptstädtisches Journal' has its more specifically German basis, and it is the least comic of the group. The 'diary' is that of one of Hitler's generals who, now that the new Bundeswehr has been created, is looking forward to serving under Defence Minister Strauss; his is the mentality of an officer who measures honour in terms of men lost in action, who cannot understand the function of a political opposition and who is hoping to install some 'healthy maidens from the civilian population' ('gesunde Mädchen aus dem Volke' — the German is more ideological than any English translation can be) in his Academy for Military Reminiscences in order to sweeten the evenings for his comrades.

Five years after *Haus ohne Hüter* Böll's fourth novel, *Billard um halbzehn*, (1959), appeared. In some ways it follows on from its predecessor. Both introduce three generations of one family, a grandmother who wishes to assassinate a former Nazi, characters who are trapped in their own memories, unable to find a meaningful relationship to the present day. *Billard um halbzehn* too is a third person narrative, whose narrator has disappeared even more completely behind no fewer than ten focalisers. Within individual chapters the focus alters between characters, and even there the narrative technique can shift from direct to indirect interior monologue and to direct speech, as in the chapters in which Robert is telling Hugo or Heinrich Lenore about their respective pasts. Most confusing of all are the chapters centred on Johanna Fähmel, who has been confined to a mental hospital since the early part of the war. This motif was to become a common one in the literature of the next few years: the narrator of Günter Grass's *Die Blechtrommel* is writing from a similar institution; in Friedrich Dürrenmatt's *Die Physiker* (1961) Möbius is attempting to conceal his discovery of the key to the universe by feigning madness, only to find that the proprietor of the hospital is herself genuinely insane; and Peter Weiss set his play

126

Marat–Sade (1964) in the asylum of Charenton. In this variation on the theme of the upside-down world we are invited to regard Johanna as saner than those outside, as she has been institutionalised for openly opposing the Nazis; her action of shooting at a former Nazi who in 1958 has become a government minister has its own moral logic — this ' "absurd" shot from a mad lady' was described by Georg Lukács as 'one of the few humanly genuine ways in which the fascist past has been dealt with in Germany' ('eine der wenigen menschlich echten Bewältigungen der faschistischen Vergangenheit in Deutschland') (Reich-Ranicki, 1968, p. 331). In the context of the later Adenauer years, however, the motif is interesting for the despair with political institutions which it implies. Schrella is 'totally unpolitical' (R 3, p. 525). The unspecified party in power is making common cause with a militarist organisation, the 'Kampfbund' (pp. 510f.) — the name is reminiscent of the paramilitary organisations of the interwar years, Stahlhelm or SA, and implies the continuity of the German militarist traditions which Bernhard diagnoses as one important achievement of the novel (Bernhard, 1970, pp. 241–54). But the 'opposition', likewise unspecified, is divided into a 'right-wing' and a 'left-wing' group which are presented as equally unpleasant (R 3, pp. 507, 529f.). Even before the SPD had adopted its Godesberg programme Böll had rejected it.

Billard um halbzehn is set on 6 September 1958. Böll undertook extensive research for the novel (Conard, 1981, pp. 132–4). Nevertheless it contains only two specific references to historical events of the time: one is the name Dulles, Secretary of State in the Eisenhower administration and known for his uncompromising anti-Communism (R 3, p. 505); the other is the banner at the railway station welcoming the returning prisoners of war from the Soviet Union (p. 451). On 3 September 1958 the *Frankfurter Allgemeine Zeitung* reported that 470 had returned to West Germany through the reception camp at Friedland; in the previous month the figure had been 333. However, the real news at the beginning of September 1958 was dominated by the crisis in the straits of Formosa, on which Dulles was repeatedly cited, and by the rapidly increasing stream of *émigrés* from East Germany. Böll places his accent on the vestiges of the Nazi past; the irony is that Schrella, a victim of Nazi persecution, actually is arrested on his return to Germany, while the men who had invaded the Soviet Union, burning and pillaging, are greeted as heroes.

Like Thomas Mann's *Der Zauberberg*, it is a 'Zeitroman' in two senses: it is a historical novel which deals with the problems of the times, and it is also a novel about the nature of time itself. The three generations of Fähmels embody three stages of German history. Heinrich's is the self-confident Germany of Wilhelm II. His profession of architect indicates his constructive, forward-looking stance. Of humble rural origins, he comes to town and wins the contract to design a new abbey against the established opposition; he marries into a patrician family and founds his own dynasty, only to be brought up short by the militarism which leads to two world wars and the death of two sons. His surviving son Robert is of Böll's own generation. Seventeen when the Nazis take power, he is forced briefly to flee to Holland because of his anti-fascist connections. Later he becomes a stress analyst whose main function during the war is to destroy buildings which block the German artillery's line of fire — one of these buildings is his father's abbey. In a sense he incorporates the post-war 'Kahlschlag' mentality, insisting that all the remnants of the past be liquidated. But his stance is almost entirely a negative one, abstract, sterile. His son Joseph is studying to be an architect like his grandfather. There is something of Walter Fendrich's nihilism in his character, when he drives full speed along a road leading to a wrecked bridge. One of the projects he is involved in is the restoration of his grandfather's abbey, but when he discovers that his father had blown it up, he resolves to abandon architecture. The new generation will turn away from the 'restoration' — where it will turn to is left open.

In this historical panorama Böll uses two major sets of symbols. The one is that of the 'buffaloes and lambs'. As we have seen, Böll viewed the nationalists and conservative Catholics as truly responsible for Nazism. A key word of the novel is 'anständig' ('decent, respectable'). In 1956 Böll had suggested that it should be struck out from the German vocabulary, as belonging to a bygone age — there had even been 'anständige Nazis' (E 1, p. 172). He may have had in mind Himmler's infamous speech to his SS men at Poznan in October 1943, praising them for having remained 'anständig' while killing a thousand civilians (Hofer, 1957, p. 114). For Carl Amery 'Anstand' ('respectability') was a central concept in the system of secondary values which had enabled German Catholics to survive the Third Reich but had prevented them from taking active steps to resist fascism and protect their Jewish fellow-citizens (Amery, 1963, pp. 20ff.). In the novel Hindenburg is the incarnation of this mentality — 'anständig, anständig' (R 3, p. 413) — , and his bull-like head inspired in Böll the image of the 'buffalo', whose 'sacrament' is taken by those who were 'only doing their duty' and whose authority survives into the Germany of the 1950s, where people like Nettlinger have retained their power. Accordingly Johanna Fähmel shoots at the minister at the end of the novel because he incorporates those very values — it will be 'not the murder of a tyrant, but the murder of a respectable citizen' ('nicht Tyrannenmord, sondern Anständigenmord') (p. 512). The 'buffaloes' of the 1930s are opposed by a group who call themselves 'lambs'. The latter image is unfortunate and misleading, as Böll later recognised, as it implies passivity on the part of the decent, unpolitical ordinary man in the street, who merely 'endures' the crimes of his social superiors, and Böll later rejected it (Lenz, pp. 66f; I, pp. 424f., 546ff.). In fact the novel is less dualistic than the 'buffalo and lamb' symbolism suggests: Robert, for example, is neither; he protects Schrella but is never a member of the group, and indeed his very 'correctness', the key term used to describe his character, has undertones of the 'respectability' of the 'buffaloes'. The 'lambs' include both those who endure, such as Schrella — but even he is imprisoned for threatening first a Dutch, then an English politician (R 3, pp. 442f.) —, and those who actively resist, such as Johanna Fähmel and Ferdi Progulske, who tries to assasinate Wakiera with a home-made bomb and is executed by the Nazis. Ferdi is the absent hero of the novel: he is alluded to again and again in the course of the story, remembered by Heinrich, by Johanna, by Robert and by Schrella as a kind of epiphany; it is for his memory's sake that Robert is not prepared to attend the rededication of the abbey (p. 489), and Hugo seems to Robert to be his son, at least 'in spirit' (p. 524). According to Böll one of the germs of the novel was his recollection of the day in 1934 (actually 1933) when four young Communists were executed in Cologne for having murdered two SA men (I, p. 16; J, pp. 31ff.; see Chapter 2). He may have forgotten this when he accepted the criticism of the lamb symbolism. The motif of violent resistance is one which cannot be ignored in a study of Böll's works; the very word 'Tyrannenmord' used by Johanna invokes such plays as Schiller's *Wilhelm Tell*.

The other major symbol is that of the Abbey of Saint Anthony itself, Böll's most striking image of West German restoration mentality; his Germany of 1958 is one in which old Nazis like Nettlinger and Wakiera have been reinstated, in which one of their victims, Schrella, is arrested on his return to the Federal Republic, and in which the monks of the abbey are ready for reconciliation with the evil forces of the past in the face of the greater dangers they perceive coming from the Soviet East. 'Nicht versöhnt' ('Not reconciled') was the title which Jean-Marie Straub gave the film he based on Böll's novel.

Nicht versöhnt (1965) is an impenetrably avant-garde film and *Billard um halbzehn* was widely regarded as the breakthrough to 'modernist' writing in Böll. Within a few years it had become the subject of three major articles (Plard, 1960; Martini, 1961; Poser, 1962). Its modernism was, however, controversial. Walter Jens deplored the pressures which he believed had forced Böll into betraying his satirical vocation (Jens, 1961, pp. 147f.). Karl August Horst, on the other hand, praised the technique which, he claimed, Böll had learned from the French novelists of the *nouveau roman* — Robbe-Grillet's *Le Voyeur* and *La Jalousie* both appeared in German in the same year as *Billard um halbzehn* — and which had enabled him to create an aesthetic construct without parallel in post-war German literature (Lengning, 1972, pp. 67–71). What appeared new in *Billard um halbzehn* was Böll's treatment of time. In these years the 'problem of time' was widely regarded as a crucial feature of modern novel-writing. Walter Jens proclaimed: 'The problem of time is *the* problem of the modern novel, and there can be scarcely a novelist of any status who has not dealt with it' ('Das Zeitproblem ist *das* Problem des modernen Romans, und es dürfte kaum einen Romancier von Rang geben, der sich nicht mit ihm auseinandergesetzt hätte') (Jens, 1962, p. 318), and Böll declared in 1960 that precisely that was one of his own preoccupations (I, p. 13). He denied that there was any radical difference in this respect between *Billard um halbzehn* and his earlier works; the 'plot' of *Wo warst du, Adam?* was already minimal and covered only a few months, while in its successors the narrated time was reduced to a few days: 'Ideally . . . a novel ought to be able to take place in one minute' ('Idealerweise . . . müßte ein Roman in einer Minute spielen können' (I, p. 19). Thus in *Billard um halbzehn* narrated time is reduced to about ten hours on Saturday, 6 September 1958; by comparison 'Bloom's Day' in Joyce's *Ulysses* covers just under twenty-four hours from the morning of 16 June 1904 to the early hours of the next day. The past is refracted in the memories of the characters or in their accounts of it to others, but rarely in a straightforward linear manner. Again montage is the governing principle, assisted by the extensive use of leitmotivs. The element of time remembered is fundamental to *Billard um halbzehn*; *Haus ohne Hüter*, at least as far as the adult characters is concerned, is in this respect too most obviously a forerunner; but even in *Wo warst du, Adam?* we find chapters which mingle past and present in the consciousness of the protagonists, and in *Und sagte kein einziges Wort* the conversations of Fred and Käte revolve round the past. Looking back in 1975 Böll admitted the novel's weaknesses, but he declared that 'in that situation, at that time at the end of the Fifties, I had to write it in that way' ('in dieser Situation, zu dieser Zeit Ende der 50er Jahre, mußte ich so schreiben')

(I, p. 547). As a contemporary observer of the times he could not remain aloof from literary developments.

One of the features associated with the *nouveau roman* is the relativisation of time: in place of temporal succession comes spatial simultaneity. 'Timelessness' is an important motif of *Billard um halbzehn*. Heinrich Fähmel's life has been spent in creating his own 'myth'. From his earliest years he knew exactly what he wanted and what he was going to do. Part of the myth consists in eating the same eccentric breakfast in the same café each morning. Johanna's life in the private world of the asylum is similarly timeless, a life without responsibilities. Robert's existence follows a comparable pattern. Every morning from nine-thirty to eleven he plays an abstract game of billiards in a hotel room, meditating on his past and reminiscing to the boy Hugo. His secretary regards him as a machine: all his movements and words seem regulated by clockwork. Listening to his stories Hugo finds it difficult sometimes to remember the year they are actually living in. The movements of the billiard balls, 'red over green, white over green', symbolise the spatiality rather than temporality of the novel. Location underlines this aspect. Everything takes place within sight of the Church of Saint Severinus, whose spire is visible even from Denklingen, the village where Hugo was born and where Johanna's hospital is situated. The window of Heinrich's atelier is a picture-frame through which he observes similar figures engaged in similar activities, whether it be the 1920s or the 1950s. Time seems immaterial when the same phrases are used to describe the scene at the river in 1935 and 1958 or even in 1907: Joseph and Marianne find the same 'bulrush stems, corks, bottles, tins of shoe polish' ('Schilfrohr, Korken, Flaschen und Schuhkremdosen') (R 3, p. 456) as Heinrich did when he first made love to Johanna there (p. 417).

However, Böll was too much of an individualist to subscribe to any school of novel-writing. As a practising, if unorthodox Catholic, he could never subscribe to a definition of 'modernism' which depended on the assumption that it was no longer possible to write like the nineteenth-century novelist Adalbert Stifter, because that presupposed 'that the world was meaningful' ('daß die Welt sinnvoll ist') (Adorno, 1954, p. 62). Böll believed passionately in the writer's duty to extract meaning, 'reality', from everyday, contemporary events (E 1, p. 71–5). In an essay of 1960 he refused to accept that there was any one 'modern novel' form. Grass and Robbe-Grillet, Camus and Faulkner, Julien Green and Graham Greene were all writing the 'contemporary novel', yet each was worlds apart from the other. It was impossible to find agreement on what was 'contemporary', let alone its novel. 'Despair' could not in itself be a defining quality of modernity, for despair could too easily become merely modish; rather he regretted the absence of 'humour' in the contemporary novel, the humour which prevents the author from taking himself too seriously, as so many novelists did. He viewed with alarm the prospect of 'the automatic novel', which would merely register the death-throes of mankind. Böll believed he had responsibility not merely towards his art, but also towards the society in which he lived (E 1, pp. 355–7). His polemic in this essay was assumed to be directed against the *nouveau roman*, and when challenged he did not deny it (I, p. 22). Elsewhere, however, he had more positive things to say about his French contemporaries (E 2, p. 22). In fact *Billard um halbzehn* is both a *nouveau roman* and its opposite. Its criticism of West German society ought to have made this clear at once. Heinrich, Johanna and Robert all leave the timeless aesthetic sphere in the course of the novel and take up a position of moral responsibility. Johanna telephones for a taxi to take her to the hotel where she will shoot at the minister, and feels 'time stream back into her face' ('Die Zeit strömte in ihr Gesicht') (R 3, p. 500). Heinrich recognises that 'irony was not enough' ('daß Ironie nicht ausreichte') (p. 370) in the face of injustice, that his myth had no purpose; he refuses to attend the rededication of his abbey, he destroys his myth and cancels his daily breakfast. And the arrival of Schrella, Robert's old school-friend, makes time 'real' again; Robert too breaks out of his timeless existence and adopts the hotel boy Hugo.

In 1961 a selection of Böll's essays and reviews appeared for the first time in book form, together with a range of short stories and radio plays from the years 1950 to 1960 (*Erzählungen Hörspiele Aufsätze*). Within a year over 100,000 copies had been sold, Böll's most spectacular success so far. In the same year, however, his most comprehensive failure occurred, when his first play for the theatre, *Ein Schluck Erde*, was premiered in December in Düsseldorf. It had to be abandoned after only three performances. In 1960 Böll had written that 'atomic suicide' had apparently already been decided on (E 1, p. 390). His play is set in the year 2500, after some such catastrophe has taken place. The descendants of the survivors live on platforms above the water, diving for earth, their most precious commodity. As usual, Böll's strength lies in his satire, and the most successful passages in the play are those where the pompous archaeologists try to work out the meaning of objects such as refrigerators and television sets which are brought up to the surface. His play is a warning to contemporaries not to sacrifice the basic elements of our lives in the name of 'the free West' or 'international Communism' (E 1, pp. 390f.). But Böll's attempt to convey these 'basic elements', such as love, bread, hunger and earth, led him to invent a new language for them: 'Möge', 'Lobe', 'Lohne'. The actors had difficulty in keeping a straight face and the audience could not take it seriously either. Böll had written earlier that it is only the details that enable one to appreciate history (E 1, p. 311); such details as the 'memory of a movement of the hand, a sound, a smell' ('Erinnerung an eine Handbewegung, an einen Laut, einen Geruch') are more effective than the reproduction of long speeches (E 1, p. 295). It was the very abstractness of his play that prevented its success. On his own admission he was not a theatre-goer (Rischbieter, p. 66). That he nevertheless here and later tried to explore the medium is a sign that he was attempting to move into a new, less literary dimension.

At the end of September 1962 Böll, together with Rudolf Hagelstange and Richard Gerlach, went on an official visit to the Soviet Union in the framework of a new cultural exchange programme between the two countries. He was very reluctant to go, as he was in the middle of writing a new novel. However, since he was the best-known West German writer in the Soviet Union — translations of his works there had sold more than 800,000 copies by the end of 1961 (anon., 1961, p. 71) — he was told that the whole enterprise would collapse without him, and in the end he agreed to take part. On his own account he was 'very bad-tempered' throughout the visit, a number of 'disagreeable things' happened, he lost the thread of his novel and had to abandon it completely (I, pp. 578, 660). Hagelstange wrote a detailed account of the visit; he relates the lively interest in Böll's work which was evident from reactions to 'Als der Krieg ausbrach', which Böll read to an audience of students (Hagelstange, 1963, pp. 45, 49f.), but also the way that officialdom tried to twist everything that was said to make it appear that Böll fully supported the Soviet line on questions of the Oder–Neisse frontier, the division of Germany, a peace treaty and the like — the text of one 'interview' with *Pravda* turned out to be a complete fabrication which created difficulties for them in Bonn (ibid., pp. 26–37). However, the visit was of great importance for Böll. He formed lasting friendships with a number of individuals, the painter Boris Birger (VG, p. 163), the literary historian Lev Kopelev (VG, p. 253) and the writer Alexander Solzhenitsyn. As a young man he had been fascinated by the novels of Dostoevsky; he now developed a lively interest in contemporary Soviet literature and its writers, one which was to prove decisive in his role as a public figure later (Vormweg, pp. 60ff.).

On his return Böll began a new novel, *Ansichten eines Clowns* (I, p. 660; but cf. FT, p. 290), which he must have written very quickly, as it began to appear in instalments in the *Süddeutsche Zeitung* on 7 April 1963. To his own surprise, it was an 'enormous success' in the Soviet Union when it was translated, although it is 'extremely provincial, very rhenish, very sectarian, concerned with a quite specific, very special German problem, that of post-war German Catholicism' ('extrem provinziell, sehr rheinisch, sehr konfessionell, mit einem ganz bestimmten, sehr speziellen deutschen Problem beschäftigt, nämlich mit dem deutschen Nachkriegskatholizismus') (I, p. 609; cf. also I, p. 426). Böll attributed this success to the fact that the structures of power in the Soviet Union were similar to those in Catholicism; 'I view the Soviet Union too as a state run by prelates, . . . the Soviet Union's structures are really clerical, and there is no country in the world where *Ansichten eines Clowns*, which deals with that particular, has been better understood than the Soviet Union, where there are scarcely any Catholics' ('Ich sehe ja auch die Sowjetunion als einen Prälatenstaat, . . . es sind ja eigentliche klerikale Strukturen in der Sowjetunion, und *Ansichten eines Clowns*, was sich ja besonders damit beschäftigt, ist in keinem Land der Welt so verstanden worden wie in der Sowjetunion, wo es kaum Katholiken gibt') (Limagne, p. 198). Conversely the novel itself, notably the scene in the GDR in which Schnier refuses to assist the East German propaganda against the West, must have been influenced by his immediate experiences in the Soviet Union. Two other personal factors contributed to the novel. One was his translation of J. D. Salinger's *The Catcher in the Rye*. Böll himself spoke later of the 'liberating' function Salinger had had for him (Lenz, p. 53). A version of Salinger's novel had appeared in German as early as 1954, but it was not until Böll's revision of this translation came out in 1962 that Salinger became well known to German readers — and Böll and Salinger together later inspired the East German writer Ulrich Plenzdorf in his story *Die neuen Leiden des jungen W.* (Plenzdorf, 1973, p. 243). Günter Blöcker was the first to point out the connection with Salinger in his perceptive review (Lengning, 1972, p. 74); Robert C. Conard and others have made more detailed comparisons (Conard, 1969; Pache, 1970). The other biographical context of *Ansichten eines Clowns* is the collapse of the periodical *Labyrinth*. The final issue was prefaced by a statement by the four editors, in which each in turn gave his gloss on the meaning of the labyrinth for the contemporary world. Grieshaber's consisted in two woodcuts, the contributions of the other three were printed in succession with no indication of authorship and it was not until Böll identified his in 1971 and it was included in his collected works in 1978 that the connection with the novel could become clear (I, pp. 159–60; Cf. *Labyrinth* no. 6, pp. 2–7). Böll interpreted the labyrinth as, for example, modern bureaucracy, of which even the Pope was a prisoner; the minotaur was the contemporary public, whose victim is Theseus the artist; the journal *Labyrinth* failed because it had no Ariadne, it was an exclusively male enterprise (E 1, p. 483). His piece was the 'plot' for the novel: it was the story of Theseus and Ariadne; Theseus–Schnier was in the labyrinth, Ariadne–Marie had cut the thread, and the labyrinth was 'political German Catholicism' ('der politische deutsche Katholizismus') (I, p. 159).

Because of the eminence that Böll had in the meantime achieved his new novel received extraordinary critical attention. In the course of a few weeks *Die Zeit* published reviews of it by no fewer than eight critics and extracts from the reviews in other journals. The reviews were mixed: many were disappointed; Günter Blöcker, however, one of Böll's severest critics, gave it an enthusiastic reception. Böll himself later spoke of weaknesses in its construction and of its occasional sentimentality (I, pp. 158f.); a great deal of weeping takes place, and on at least one occasion the time scheme breaks down (just before eight o'clock Schnier has been in Bonn for almost two hours: R 4, p. 209; half an hour later he has still been there for only 'almost two hours': p. 241). The reception of the novel seemed to confirm the congruence Böll had diagnosed between the cultural policies of the Catholic Church and of the Communist Party. Böll had hitherto been relatively favourably received in East Germany; because of the scene in Erfurt *Ansichten eines Clowns* has never appeared in the GDR. The reaction of the Catholic Church was more public. In a long article in the *Petrusblatt* Monsignor Erich Klausener accused Böll of doing what in the Weimar Republic had led directly to Hitler, undermining all authority with his cynical, rationalistic criticism. Böll responded with accusations that Klausener was 'bordellising' literary criticism and seeking a literature not very different from the 'tractor literature' of the GDR (E 1, pp. 620f., 561, 569). The novel caused a radical downgrading of Böll's status in a Catholic literary history (Nägele, 1976 b, pp. 52f.) and it was boycotted by some Catholic bookshops (FT, p. 289). One reason for the Church's alarm was that this was the third time within as many months that it had found itself under attack. Rolf Hochhuth's play *Der Stellvertreter*, premiered on 20 February 1963 in West Berlin, had accused Pope Pius XII of sacrificing the Jews in order to protect the Church's immediate political interests, an anti-Communism for which Hitler was a not unwelcome ally; and in May of the same year

Carl Amery's *Die Kapitulation*, for which Böll provided a postscript, aroused almost as much debate (cf. E 2, pp. 143f., 249). Böll himself believed that his novel helped to raise Catholic awareness politically and socially (I, p. 158). Not least because of all the publicity, it had sold over 100,000 copies before the year was out.

Böll's earlier novels, notably *Und sagte kein einziges Wort* and *Billard um halbzehn*, had already contained strong criticism of his Church. What made *Ansichten eine Clowns* so much more threatening was partly the specificity of its setting. Hitherto Böll's novels were set in anonymous or fictitious towns; although the time of their action can be determined down to the month, even day, allusions to historical events and even historical figures are curiously sparse. By contrast, the opening words of *Ansichten eines Clowns*, 'It was dark already when I arrived in Bonn' ('Es war schon dunkel, als ich in Bonn ankam'), are brutally direct. At the end of *Billard um halbzehn* Johanna Fähmel shoots at an anonymous minister; in *Ansichten eines Clowns* Schnier inveighs against Strauss, Erhard and Adenauer, extols Alec Guinness and Pope John XXIII, and distances himself from both CDU and SPD. Accordingly many thought they recognised themselves in Böll's gallery of characters (Rischbieter, p. 68). For the first time Böll introduces a politically committed socialist, Marie Derkum's father. Derkum despises the SPD even more than the CDU — on the other hand the incident in which a dog sniffs at a SPD political poster, but pees on the CDU one may suggest that Böll — just — might give the SPD another chance.

It is a first person narrative, like *Das Brot der frühen Jahre*. But while the latter is a conventional autobiography, in the sense that its narrative stance is restrospective — Fendrich is focalising his own past — *Ansichten eines Clowns* is more akin to *Und sagte kein einziges Wort*: Schnier is narrating as he experiences. Like the Bogners he does not appear to be addressing any reader, his novel is monological. The ending is inconclusive. The reader knows no more than Schnier whether Marie will arrive and take pity on him as he busks outside the railway station. The narrative time covers about three hours, and past events are narrated restrospectively as Schnier meditates on how he has reached his present state. In this reduction of narrative time, *Ansichten eines Clowns* goes further than any of Böll's novels and most closely fulfils his then ambition of telling a novel 'in one minute' (I, p. 19). At the same time Böll restricts the location of his novel even more radically than with *Billard um halbzehn*, to Schnier's flat in Bonn, the centre of the 'labyrinth', from where he communicates with the outside world only by telephone.

Schnier has much in common with Salinger's Holden Caulfield, as has been pointed out. Both are in conflict with their parents, both have dead siblings whom they remember with something approaching hero-worship, both are outsiders, who reject the 'phonies' and hypocrites they encounter. But Schnier is also in a sense a reincarnation of Walter Fendrich. He too is an angry young man, at twenty-seven a little older than Fendrich and rather less violent. His relationship with Marie is a development of the earlier story. Schnier too takes it into his head one evening that he has to sleep with Marie, although they have scarcely spoken to each other before. Her weak 'Go' is as unconvincing as Hedwig's (R 4, p. 95; R 3, p. 122); just as Hedwig is to abandon her studies, Marie, who is about to take her final school examinations, resolves not to return to school after her night with Schnier. Walter and Hedwig do not wait for marriage and the story ends with their first night together; Hans and Marie live together for five years and the novel begins after she has left him. Hans refuses to marry her because he cannot accept her Church's insistence that he should promise in writing that their children will be brought up as Catholics. As in *Und sagte kein einziges Wort* Böll is suggesting that marriage turns personal relationships into a legal contract (I, pp. 550–5). Hans regards Marie as his wife; she is committing adultery, even bigamy with Züpfner whatever the legal status of their marriage may be — Böll called it 'the novel of a marriage' ('Eheroman') (FT, p. 290). In his figurative 'fight' (R 4, p. 83) with the Minotaur of the Church, the telephone is his 'weapon' (p. 77), with which he attacks in succession the Church's dignitaries and their allies and his parents. Many of Böll's targets recur here: the Church's alliance with the military, with industry, with the culture industry, and the insensitivity of the wealthy prelates towards the poor. In one crucial way Böll goes further than before: Schnier is an agnostic, where Böll's earlier victims were believers. The novel's epigraph is the verse: 'To whom he was not spoken of, they shall see: and they that have not heard shall understand' ('Die werden es sehen, denen von Ihm noch nichts verkündet ward, und die verstehen, die noch nichts vernommen haben') (Romans 15.21). It implies that Schnier, the unbeliever, is closer to Christ than the practising Christians themselves; salvation can only come from outside the Church.

Schnier is also, however, an embodiment of the artist as clown. This too was foreshadowed by Böll's declaration on the end of *Labyrinth*: 'The public as such would take on the role of the Minotaur, the downwards pointing thumb the sign of its absolute authority; the artiste, the entertainer, the artist in the surprising role of the victim' ('Die Öffentlichkeit als solche wäre in der Rolle des

Minotauros, der nach unten weisende Daumen das Zeichen ihrer absoluten Herrschaft; der Artist, der Gaukler, der Künstler, überraschenderweise in der Rolle des Opfers') (E 1, p. 483). His art is that of the satirical mime, ridiculing the General and social behaviour such as the meeting of a Board of Directors and arrivals and departures at railway stations. Jochen Vogt has pointed out the traditional motif of the 'fool who holds up a mirror to an apparently well-ordered world, revealing its wrongheadedness, its folly' ('Narr, der einer scheinbar wohlgeordneten Welt den Spiegel vorhält, in dem ihre eigene Verkehrtheit, Narrheit offenkundig wird') (Vogt, 1978, p. 81). At the close of *Das Brot der frühen Jahre* Fendrich wishes to 'go back' — to what he does not know. At the close of *Ansichten eines Clowns* Schnier leaves the isolation of his flat, and goes off to sing political songs to his own guitar accompaniment on the steps of the railway station. It is true that since it is carnival time and everyone else is in fancy dress his peculiar form of protest goes largely unnoticed — Böll is under no illusions about the effectiveness of such behaviour. But here the artist has left the 'comfortable prison' of the 'museum' into which West German society has placed him (E 1, p. 393) and is looking for new, more telling ways of reaching his public. Schnier's last words are splendidly defiant: 'and continued to sing' ('und sang weiter') (R 4, p. 303). The 'resignation' which Vogt diagnoses (Vogt, 1978, p. 79) is nowhere to be seen; Böll himself was moving away from the inwardness of his early works.

6

The End of Humility (1963–1969)

The years 1963 to 1969 were of crucial importance in the development of West German society. It was in these years that a generation
came of age which had been born after the end of the war, one which
had no reason to feel guilty about the Nazi past. West German
prosperity had been created by what Böll never ceased to criticise as
a purely materialist outlook; the new generation took this prosperity
for granted and developed ideals of its own. The Federal Republic
had been created and run by sexagenarians and older; Adenauer's
retirement from government in October 1963 could have meant the
rejuvenation of West German politics; that initially it did not was
one important reason for the upheavals of the later 1960s, in which
the new generation showed itself sceptical towards its elders, sceptical of the institutions which they had created, and sceptical of most
traditional authority, whether it was the power structures in the
schools and universities, the American 'friends' stationed in Germany for their 'protection', or the parents with their obscure pasts.
A new wave of Nazi trials began. Initially the Allies had been
responsible for bringing the chief Nazi criminals to justice; in the
1950s it had seemed that this episode was largely over; but as more
information came from sources in Eastern Europe, from the returning prisoners of war and from the archives of the Allies themselves, it
became apparent that it was not. The trial of Adolf Eichmann in
Jerusalem in 1961 was an enlightening and sombre event (E 1, pp.
451ff.). The two Auschwitz trials in Frankfurt (1963–6) and the
Treblinka trial in Düsseldorf (1968) called in question the moral
stature of those who had lived as adults under Hitler. The direct
American involvement in the war in Vietnam from August 1964
onwards, when the United States was perceived to be supporting a
corrupt and brutal regime in the South, led many to question the
moral stature of the liberators of 1945.

It was in the universities that the new questioning mood became
immediately obvious. The population 'bulge' of the immediate
post-war years reached the universities in these years, encountering
an institution which had basically remained unchanged since the
nineteenth century. Too few professors jealous of their power and

139

status, overcrowded lecture rooms, impersonal teaching, a student population heavily weighted towards the middle classes — as Böll pointed out it was a microcosm of unjust social structures (E 2, pp. 355–6, 388) — all this inspired students to question institutions in general. A short story of 1962, 'Keine Träne um Schmeck' ('No tears for Schmeck'), reads as a prophecy of what was to come. Müller, a working-class student of sociology, 'a rarity . . . the great miracle . . . one of those of whom there are only five per hundred . . . really and truly the son of a working-class man studying at a West German university' ('eine Rarität . . . das große Wunder . . . einer von denen, von denen es nur fünf auf hundert gibt . . . tatsächlich der Sohn eines Arbeiters, der an einer westdeutschen Universität studiert') (R 4, p. 55), is preparing a dissertation on the 'sociology of the loden coat' and hoping that Professor Schmeck will give him a post as junior assistant; he finds in the middle of a lecture that the professor has appropriated his ideas and even phrases from the outline he had submitted. Müller and his girlfriend determine that violence is their only redress, waylay Schmeck one night, but find that he is accompanied by a large dog; instead Müller determines to go over to Schmeck's rival and write a dissertation on Schmeck himself. In the years that followed, not all students were to be put off by the large dog.

In all this there was an international dimension which had been lacking up to now. The second half of the 1960s witnessed worldwide changes, which were followed with great interest by the West Germans and were mirrored in the Federal Republic itself. The Civil Rights movement in the United States, later that in Northern Ireland and the rise of the Palestine Liberation Organisation could all in various ways be viewed as movements for emancipation; by contrast the assassination of prominent liberals in the USA, President Kennedy in 1963, his brother Robert and the Civil Rights leader Martin Luther King in 1968, the 1967 putsch by the Colonels in Greece, the oppressive regime of the Shah in Iran, the crushing of the Czechoslovak attempt to realise a 'socialism with a human face' by the invasion of the Warsaw Pact armies in August 1968, the civil war in Nigeria, and above all and continuously the war in Vietnam — all these processes and events were the inspiration for protests, demonstrations, petitions, but not only in West Germany. And the student unrest which reached its climax in 1968 found its equivalent in France and the United States too. In West Germany the student protest movement crystallised around a visit of the Shah of Iran to West Berlin. On 2 June 1967 in the course of what had begun as a peaceful demonstration an unarmed student, Benno Ohnesorg, was shot dead by a policeman. The effect was the mobilisation of even greater numbers of students and a radicalisation of their attitudes.

Adenauer was replaced by his Economics Minister Ludwig Erhard, the man popularly regarded as the architect of West German prosperity, in October 1963. In his review of Adenauer's memoirs, Böll commented that the Federal Republic had been designed to fit Adenauer; it would be difficult to shape it for others (E 2, p. 177). In spite of the sniping which took place within his own party and that of his coalition partners, Erhard led the CDU/CSU to victory in the elections of 1965, and the coalition with the FDP continued. Erhard declared in his first policy statement that 'the post-war period was at an end'. What *was* at an end was the steady growth of the West German economy, and the years 1966 and 1967 witnessed a minor recession which was widely perceived as a serious setback. At the same time the neo-Nazi NPD with its programme of hostility toward the foreign workers who had flocked to West Germany during the time of economic expansion, began to win seats in local parliaments. Disagreements within the coalition led to its break-up in October 1966; after complicated negotiations Erhard resigned, and a 'Grand Coalition' of CDU/CSU and SPD was formed, in which Kurt Georg Kiesinger (CDU) became Chancellor and Willy Brandt (SPD) his deputy and Foreign Minister. The governing parties in the Federal Parliament now held 447 seats, the opposition, consisting solely of the FDP, forty-nine.

The Grand Coalition was a grave disappointment to many of the SPD's supporters. Günter Grass and Rolf Hochhuth had been active in the 1965 campaign; in West Berlin a bevy of writers, some established figures like Peter Härtling, others still to make their mark like Peter Schneider and Gudrun Ensslin, had helped to devise slogans and write speeches for the SPD's candidates. The gulf between writers and the ruling conservative party had deepened. Böll had not been one of those who supported the SPD publicly in 1965. In 1963 he had suggested that there was so little to choose between the parties that West Germany might as well be a 'one-party state' (E 1, p. 534). In the election year he criticised the Gruppe 47 for becoming too closely identified with the SPD, which had been demanding a return to Germany's frontiers of 1937, which had betrayed the campaign for nuclear disarmament and which was already seeking a Grand Coalition; such a coalition would be 'absolute political promiscuity' (E 2, p. 171). Elsewhere he declared: 'The CDU has destroyed Christianity in this country, the SPD socialism' ('Die CDU hat in diesem Land das Christentum, die SPD hat den Sozialismus zerstört') (Selbstinterview, p. 601). Now the

SPD had actually agreed to serve in a government which included the Franz Josef Strauss who had been responsible for the *Spiegel* affair; its leader was the first Chancellor of the Federal Republic to have been a Nazi — Kiesinger had even joined the party as an adult in 1933: 'When I imagine that if I had campaigned for the SPD in 1965, then I would have practically been campaigning for Herr Kiesinger and Herr Strauss, that frightens me' ('Wenn ich mir vorstelle, daß ich also, wenn ich 1965 für die SPD geworben hätte, praktisch für Herrn Kiesinger und Herrn Strauss geworben hätte, dann wird mir bang') (Beth, 1980, p. 188). Kiesinger was for Böll an 'affront', there were other CDU politicians who had at least as much ability and a more creditable past (I, p. 573), and when in November 1968 Beate Klarsfeld publicly boxed Kiesinger's ears in protest, Böll sent her flowers, something which incurred the displeasure of Günter Grass, who suggested that behaviour of this kind was encouraging violence (Grass, 1968). Böll defended himself; he had done it not least in memory of his mother, who had strengthened his hatred of the Nazis, 'especially the kind represented by Dr Kiesinger: the well-groomed, middle-class Nazis, who dirtied neither their fingers nor their slates and who now continue after 1945 to parade shamelessly across the countryside' ('ganz besonders jene von der Sorte, zu der Herr Dr. Kiesinger zählt: die gepflegten bürgerlichen Nazis, die sich weder die Finger noch die Weste beschmutzten und die nun nach 1945 weiterhin schamlos durch die Lande ziehen'). He had had enough of being the 'conscience of the Federal Republic', being used to bring his country credit abroad but powerless to alter events at home; writers like Grass and Böll were 'idiotic front-men' ('Vorzeigeidioten') (E 2, pp. 345f.).

In retrospect the Grand Coalition brought its benefits for the SPD. By serving its apprenticeship as junior partner in a coalition with the Christian Democrats it demonstrated that it was a responsible political party which could be entrusted with government, and this was one factor which enabled it to take power in 1969. With Brandt as Foreign Minister it was able to initiate new steps to improve relations with Eastern Europe, the 'Neue Ostpolitik' which, under the slogan 'Wandel durch Annäherung' ('change through *rapprochement*'), abandoned the Hallstein Doctrine, established diplomatic relations first with the various countries of the Eastern bloc, later with the German Democratic Republic itself. But the two main reasons for the formation of the Grand Coalition were to carry out economic reforms, and to enact legislation to enable the Federal Republic to take over one of the last remaining rights held by the Allied Powers of Occupation, that to deal with political emergencies.

It was over the latter issue that the students joined forces with those outside the universities who were concerned about the undemocratic turn that the Federal Republic seemed to be taking: first a Grand Coalition which seemed designed to thwart parliamentary opposition, then legislation which was ominously reminiscent of that which had brought Hitler to power in 1933. The 'Extra-Parliamentary Opposition' (APO) was born, with which Böll was to identify himself (Riese, p. 24).

The year 1968 was one of especial turmoil. In February there was a large demonstration against the American involvement in Vietnam, aimed at persuading the government at least to condemn the American actions in public. There was no response. At this point some of the protesters began to use violence, violence directed initially at property — at the beginning of April a department store in Frankfurt was set on fire by a group which included Gudrun Ensslin and Andreas Baader. On 11 April the charismatic student leader Rudi Dutschke was shot and seriously wounded. There was evidence to connect the shooting with the hostility shown to the students and their demands by the right-wing popular press owned by Axel Springer. Springer owned the largest publishing group in Europe. In 1968 his publications accounted for almost 40 per cent of West Germany's newspaper circulation, 65 to 70 per cent in Hamburg and West Berlin. He had a monopoly of Sunday newspapers; his sensationalist *Bild-Zeitung* had a circulation of 3.75 million and a readership of more than twice that figure. A commission was set up in 1967 to investigate the problem of press concentration and recommended restrictions; it was boycotted by Springer (Sandford, 1976, pp. 30ff.). In October of the same year 106 members of the Gruppe 47, including Böll, announced their intention of boycotting all papers owned by Springer in protest against press concentration, which was endangering the freedom of information. Springer's right-wing views permeated editorial policies and more; after the erection of the Berlin Wall in 1961 he threatened to cease to supply newsagents who continued to sell newspapers which printed East German radio and television programmes (Müller, 1968, pp. 327ff.). In 1966 his editor William Schlamm had accused Böll, Enzensberger and Richter of being controlled from Moscow (ibid., pp. 288f.). From the outset the ideals and behaviour of the long-haired students had been ridiculed in his papers. The shooting of Dutschke was followed by three days of unrest on the streets of university towns. On 13 April a group of fourteen prominent citizens, including Böll, protested publicly: 'Fear and unwillingness to take the arguments of the student opposition seriously have created a climate in which the

143

deliberate defamation of a minority must necessarily incite to violence against it' ('Angst und mangelnde Bereitschaft, die Argumente der studentischen Opposition ernst zu nehmen, haben ein Klima geschaffen, in dem die gezielte Diffamierung einer Minderheit zur Gewalttätigkeit gegen sie aufreizen muß'); they demanded a public debate on the role of the Springer press, and proclaimed their solidarity with the students while appealing to them to desist from violence. The fourteen consisted mainly of academics, including Theodor W. Adorno, Walter Jens, Golo Mann and Alexander Mitscherlich (*Die Zeit*, 19.4.1968, p. 5). On 19 April Böll wrote to the *Kölner Stadt-Anzeiger* defending the students, their aims and their methods; their only leverage lay in public demonstrations since the mass circulation newspapers owned by Springer were closed to their case; again, however, he appealed to the students to desist from violence (E 2, pp. 283–4).

One month after the shooting of Dutschke some 30,000 people demonstrated in Bonn against the Emergency Legislation, which was entering its last stages. Böll was one of the speakers; he compared the bill to the decision to rearm the Federal Republic; the definitions were vague; the latest version had not been properly published; he contrasted the soft treatment given to demonstrating farmers with the violent reaction in the media and parliament to radical students and forecast that the new legislation would be misused on behalf of materialist interests (E 2, pp. 287–90). By now his appeal to the students to abstain from violence was being met with jeers (I, p. 723). At the end of May he took part in a debate, in which he repeated many of these accusations; the CDU was being identified with the government, the government with the State (E 2, pp. 291–2). Böll had hoped that the SPD would be persuaded to turn back; but the legislation was passed and came into effect on 24 June.

The gloomy forecasts of Böll and his friends were not on the whole fulfilled. The invasion of Czechoslovakia in August 1968 caused many of the radicals on the left to think again about revolutionary socialism. In September a new Communist party, the DKP, was actually allowed to form in the Federal Republic. On the 5 April 1969 West Germany's first Social Democratic president was elected, Gustav Heinemann. In his address on the Emergency Laws Böll had forecast that the SPD would be obliterated in the parliamentary elections of 1969 if it did not withdraw from the embrace of the CDU (E 2, p. 288); in the event, it increased its share of the vote, albeit by just over 3 per cent, and although the CDU/CSU remained the largest party in parliament, a coalition between SPD and FDP was agreed and Willy Brandt was elected chancellor on 21 October.

In keeping with these developments, from 1963 onwards West German writers showed an increasing political awareness. Initially this was most obvious in the theatre. Rolf Hochhuth's *Der Stellvertreter* was provocatively polemical and caused questions to be asked in parliament. His later plays, *Soldaten* (1967) on the bombing of Dresden and *Guerillas* (1970) on American neo-colonialism in Central America were almost as controversial. Peter Weiss's *Marat-Sade* (1964) created a new form of theatre, in which topical ideas relating to political and sexual emancipation were argued out on stage within a complex framework of play within play within play. Both *Der Stellvertreter* and *Marat-Sade* were European successes. In 1961 the Gruppe 61 had been formed to provide a forum for working-class writers to discuss their work. 1963 saw the first popular success by a member of the group, the novel *Irrlicht und Feuer* by Max von der Grün; at the same time it brought a court case on the author from industrialists who believed themselves slandered in the way the novel presented exploitation and unsatisfactory safety measures in industry; the trade unions were equally unhappy about the depiction of their behaviour (E 2, p. 76). And in the same year Böll's own *Ansichten eines Clowns* caused an uproar in Catholic circles.

The last meeting of the Gruppe 47 took place in November 1967. It was an unhappy affair, disrupted by students, who believed that instead of discussing literature the assembled writers should be practising solidarity with them and ironically chanted 'Dichter, Dichter' ('Poets, poets') outside the meeting place — some of the writers in fact went out to join them. Böll was not present; he had become an infrequent attender over the past ten years and although he had agreed along with Grass to put up the money for that year's prize he had urged Richter to disband the group (Richter, 1986, pp. 66ff.). The occasion underlined a central preoccupation of the times, the relation between literature and political involvement. In 1962 Hans Magnus Enzensberger had still been insisting that the only possible political function of a poem must be its refusal to have any political function (Enzensberger, 1962). In 1965, however, he founded the journal *Kursbuch*, which was to become one of the bibles of the student movement, a journal which published poems, plays and essays on literature but which was above all devoted to *theory*, social theory, political theory, literary theory. Böll's 'Brief an einen jungen Nichtkatholiken' appeared there in September 1966, a pendant to his earlier 'Brief an einen jungen Katholiken'. The young non-Catholic was Günter Wallraff, the piece was to be the preface to the latter's account of his experiences with the Bundeswehr as a conscientious objector. Böll had earlier accepted a contribution by Wallraff for *Labyrinth* before that journal folded (I, p. 676); later he wrote a preface for a Swedish edition of Wallraff's *Dreizehn unerwünschte Reportagen* (E 2, pp. 490–3); and when Wallraff was taken to court in 1976 by the Gerling concern Böll was called as witness in his defence (I, pp. 675–81). Wallraff belonged to the Gruppe 61; his speciality was a literary reporting whose authenticity came from the fact that instead of describing his subject from outside like a conventional journalist, he would smuggle himself into the business as an ordinary employee, and report from within — he was a receptionist with the Gerling concern, and later was to infiltrate *Bild* itself. One of the demands of the students demonstrating at the 1967 meeting of the Gruppe 47 was that Wallraff be awarded its prize: he, unlike the 'Dichter' at their debates, was clearly committed and apparently effective. Wallraff's was only one kind of documentary literature. Erika Runge's *Bottroper Protokolle* (1968) recorded interviews with working-class people. Peter Weiss's 'oratorio' *Die Ermittlung* (1965) consisted of excerpts from the transcripts of the first Auschwitz trial; his play *Viet Nam Diskurs* (1968) 'documented' the history of the Vietnamese people in relation to their current struggle against American aggression. In November 1968 *Kursbuch* proclaimed the 'death of literature'. Karl Markus Michel declared that contemporary literature, where it was 'realistic', as in the works of the Gruppe 47, had failed the students, and where it was 'modernist' its progressiveness had been merely formal (Michel, 1968); and Enzensberger himself, taking back what he had written six years earlier, accused literature of being 'elitist', an 'alibi in the superstructure', salving writers' consciences without influencing society; in the current situation writers could have only two tasks: to fight the cultural apparatus and to document the struggle of the workers in the factories and of the peasants in Vietnam (Enzensberger, 1968).

Some of these developments are foreshadowed in Böll's *Entfernung von der Truppe*, his first publication of substance after *Ansichten eines Clowns*. It was serialised in the *Frankfurter Allgemeine Zeitung* between 27 July and 10 August 1964. Böll called it a 'very subjective affair . . . almost autobiographical' ('eine sehr subjektive Sache . . . fast autobiographisch') (I, p. 327). It is a first person narrative and again told by someone who cannot forget the past. Wilhelm Schmölder, the narrator, calls his text a 'chapel for the dead' (R 4, p. 296) in memory of two brothers Bechtold and their sister, to whom the narrator was briefly married before she died in a bombing raid. Its story is reminiscent of that of the classical novella, centred on

146

Schmölder's extraordinary encounter with Engelbert Bechtold as they were on latrine cleaning duty in 1938; within fifteen minutes Engelbert had told him he ought to marry his sister Hildegard, and a fortnight later Schmölder was greeted by the family with a chorus from Bach's *St Matthew Passion* and their union was sealed. However, more than with any other of Böll's stories it is impossible to give an adequate account of the plot. Not only does the narrator constantly switch back and forward in time, to such an extent that the satirical magazine *Pardon* produced a comic-strip version with arrows to make the chronology explicit (*Pardon*, 4, 1965, no. 3, pp. 34f.), but he deliberately leaves much to the imagination of the reader. Characters are sketched in and then dropped: the doctor who helped the narrator to feign an eye defect; the nuns in Rouen whom he helped to get coal; the Jewish woman in Romania who was sorry for him because he came from such a 'poor nation'.

Entfernung von der Truppe is the earliest example in Böll's works of what might be called 'post-modernist' fiction. One of the central concepts of modernism was that of the autonomy of the work of art. Archibald McGleish's dictum, 'A poem should not mean / but be', is its most concise expression; Gottfried Benn's *Probleme der Lyrik* is its most coherent exposition in the German-speaking world — poetry is the art of the anchorite, the poet is conversing only with himself. Enzensberger's essay of 1962 belongs to this tradition: any political message a poem may contain must be an indirect one, the very fact that it is a poem at all is the political message. Böll's works of the 1950s share many of the features of this kind of modernism: the absence of the overt narrator who in pre-modernist fiction acts as a bridge between the world of the text and the world of the reader; the spatialising technique which reduces narrated time to a minimum and creates an aesthetic pattern based on colours and leitmotivs; the avoidance of references to historical events and historical places — all these devices serve to disguise the fact that the novel is a construct within the reader's reality. Clearly Böll, however, could never be content with a literature which came perilously near to 'l 'art pour l' art'. Both *Haus ohne Hüter* and *Billard um halbzehn* end with a rediscovery of 'real' time, and *Ansichten eines Clowns* introduces direct references to historical events and people of the reader's own world. *Entfernung von der Truppe* goes much further. The narrator expressly breaks with the concept of the autonomous work of art when he compares his text to a child's painting book in which dots have to be joined together and shapes filled with colour (R 4, pp. 275–7); the reader is invited to insert appropriate details as on the order form in a shop (p. 270). Where in the earlier novels flashbacks

147

were part of the aesthetic economy, here the narrator himself draws
attention to them, reassuring his older readers that every school-
child now knows that these are called 'changes of narrative level'
(p. 299). And, anticipating the documentary fashion but also perhaps after the model of Alfred Döblin's novel *Berlin Alexanderplatz*
(1929), he introduces into his fictional narrative historical documents, newspaper cuttings and reports from 22 September 1938,
some apparently trivial, such as the weather forecast, sports news or
a conference of the heating and ventilation trades, others more
ominous, a report on the building of Germany's Western fortifica-
tions, the publication of regulations for fire-fighting in case of an
air-raid and the arrival of Neville Chamberlain in Bad Godesberg.
Where the earlier works set up the pretence that the narrative had
neither a producer nor a recipient, *Entfernung von der Truppe* addresses
a 'patient reader' (p. 273). Its opening paragraph parodies the
beginning of Thomas Mann's *Doktor Faustus*: in both a first person
narrator feels obliged in two long and tortuous sentences to say
something about himself before going on to the proper topic of his
narrative, both break off in full rhetorical flow. Parody too is a
feature of self-conscious post-modernist writing. Whereas Zeitblom
in the earlier work can finally only hope that God will have mercy on
his 'poor fatherland', Schmölder is expressly attempting to activate
his reader: '*Moral* You are urgently advised to go AWOL' ('*Moral* Es
wird dringend zur Entfernung von der Truppe geraten') (p. 321).
The 'troops' from which the reader is urged to 'absent' himself are
all forms of organisation, from the military to the churches and
ultimately, as with 'Nicht nur zur Weihnachtszeit', the State itself:
emigration is a last resort. For the story is not merely concerned to
remind the readers of the past, but to warn against opportunism in
the present and to encourage non-conformism.

Und sagte kein einziges Wort devoted a whole chapter to a housewife
cleaning her flat; *Das Brot der frühen Jahre* was about a man who
serviced washing-machines; *Entfernung von der Truppe* describes the
lowliest occupation of all, latrine-cleaning. It was just at this time
that Böll in his Frankfurt lectures was saying that: 'Literature
apparently can choose as its subject only what society rejects as
refuse' ('Die Literatur kann offenbar nur zum Gegenstand wählen,
was von der Gesellschaft zum Abfall, als abfällig erklärt wird') (E2,
p. 71).

Böll had been invited to become Guest Professor of Poetics at the
University of Frankfurt in the summer semester of 1964. The Chair
of Poetics had been established in 1959 to give contemporary writers
the opportunity to air their views on literature and its function in a

series of lectures and to discuss these views in seminars with students. Böll was the first novelist to be honoured in this way; his
predecessors were Ingeborg Bachmann, Karl Krolow and Helmut
Heißenbüttel. Böll gave four lectures between 13 May and 8 July
1964. They were published in 1966. They are of uneven quality; in
the last of them Böll admitted that he had undertaken more than he
had been able to deliver. His aim was to outline an 'aesthetics of the
humane' ('Ästhetik des Humanen'), and he defined the humane in
terms of 'dwelling, neighbourhood and homeland, money and love,
religion and meals' (E 2, p. 34). For only some of these themes did
he have time. Besides his concern for society's 'refuse' — the
outsiders, the lowly, the 'wash-houses' of an earlier essay — he
defended the concept of provincialism against its contemporary
detractors. Many of the ideas thrown up in these lectures are
interesting for the light they shed on some of his own works: his
'aesthetics of bread' (p. 83), for example, his definition of humour
and his rejection of that household author of the German philistines
Wilhelm Busch (pp. 87ff.), and his notion of a 'trinity of the female'
('Trinität des Weiblichen') (p. 86). Böll's own tastes in literature
emerge clearly, as he extensively quoted other writers to illustrate
his ideas. Günter Eich, Ingeborg Bachmann, Thomas Mann and
Franz Kafka are important, but the two writers most frequently
cited are H. G. Adler and Adalbert Stifter. Adler, a Jew from Prague
and living in London had written the novel *Eine Reise*, which Böll
reviewed in 1963 (E 1, pp. 551ff.); later Böll reviewed Adler's
documentation of the deportations of the Jews, *Der verwaltete Mensch*
(E 3, pp. 120ff.), extracts from which he included in his *Mein
Lesebuch*. Stifter's prominence was perhaps the least expected; the
nineteenth-century writer of the Bohemian forests and the 'gentle
law of nature' seemed worlds apart from the social critic and
city-dweller Böll. Böll read Stifter against the grain: his serenity
masked the 'desperation' at the heart of his 'dream of continuity,
culture, dwelling' (E 2, p. 70); and there is something of this
'desperate silence' (p. 58) to be found in the description of the
Hungarian countryside around Berczaba in *Wo warst du, Adam?* In
1970 Böll published an ironic 'epilogue' to Stifter's *Der Nachsommer*,
in which the snobbishness, elitism and inhumanity on which Stifter's world view was based are made explicit (Wirth, 1972; Conard,
1981, pp. 82ff.).

In the context of Böll's biography as a 'contemporary' two further
points stand out. The lectures were evidently composed in the wake
of the hostile reception of *Ansichten eines Clowns* and there are numerous polemical sideswipes at the politicians and lobbyists whose

interests are diametrically opposed to those of the writer: the former were concerned to restore authority, law and order, while literature went a different way, in search of language and the humane (E 2, p. 76). And his words to the students in his audience, the citizens of the future, encouraging them to create a new Germany, 'a state which one may be homesick for and which will appear as something humane when literature is written about it' ('Staat . . . nach dem man Heimweh haben, der als Humanum in der Literatur erscheinen wird') (p. 75), again anticipate developments which began only a couple of years later.

Two years after his Frankfurt lectures Böll was invited to give an address at the opening of the new theatre in Wuppertal on 29 September 1966. His third 'Wuppertal Speech' contained more provocative ideas than the lectures; for example, he pointed out that one of the functions of literature was to break social taboos; once society caught up with literature in this respect, it invariably found that literature had already advanced further on. His address provoked no little controversy. In the first place he insisted that the freedom of art had constantly to be tested and reasserted; art *was* freedom, it could not be given freedom, only prevented from manifesting its freedom; and since it was impossible to say in advance where the limits of its freedom were, it had to 'go too far', only when it overstepped the limits imposed on it by society was it being itself. This was provocative enough, but Böll 'went further'. He coupled his eulogy of art, 'the only perceptible form of liberty on earth' ('die einzig erkennbare Erscheinungsform der Freiheit auf der Erde') (E 2, p. 228), with a denunciation of the West German state. While he himself as artist needed no state, only a certain 'provincial administration' to light the lamps and deal with the refuse (pp. 230f.), others did, and since at present he could see no state but in its place 'only a few rotting remnants of power' ('nur einige verfaulende Reste von Macht') which were being defended with the energy of rats, he feared that some day a political messiah might emerge to 'restore order' (p. 229). This allusion to the restoration of 'order' by Hitler after the 'disorder' of Weimar was followed by ironic commentaries in the conservative press and for some days the letters columns of *Die Welt*, *Frankfurter Allgemeine Zeitung* and *Die Zeit* were filled with reactions from readers, some hostile, some supportive.

What Böll meant by the 'invisibility' of the State and by the need for art to 'go too far' becomes clearer from *Ende einer Dienstfahrt*, the short novel which was serialised, ironically enough, in Axel Springer's *Die Welt* — this was before the boycott — prior to the address in

Wuppertal, and which appeared in book form in the same year. Böll described its genesis in unusual detail. It was written between the end of 1965 and May 1966. With visits to Ireland, France, Holland, the GDR, Belgium and the Soviet Union, and an intensive study of Dostoevsky for a television feature on the Russian novelist to be broadcast in 1969, 1966 was an especially hectic year for him (E 2, p. 402; H, pp. 537ff.). Dostoevsky seems hardly to have influenced *Ende einer Dienstfahrt*; on Böll's account three elements contributed to its composition (E 2, p. 253). One was a story that from time to time army jeeps had to be sent on official journeys merely to register sufficient mileage for their regular servicing; this may have been the 'authentic detail' for which Böll in his defence of Wallraff said he had once had to bribe a soldier (I, pp. 675f.); it confirmed his conviction that the army was an absurd institution. A second was his perception that the freedom of art in Western society was the freedom of the 'padded cell', what he had earlier called the 'museum', that is that anything was acceptable provided it was defused by being called 'art'. And the third consisted in the contemporary 'happenings' and the activities of the Provos in Amsterdam. The Provos were an early example of the youth protest movement; in 1965 they had begun to break rules and taboos in a more or less witty fashion, creating traffic jams, for example, by driving along one-way-streets in the wrong direction — this was to be an important motif for *Gruppenbild mit Dame* and *Fürsorgliche Belagerung*. 'Happenings' were rather older; they reached West Germany in 1962, when at the Wiesbaden 'Fluxus Festival' events had included the demolition of concert pianos; in one case the instrument was dismantled and the individual parts auctioned off (Becker/Vostell, 1965, pp. 147, 180) — again this was a motif which Böll took up, much later, however, in *Frauen vor Flußlandschaft*. A notorious occasion was in Aachen, when a 'happening' organised by Joseph Beuys on 20 July 1964, the twentieth anniversary of the attempt to assassinate Hitler, the day which is commemorated as the Day of Resistance, began with a distorted tape-recording of a speech by Joseph Goebbels. Infuriated students stormed the platform and one of them punched Beuys on the nose; a photograph exists in which Beuys with bleeding nose holds a crucifix in what appears to be a beer mug perched on a book (ibid., p. 283) and this may have inspired the 'one minute piece of art' in *Die verlorene Ehre der Katharina Blum* (R 5, pp. 467f.). One of the many paradoxes of avant-garde art was Beuys's indignation at the disturbance (Becker/Vostell, 1965, p. 326) — the object had presumably been to provoke 'resistance'. One of Beuys's ideas was what he called the 'expansion of art into life', the removal of the barriers between art and life which modernism had created (Ohff, 1973, p. 171), and 'happenings' were one of the forms he employed to this end. Böll knew Beuys personally and admired his public commitment, although he was sceptical about some of the more 'mystical' elements in his friend's outlook (I, p. 156; Rischbieter, p. 67). Together they founded a 'Free international college of creativity' in 1974, and Böll published a poem on the occasion of Beuys's sixtieth birthday in 1981. Wolf Vostell was the other major exponent of 'happenings' in West Germany. His 'In Ulm, um Ulm und um Ulm herum' ('In and around Ulm' — a standard German tongue-twister) took place on 7 November 1964; at one stage the 250 spectator–participants were taken to the Federal Air Force's base at Leipheim, where they were entertained to a 'concert' given by three stationary jet fighters with engines running full blast. A month later questions were asked in the Federal Parliament about this apparent misuse of air force facilities (Becker/Vostell, 1965, pp. 386ff., 410ff.). *Ende einer Dienstfahrt* contains an allusion to this incident (R 4, pp. 492f.).

In contrast with *Entfernung von der Truppe*, which has been probably Böll's least popular work of prose fiction, *Ende einer Dienstfahrt* is one of his most accessible, entertaining and — at least on the surface — unproblematic stories. Böll intended it as a 'chocolate', but one with a poisoned centre (E 2, p. 253). It is a courtroom novel, with all the possibilities for drama and tension that that implies. (In 1955 Böll had observed a famous murder trial for the *Frankfurter Allgemeine Zeitung* — E 1, pp. 156–8 — , and for the novel he engaged in extensive research on the legal system — E 2, p. 254.) Two men, Johann and Georg Gruhl, father and son, are accused of setting fire to an army jeep with which Georg, who is on compulsory military service, had been entrusted: the trial lasts a day, at the end of which they are given a six weeks gaol sentence and ordered to pay compensation for the jeep. As they have already spent that time in custody they are able to leave the courtroom as free men. In the course of the hearing a succession of witnesses are called, many of them colourful personalities with idiosyncrasies which are sometimes ridiculed, sometimes indicate an individuality which bureaucracy has not yet been able to suppress — a tax inspector and a traffic expert who get carried away by their respective hobby horses, or an elderly priest who turns out to be much more liberal in his views on theology than a young army lieutenant. It is all very good-humoured, the Gruhls have been well treated in custody, Georg has even managed to get his girlfriend pregnant there, and their fine will be paid by Agnes Hall, a wealthy spinster, who alters her will to put up a sum for the annual burning of an army jeep.

The harmoniousness of the story is underlined by the narrative technique. The novel begins: 'At the magistrate's court in Birglar in the early autumn of last year a case was heard of whose outcome the general public heard very little' ('Vor dem Amtsgericht in Birglar fand im Frühherbst des vorigen Jahres eine Verhandlung statt, über deren Verlauf die Öffentlichkeit sehr wenig erfuhr') (R 4, p. 353). All of Böll's longer narrative works up to now, whether they were first or third person narratives, had begun personally and without any explanation of context, the reader had found himself confronted with a piece of text which he had gradually to decode. Here we are given details of place and time and the privileged position of knowing what the general public was not allowed to know. The narrator is extra-diegetic, anonymous, impersonal, 'ominiscient' in the sense that he knows everything that the reader needs to be told, including the unexpressed thoughts of some of the characters, and especially what the powers that be are trying to cover up. The narrative focus is for most of the story external to the characters, although there is a section in the middle where we follow them in turn as they make their respective ways to their eating places. The technique is intriguingly pre-modernist, indeed it is reminiscent of that of the early nineteenth-century writer Heinrich von Kleist, whom Böll so much admired; the handling of the story, which opens with a succinct outline of the remarkable events and having whetted the reader's interest goes on to explain them, is another feature of Kleist's stories. The geographical location is fictionalised, but Böll gives it the name Birglar in true old-fashioned style to indicate what is going on — 'birg' comes from 'bergen', to hide (Reid, 1974).

So much for the chocolate coating; what about the poisoned centre? In *Ende einer Dienstfahrt* Böll presents two main aspects of society, the legal system and the army, with subsidiary darts at the taxation system. The latter was the subject of an article for *Die Zeit* in 1963, when value-added tax was being introduced to the Federal Republic. Böll pointed out that writers would be severely disadvantaged: requiring no material other than paper and pencil, having no overheads such as wages for employees, unable to invest in expensive capital equipment, both of which they could offset against tax, they were nevertheless to be taxed on the same basis as industrial firms, *de facto* at a higher rate (E 1, pp. 557–60). In the novel Gruhl senior, a cabinet-maker like Böll's father, has been ruined by the tax system for precisely the reasons Böll set out in his article, and the accountant Grähn can only shake his head with astonishment that he has survived at all. Grähn admits that it is 'absurd' that Gruhl should go bankrupt with an annual profit of 40,000 marks; taxation policies were aimed at creating 'absurd' expense accounts. In order to survive Gruhl is forced into equally absurd stratagems, such as insisting on being paid in kind — on one occasion this consisted in twenty kilograms of butter, which the bailiff confiscated only to find that it went rancid in a thunder-storm, whereby Gruhl threatened to take him to court in turn for failing to look after his property. Absurdity is repeated in the case of the army and the law. With the former it is illustrated by the incident which sparked off the story for Böll. Private Kuttke, a colleague of Georg Gruhl's, explains in his evidence that he became a professional soldier because 'life in the army contained just that kind of concentrated boredom that he desired' ('das Leben bei der Bundeswehr enthalte genau die Art konzentrierter Langeweile, nach der er begehre') (R 4, p. 463); Georg had '*suffered* under that "quaternity of the absurd"; meaninglessness, unproductivity, boredom, indolence, which he, Kuttke, regarded as absolutely the *only meaning* of an army' ('habe *gelitten* unter dieser "Quaternität des Absurden"; Sinnlosigkeit, Unproduktivität, Langeweile, Faulheit, die er, Kuttke, geradezu für den *einzigen Sinn* einer Armee halte') (p. 464). The absurdity of the law is to be found in the element of ritual which Böll emphasises in his depiction of its procedures. From the beginning the theatricality of the occasion is stressed: the mood in the courtroom is similar to that at the premiere of an amateur production. Defence and prosecution are at each other's throats in the courtroom — outside they are the best of friends. Kugl-Egger even suffers a slight heart attack during the proceedings in his rage over the way he believes he is being cheated of his prey, but his behaviour afterwards is calm and humane. What disrupts the workings of the court is behaviour which disregards these conventions, as when Gruhl senior absent-mindedly lights his pipe or Agnes Hall addresses the presiding magistrate by his first name — on both these occasions chaos ensues.

Against the absurdity of the system Böll sets the freedom of art. In various guises art plays a major role in the novel. 'Conventional' art is represented by Tervel, a young painter who has been allowed to exhibit his works in Birglar's treasury office. They consist of a cycle called 'The sacrament of marriage', one of which depicts a naked young man lying on top of a naked young woman whose breasts are gas-burners. The organiser of the exhibition is afraid of adverse reaction from Birglar's ratepayers, but none of them takes any notice; the judgement of the critics is either negative or neutral. For the conventional artist society is indeed a padded cell. Gruhl senior is a joiner, but he has come to specialise more and more in the restoration of antique furniture, which he does with great sensitivity. Grähn compares his situation with that of the artist; Böll himself preferred to stress the craftsmanship side to his profession (I, p. 355). The artist as citizen is in an underprivileged position, however much he may be respected and encouraged as artist. But finally there is the 'happening'. Gruhl junior describes himself explicitly as an artist. The burning of the jeep was a 'happening' — the craftsman Gruhl senior was his assistant. The art historian Büren who is called as witness confirms that it was indeed a work of art; he could find in it elements of five different arts: architecture, sculpture, literature, music and dance. The 'musical' effects were obtained by the insertion of boiled sweets into the petrol canisters with which the jeep was set on fire; the literary dimension consisted in the Gruhls' reciting the litany for All Saints; that of dance was their rhythmically tapping their pipes together; and so on. In the end this description of the event is accepted by the presiding magistrate, and the judgment is given as outlined. Is then the 'happening' as innocuous as the works of Tervel? Hardly so. In the first place an actual piece of army property has been destroyed and a protest against militarism has been registered. And the very fact that the affair has been so carefully hushed up implies that the State is *not* able to digest art of this kind quite so easily.

Böll himself was disappointed at the reception of the novel. Critics and readers, he felt, had missed the 'invitation to action' implied in the burning of the jeep, which he regarded as a practical form of resistance (I, pp. 155–6). His critics have suggested that his novel is too cosy to be genuinely provocative (Conard, 1981, pp. 157ff.). There is in fact a contradiction between his stated aim and his disappointment with the result, just as there was a contradiction between Beuys's stance and his reaction to the personal attack it provoked. For one of Böll's purposes was to reveal the 'padded cell', the innocuousness of *all* art, including 'happenings', in the contemporary scene. As the final example of art there is the novel itself. The early years of the student movement were marked by some humorously irreverent behaviour towards the institutions of authority. *Ende einer Dienstfahrt* may well, as Peter Schütt suggests, have been an anti-authoritarian factor of some influence (Beth, 1980, p. 175), may therefore have been more provocative than Böll suspected. The old-fashioned narrative technique itself points to a further aspect of society, the way in which events are manipulated from behind the scenes. Throughout the trial the strings are being pulled by a mysterious Grellber, to whom the observer Bergnolte has to report. Grellber is addressed by Bergnolte as 'Herr Präsident' (p. 487);

presumably he is the State's chief officer responsible for justice; it emerges at the end that he has important contacts in the army, in parliament, in the Church and with the press, as well as being responsible for the administration of justice. Because of the latter two he is able to ensure that the case is tried in the most discreet manner and that the details are not publicised by the press. There is something Kafkaesque about this side to the story, and it points forward to Böll's later *Die verlorene Ehre der Katharina Blum*. By telling the story in a non-Kafkaesque manner, by introducing a narrator who *does* know what is going on and who by implication is not on the side of a secretive bureaucracy since he is prepared to publicise what is not to be publicised, Böll is, following his Wuppertal address, 'breaking taboos'; his art is going further than the State would wish. The narrator is a Günter Wallraff perhaps, the link between the world of fiction and the world of the reader and he is clearly on the side of the reader. The modernist perspectivism or subjectivism of Böll's earlier works implied the individual's isolation in a hostile society. By breaking with the conventions of modernist fiction he was also breaking with their assumption that the individual was helpless and condemned to passivity. For the other outstanding feature of *Ende einer Dienstfahrt* is that for the first time in Böll's fiction the victims are *not* alone. The Bachs and the Fähmels were families; they could at best draw into their community individuals from outside. The Gruhls belong to a community, one which is formed not least by its local dialect; even in gaol they have their sympathisers and helpers and it is the members of the Establishment like Bergnolte who are the real outsiders. In his Frankfurt lectures Böll attacked the mentality which criticised provinciality; here the provincial town of Birglar *contains* (another meaning of *bergen*) genuine humanity and solidarity. In this respect too there is something post-modernist about *Ende einer Dienstfahrt*.

Between *Ansichten eines Clowns* (1963) and *Gruppenbild mit Dame* (1971) Böll published no large-scale works and it was felt by some that he was losing his central position in German literature. Marcel Reich-Ranicki, for example, wrote that Böll, who had once spoken in the name of a whole generation, now seemed unable to 'keep in step' with developments (Reich-Ranicki, 1963, p. 141), an accusation which prompted the sarcastic response from Böll that he had never been able to 'keep in step', not even in the army, and did not propose to do so now (E 2, p. 20). In fact, as I have attempted to show, Böll remained very much of his time. The Festschrift brought out by his publishers to celebrate his fiftieth birthday, *In Sachen Böll*, contained forty-two contributions, some eulogies, others critical, by German-

156

ists, fellow-writers, journalists and politicians and covered every
aspect of his interests. It is a nice touch and one that is indicative of
the confused public image of Böll at the time that the collection
begins with a piece by Theodor W. Adorno and ends with one by
Georg Lukács, representatives of diametrically opposite and indeed
hostile theoretical schools, the former the apostle of a radical modernism, the latter the proponent of a socialist realism moulded on
the traditions of the nineteenth century (Reich-Ranicki, 1968). Both
approved of Böll.

Böll was modifying his orientation all the time, developing new
interests, becoming more of a public figure and a controversial one
at that. It is no coincidence that his most substantial book of these
years was the 510-page collection of essays, speeches and reviews
published in 1967 as *Aufsätze Kritiken Reden*. His contributions to the
debates on the Emergency Legislation in 1968 have been mentioned.
He described this moment as a caesura in post-war German journalism: for the first time he had delivered an address which had not been
bought beforehand for publication by one of the newspapers, such
was the delicate nature of the occasion (E 2, p. 295). In 1967 he was
awarded West Germany's most prestigious literary prize, the Georg
Büchner Prize. In his address he drew numerous parallels between
Büchner's time and the present: the shooting of Benno Ohnesorg
earlier that year repeated an earlier officially sanctioned 'murder',
that of Büchner's fellow-student and revolutionary, Minnigerode
(E 2, p. 277); it was Büchner who wrote that violence was endemic
to the political circumstances of 1833: 'They accuse the young
people of using violence. But are we not in an eternal state of
violence?' ('Man wirft den jungen Leuten den Gebrauch der Gewalt
vor. Sind wir denn aber nicht in einem ewigen Gewaltzustand?')
(p. 280; Büchner, 1833, p. 416). In August 1968 Böll was invited to
Prague by the Czech Writers Union; he arrived on 20 August, and
the following day the armies of the Warsaw Pact countries invaded.
He gave numerous interviews, including one with *Literární Listý*,
published illicitly in Czechoslovakia on the 24th, in which he
expressed his support for the Czech model of a democratic socialism
and condemned the invasion as the 'moral bankruptcy' of Moscow
centralism (I, pp. 69–76; E 2, pp. 305–16; *Die Zeit*, 30.8.1968, p. 4).
But Böll's position at this time is perhaps best summed up by the
title he gave his address to the first congress of the newly formed
West German Writers Union on 8 June 1969: 'The end of humility'
('Ende der Bescheidenheit') (E 2, pp. 374–86). Böll was one of the
initiators of this new association; his concern was, as in the early
article on VAT, with the plight of his less financially successfully

colleagues in their struggle against unscrupulous publishers and with the State itself. His words included a challenge to the State: 'We owe this state nothing, it owes us a great deal; may it therefore expect that in future it can no longer keep us divided and splintered by means of a pseudo-cult of genius or even a pseudo-cult of individuality, enabling it to pick us off one by one' ('Wir verdanken diesem Staat nichts, er verdankt uns eine Menge; mag er also darauf gefaßt sein, daß er uns nicht länger auf dem Umweg über einen Pseudo-Geniekult oder auch nur auf dem Umweg über einen Pseudo-Individualitätskult zerspalten und zersplittert halten und einzeln abfertigen kann') (p. 385). Böll, who was still best known for the individuality of his 'little men', the victims of an all-powerful bureaucracy, was now preaching the strength of solidarity.

7

Citizen for Brandt (1969–1976)

'The Federal Republic has been transformed since the start of the social–liberal coalition, along with the world around it' ('Die Bundesrepublik hat sich seit Beginn der sozial–liberalen Koalition gewandelt, mit ihr die Welt um sie herum'), Böll declared at an election meeting in Cleves in 1972 (E 2, p. 599). In many respects the years 1969 to 1976 were for the Federal Republic years of triumph. Hitherto the West Germans had been admired for their material progress; now they seemed to have achieved equal moral status with the other nations of the world. It was in this period that West Germany was admitted to membership of the United Nations, that their Chancellor was awarded the Nobel Peace Prize and that one of their authors received the Nobel Prize for Literature. Thirty-six years after the Berlin Olympics, when Hitler had demonstratively refused to invite the black athlete Jesse Owens to a reception, Germany once more played host to the world's athletes, determined to mark the contrast between then and 1972. That the Munich games ended in a blood-bath was scarcely the fault of the West Germans; but it did point to world problems from which they were not excluded. Some of these problems seemed to be on the point of being solved: in April 1975 the Americans abandoned Saigon and the Vietnam War came to an end; and at the beginning of August of the same year in Helsinki thirty-five nations signed the Final Act of the Conference on Security and Cooperation in Europe, formally accepting the territorial changes which had followed the Second World War and, as they hoped, laying the basis for peaceful cooperation and internal liberties. Something of the initial optimism of these years is conveyed in an address which Böll gave in 1970:

> I see this current international restlessness, from the factories into the most holy Offices, from the academies right into the apprentices' hostels, in armies and prisons, in churches, schools, families, in art and in anti-art — I see this restlessness as a grand attempt to abandon or to destroy the old contexts, as a preliminary stage or precondition of fraternity.

> (Ich deute mir diese internationale gegenwärtige Bewegtheit von den Fabriken bis in die heiligsten Offizien, von den Akademien bis in Lehr-

159

lingsheime hinein, in Armeen und Strafanstalten, in Kirchen, Schulen, Familien, in der Kunst und in der Antikunst — ich deute mir diese Bewegtheit als den großen Versuch, die alten Rahmen aufzugeben oder zu zerstören, als eine Vorstufe oder Vorbedingung zur Brüderlichkeit.)

On 5 March 1969 Gustav Heinemann was elected third president of the Federal Republic. Heinemann was the candidate of the SPD; he had been a member of Adenauer's first cabinet, but had resigned from the CDU in protest against his leader's initiatives to set up a new West German army in 1950. When his term of office ended in 1974 Böll eulogised him as a 'radical', who had fearlessly laid bare the roots of the nationalist consciousness and, like many a writer — especially Böll himself — had reaped opprobrium from the right for his pains (E 3, pp. 140–3). Heinemann had been elected with the help of the FDP; his election pointed forward to the coalition which SPD and FDP were to form after the parliamentary elections of September of the same year and which was to last until 1982. Exactly twenty years after the founding of the Federal Republic the government was led for the first time by a Social Democrat, Willy Brandt. The coalition's majority was a narrow one of six, and defections over the years made it necessary to hold new elections prematurely in 1972. This time, however, the SPD, with almost 46 per cent of the votes, overtook the CDU/CSU, obtaining the electorate's approval for the coalition's policies with a comfortable majority.

Böll suggested in 1975 that it was difficult for foreigners to appreciate the sensational nature of Brandt's victory; other democracies were accustomed to the regular pendulum of power between opposing parties; the change was a 'counter-movement against the development which began in 1949' ('Gegengewicht gegen die Entwicklung, die 1949 begonnen hat') (I, p. 510). He even made speeches on behalf of the SPD in the 1972 election campaign as one of the prominent 'citizens for Brandt' ('Bürger für Brandt') (E 2, pp. 599–604), he addressed the SPD's party congress in Dortmund (E 2, pp. 605–8) and contributed to the SPD's electoral newspaper (E 2, pp. 609–12). He put the manuscript of *Entfernung von der Truppe* up for sale in aid of the SPD's election funds — it fetched 10,000 marks (*Die Zeit*, 13.10.72, p. 2; I, p. 312). In 1974 he again addressed a meeting of the SPD's parliamentary party (E 3, pp. 111–14). In view of his earlier scorn for the Social Democrats, this volte-face may seem surprising. It was due almost entirely to the personality of Willy Brandt himself. Even in 1971 Böll had still been sceptical about the electoral effect of speeches by celebrities like Günter

Grass, who had been campaigning tirelessly for the SPD for many years; if he thought he could win votes for the SPD in that way he would certainly do so, because 'I am concerned for this state, its progress, and for the stabilisation of the SPD' ('ich bin interessiert an diesem Staat, an seinem Fortschritt und an der Stabilisierung der SPD'), but only 'because it has Willy Brandt — that's the only reason' ('weil sie Willy Brandt hat — nur deshalb') (I, p. 162). In 1972 Grass persuaded him to overcome his scepticism and join the Social Democratic campaign (I, pp. 602f.). In that year he wrote an essay on Brandt, in which he stressed above all his plebeian origins: illegitimate, a 'man of the people', the first German chancellor to break with the 'Herrenvolk' tradition. One thing Böll could never forgive Adenauer was his attempt to discredit his Social Democratic opponent by sneering at his illegitimacy and at the fact that he had emigrated from Nazi Germany. He also admired Brandt's defence of the radical youth wing of his party (E 2, pp. 535–41). But the decisive political factor for Böll in his opting for the Social Democrats was Brandt's *Ostpolitik*, what he called the 'cleaning up of what was left over from 1945 in Europe' ('Bereinigung der Reste von 45 in Europa') (I, p. 587).

These two aspects of Brandt's period in office, the search for reconciliation with Eastern Europe and the question of 'radicalism' in public life, profoundly affected Böll. From the beginning, when in November 1969 the Federal government signed the international treaty outlawing the proliferation of nuclear weapons, Brandt made it clear that he was determined to efface the image of militaristic, revanchist Germany. Meetings with his opposite number in East Germany, Willi Stoph, in March and May 1970 were the first ever to take place between the leaders of the two German states. There followed a series of treaties with the Soviet Union, with Poland, with Czechoslovakia, in which the respective sides accepted the existing frontiers and renounced the use of force in settling outstanding differences; the most spectacular and moving event in this connection was Brandt's visit to Poland in December 1970, during which, quite spontaneously it seems, he knelt down before the monument to those killed in the Warsaw ghetto — it was subsequent to this that he was awarded the Nobel Peace Prize in October 1971. Finally, the most difficult task of all, a Basic Treaty was signed with the GDR, in which the two Germanies, while not going to the extent of exchanging ambassadors, recognized each other's rights within their respective territories and promised to encourage normal relations. This was followed by the entry of the FRG and the GDR to the United Nations in 1973. Incomprehensibly for most foreigners and certainly for Böll (E 2, p. 600), all of these *démarches* were opposed by the CDU/CSU leadership, who even took the government to court over the Basic Treaty with the GDR in 1973, on the grounds that recognition of the East German regime was at odds with the written constitution.

Brandt won his case at the Constitutional Court. More problematic were the domestic issues concerning the aftermath of the student unrest of 1968. The student movement and the Extra-Parliamentary Opposition had disintegrated into countless, mutually hostile splinter groups. Many returned to the Social Democrat fold, where the 'Young Socialists' ('Jusos') formed a ginger group, even an inner opposition to the more conservative establishment and provided ammunition to the Christian Democrats when they wished to represent the SPD as 'socialist'. Others, including the 'Red Army Faction' (RAF) or 'Baader–Meinhof Group' and the 'Movement of 2 June' (the date of the shooting of Ohnesorg in 1967), despairing of democratic, peaceful means of changing society, turned to violence. This was initially directed against property: arson attacks on two Frankfurt stores, on the central administrative office of the Free University and on the Kennedy Library in West Berlin. However, in 1970 when Ulrike Meinhof and others liberated Andreas Baader from captivity, a librarian, Georg Linke, was shot and seriously injured, and from then on weapons were increasingly used. The group claimed that the shooting of Linke was unplanned, and had they anticipated it they would have used different tactics; thereafter it had been the police who fired the first shots and who appeared to have orders to shoot to kill. In 1971 both Petra Schelm and Georg von Rauch were shot dead by police in unexplained circumstances — in 1974 Böll gave evidence on behalf of the poet Erich Fried, who had been taken to court for describing the latter shooting as 'preventive murder' ('Vorbeugemord') (E 3, pp. 88ff.). On other, separate occasions in 1971 two policemen died. In May 1972 a bomb attack on a United States army barracks in Heidelberg killed one American serviceman and injured sixteen others; a week later an explosion at the headquarters of the Springer newspaper concern in Hamburg injured seventeen people. Within a few weeks, however, the five most wanted urban terrorists had been arrested, Andreas Baader, Holger Meins, Jan Carl Raspe, Gudrun Ensslin and Ulrike Meinhof. The first phase of urban terrorism had ended. When the actual incidents are listed it seems hard to see these activities as anything other than a ludicrously romantic and unreal attempt to repeat the Cuban exploits of a Che Guevara in the most unpromising, because stable and prosperous, society of Western

Europe. When compared to the simultaneous rioting and bombing in Northern Ireland, for example, the situation in West Germany was downright calm. What was peculiarly unpleasant was the way in which these on the whole isolated incidents were exploited by the right-wing mass media, which sensationalised each of them and attempted to whip up public hysteria; this, they hoped, would undermine the Brandt government.

Böll followed events with increasing alarm. In 1970 he had been elected president of the West German branch of PEN — in this function he proposed Alexander Solzhenitsyn for the Nobel Prize for Literature (I, pp. 118f.). At the beginning of November he addressed a meeting of Amnesty International, singling out the atrocities which were being committed against political prisoners in Greece (E 2, pp. 442–7). In the following year he became president of PEN International, the first German ever to take up this office, a further honour for the Federal Republic. In this capacity he found himself inevitably involved in semi-public activities on behalf of writers the world over who were in difficulties with their governments. Just how much influence the PEN Club can have on the policies of governments is unclear; because of his high reputation in the Soviet Union and his numerous personal contacts there Böll was hopeful that he might be able to help Soviet dissidents such as Vladimir Bukovski, Andrey Amalrik and Solzhenitsyn. When his term of office ended, however, he had to admit that relations between the Soviet Writers Union and PEN had not improved — the results of Brandt's *Ostpolitik* had not spread to the cultural sphere and it seemed easier for industrialists to do business with the Soviet Union than for writers (I, p. 287). In fact, as he said elsewhere, it was impossible to gauge the effects of public appeals and behind-the-scenes negotiations. The East German poet Peter Huchel, who had been living in a kind of internal exile since he was stripped of his editorship of the journal *Sinn und Form* in 1962, was permitted to settle in West Germany in 1971 and Böll may have had some influence in his case (I, pp. 577f.); Andrey Sakharov believed that Böll had helped him in 1973 (I, p. 436); Amalrik was in the end released from prison (E 3, p. 87); and when in January 1974 Solzhenitsyn was allowed to leave the Soviet Union, it was with Böll and his family that he initially stayed (I, pp. 283–6). This context helps to explain Böll's intervention on behalf of Ulrike Meinhof at the beginning of 1972, which resulted in an unparalleled outbreak of demagogic hysteria. Ulrike Meinhof too had been a writer, originally a journalist, and her television play on education in orphanages, *Bambule*, which Böll thought highly of, had never been

163

transmitted (E 2, p. 547; I, pp. 212, 225).

It was not primarily because Ulrike Meinhof was a writer that Böll intervened. Shortly before Christmas 1971 *Bild* had a front page banner headline: 'Another Baader–Meinhof gang murder' ('Baader–Meinhof–Bande mordet weiter'). A policeman had been killed during a bank raid by unknown robbers. *Bild* presented the event as if the Baader–Meinhof group had already been tried and found guilty, when in fact the police had no evidence to link them with the crime. The Press Council later found the newspaper guilty of irresponsible reporting. Böll did not wait for that, however. He wrote a furious article for *Der Spiegel*, which appeared on the 10 January 1972 under the title 'Will Ulrike Gnade oder freies Geleit?' ('Does Ulrike want pardon or free conduct?'), and in which he pointed out the absurdity and hopelessness of the group's position, quoted some of the factors which had led to their 'declaration of war' on West German society and suggested that while it would be sensible for Ulrike Meinhof to give herself up to the police, in the hysterical atmosphere which Springer and his newspapers were creating there was no likelihood of her obtaining a fair trial. His article was intended as an appeal for calm to give the terrorists the opportunity to reconsider their position before further blood was shed. In the event it did precisely the opposite. A fortnight earlier on television Böll had defended Saarland Radio's literary editor Arnfried Astel, who had been sacked for publishing an epigrammatic poem implying that the measures announced in connection with the Bundeswehr's summer manoeuvres made anything that the Baader–Meinhof group had done seem relatively harmless (I, 194–6); on the day on which his *Der Spiegel* article appeared he had been interviewed on television in connection with the Soviet dissidents and had appeared reluctant to intervene — too much publicity might be counter-productive, he believed (I, pp. 197–202). His critics now accused him of being 'blind on the left eye'; he was an opportunist, wishing to safeguard the continued sales of his books in the Soviet Union — or else he was a subversive revolutionary, who sympathised with the aims of Baader and Meinhof. *Bild* accused him of using the language of Joseph Goebbels. On television Ulrich Frank-Planitz described him as one of Germany's 'drawing-room anarchists' and Gerhard Löwenthal declared that 'those who sympathise with this left-wing fascism, the Bölls and Brückners [Professor Peter Brückner had been suspended from his post at the Technical University of Hanover for having allowed Ulrike Meinhof to spend a night at his home] and all the other so-called intellectuals are not a jot better than the spiritual pacemakers of the Nazis who brought so much misfortune over our country once before' ('die Sympathisanten dieses Linksfaschismus, die Bölls und Brückners und all die anderen sogenannten Intellektuellen sind nicht einen Deut besser als die geistigen Schrittmacher der Nazis, die schon einmal so viel Unglück über unser Land gebracht haben')(Grützbach, 1972, p. 104). In the illustrated magazine *Quick* Wilfried Ahrens declared 'The Bölls are more dangerous than Baader–Meinhof' ('Die Bölls sind gefährlicher als Baader–Meinhof'), quoted Böll's 1966 words on the 'rottenness of the State', and stressed Böll's friendship with Willy Brandt (ibid., pp. 147f.). By the end of February 1972 Frank Grützbach had been able to compile a 192-page paperback documenting the affair with a mere 'selection' of between one-fiftieth and one-sixtieth of the available material. Böll was in the Soviet Union at the time, engaged on delicate negotiations on behalf of the dissidents there, and his efforts were not helped by the controversy (EZ, p. 16). Paradoxically the West German Communists were accusing him of being manipulated by the CIA in his intervention on behalf of Amalrik (E 3, pp. 531f.; E 3, pp. 58ff.).

It did not end there. During the election campaign Böll encountered voices advising him to 'emigrate' (E 3, p. 172). Between June 1972 and November 1977 police searched his property or that of his family on four occasions in search of weapons and wanted criminals; on one of these occasions, 7 February 1974, news of the search of his son's flat in West Berlin appeared in Springer's *BZ* before it had actually occurred (I, pp. 700, 744). In the parliamentary debate on internal security on 7 June 1972 he heard his name mentioned at least six times as he travelled home in his car (E 2, pp. 569f.). The witch hunt had reached such a level that his publisher Reinhold Neven DuMont appealed for help and in July over 100 prominent German writers signed a declaration of support for Böll's position (Wagenbach, 1979, p. 286). But even in November 1974, when the President of the West Berlin Supreme Court Günter von Drenkmann was assassinated, an act which Böll immediately condemned, the journalist Matthias Walden was able to go on television and, referring once more to Böll's words of 1966, accuse him of having 'manured the soil' on which violence flourished. Böll took Walden to court, lost his action in the first instance, won it on appeal in 1976 (E 3, pp. 208 ff.), lost it again in the Federal Appeal Court in 1978, but finally won it in the Constitutional Court in 1981.

Looking back Böll agreed that he had been naïve and possibly clumsy in some of his original formulations — the term 'Gnade', which in German means both 'pardon' and 'grace', was misleading (E 2, pp. 559–61). The title of the article was unfortunate; it was not in fact his but *Der Spiegel*'s formulation. At least part of the reason for the press campaign had to do with Brandt's *Ostpolitik*, he believed, which the right was opposing. Had he intervened on behalf of Bukovski, for example, the reaction in the Soviet Union would have been negative, because of the right-wing voices involved (I, p. 207) — when Amalrik was released the news was given far less prominence than when he was arrested (E 3, p. 87). The Radicals legislation which the hysteria of late 1971 and early 1972 provoked was, however, something he found it difficult to forgive the SPD government. On the 28 January 1972 a joint decision of Brandt and the prime ministers of the provincial states decreed that anyone whose loyalty to the 'free and democratic basic order of the State' ('freiheitlich demokratische Grundordnung') was in doubt could be refused a post or dismissed from his or her post in the public services. This was the so-called 'Radicals Decree' ('Radikalenerlaß'), which its opponents immediately labelled 'Berufsverbot', in allusion to the National Socialist laws which prevented Jews from holding public office. It was the most controversial legislation of Brandt's administration and he is known to have regretted it. Public employment included teaching, the post office, the railways — the number of potential refusals was large. The new Communist Party, the DKP, had been legalised in 1968, but membership in a legal party now could debar one from the employment for which one had trained. The Constitution granted all citizens freedom of conscience — but some seemed freer than others. And, as was frequently pointed out, those who had been members of a party which had demonstrably brought disaster on Germany, the Nazis, remained at their posts as teachers, civil servants, postmen and railway workers — they might even, like Hans Filbinger, become prime minister of the state of Baden-Württemberg, where the new legislation was invoked most readily. By 1978 it was estimated that over 2 million persons had been investigated, 611 of whom had been rejected as candidates for employment in the public sector, although this may well be an underestimate (Conard, 1981, p. 207; cf. also E 3, p. 380).

Numerous writers protested. Peter Schneider's semi-autobiographical novel . . . *schon bist du ein Verfassungsfeind* (1975) demonstrated some of the illogicalities of the legislation. Alfred Andersch's poem 'Artikel 3 (3)', which made the parallel with the Third Reich explicit, created a public scandal when it was banned from a television programme in 1976 (Andersch, 1976). Böll spoke out frequently against the measures. On Christmas Day in 1973 he described them on radio as 'unworthy of the Federal Republic of Germany'; in no other West European democracy would such

166

legislation be possible; it was stifling public debate: 'The Radicals Decree is preventing any radical political and intellectual, theoretical and practical discussion of problems; it is discouraging teenagers and young people who wish to work in the public sector, it is forcing them into a humiliating opportunism or hypocrisy. It is a decree against hope, it prescribes hopelessness and paralysis' ('Der Radikalenerlaß verhindert radikale politische und geistige, theoretische und praktische Auseinandersetzung mit Problemen; er entmutigt Jugendliche und junge Leute, die im öffentlichen Dienst arbeiten wollen, er zwingt sie zu demütigender Anpassung oder zur Heuchelei. Es ist ein Erlaß gegen die Hoffnung, er verordnet Hoffnungslosigkeit und Lähmung') (E 3, pp. 75f.). In 1974 he suggested that legislation against radicals ought logically to ban the arts, the law and the Gospel (E 3, p. 149). Two years later he suggested that it was fulfilling George Orwell's vision of the totalitarian State (E 3, p. 383). The political culture of the 1920s had been destroyed by the Nazis and the virulent anti-Communism of the Adenauer years; from 1967 onwards there had been signs of new growth but the new laws had swept it away (E 3, pp. 410f.). Provocatively he described Gustav Heinemann as a 'radical in public service' ('Radikaler im öffentlichen Dienst') (E 3, pp. 140ff.), and returned to the theme in 1983 when he entitled an essay on Thomas Aquinas, 'Radikaler in Gottes Dienst' ('Radical in God's service') (EZ, pp. 158–64). The short satire 'Du fährst zu oft nach Heidelberg' (1977) is his most direct literary presentation of the theme: an unpolitical student is refused a teaching post because of his humanitarian help for two exiles from Chile. But Böll also intervened in individual cases of persons whom he believed had been unjustly treated. In 1978 he wrote to the Minister of Education of North-Rhine-Westphalia on behalf of Regina Herberg, who had lost her teaching post because she had organised a discussion with her pupils on, among other things, an article by Böll. This is the topic of his contribution to a volume of which he was co-editor, *Briefe zur Verteidigung der bürgerlichen Freiheit* (Reinbek, 1978, pp. 12–24), which is devoted largely to the Radicals Decree and its effects.

The decree did not in any case result in less violence in West German society. Indeed, if the Baader–Meinhof group had any rational strategy it was to force the State into taking ever more draconian measures which would demonstrate its own illegitimacy. In December 1974 Böll was awarded the Ossietzky medal by the International League for Human Rights (Carl von Ossietzky was a pacifist journalist who had been imprisoned for treason during the Weimar Republic and died in a concentration camp under the

Nazis; he received the Nobel Peace Prize in 1936). The ceremony was boycotted by the local CDU. In his address Böll described the current mood as one of 'madness': 'If things go on like this, in six months the Baader–Meinhof group will have reached its target, not because of us, who are perhaps committing the criminal sin of differentiating, but because of the rabble-rousers on the right who are just as interested in confrontation as the Baader–Meinhof group' ('Wenn das so weitergeht, wird die Baader–Meinhof-Gruppe in einem halben Jahr ihr Ziel erreicht haben, nicht durch uns, die wir möglicherweise die kriminelle Sünde der Differenzierung begehen. sondern durch die Scharfmacher auf der Rechten, denen an der Konfrontation so viel liegt wie der Baader–Meinhof-Gruppe') (E 3, pp. 169f.). The second phase of urban terrorism was much more bloody than the first and Böll's predictions seemed fulfilled. It began when Holger Meins died on 9 November 1974 after two months on hunger strike. The following day Gustav von Drenkmann was assassinated in West Berlin. At the end of the month a CDU politician survived a further assassination attempt. On the 27 February 1975 Peter Lorenz, a West Berlin CDU deputy, was kidnapped; he was freed a week later after the government had released five members of the Baader–Meinhof group from prison and allowed them to fly to South Yemen. On 24 April the West German embassy in Stockholm was occupied and its personnel taken hostage with the demand that twenty-six prisoners be released; when the government refused, two hostages were killed and the embassy set on fire; five terrorists were captured, one had been shot. It is a measure of the hysteria of the time that a play by Jean-Paul Sartre was banned in 1975 in West Germany because Sartre had visited Baader in prison (I, p. 430). The trial of Andreas Baader, Gudrun Ensslin and Jan Carl Raspe began on 21 May in the top security prison of Stammheim, which had been built specially to house them. A year later, on 9 May 1976 Ulrike Meinhof committed suicide in the same prison, possibly because of the inhumane isolation to which she had been subjected. Many left-wing intellectuals, not including Böll, suspected that she had been murdered, and there was unrest in a number of cities.

Brandt resigned as chancellor on 6 May 1974. It was not the 'radicals' who brought about his downfall but the cold war, which continued in spite of his *Ostpolitik* — one of his assistants was found to be an East German spy. He was succeeded by the more pragmatic Helmut Schmidt and Böll's sympathies for the SPD rapidly cooled. In the election year 1976 he continued to write pamphlets against the CDU/CSU in a regular series of contributions for *Konkret* (E 3, pp. 350–2, 364–70, 380–3). But he also was suggesting ironically that there was no need for a change of party since the SPD was as friendly towards industry and capital as any CDU government could be (E 3, p. 360) and by the end of October he was using vocabulary to describe the two major parties in terms similar to those of his 1963 article 'Was heute links sein könnte': the Federal Republic was a 'country in which left and right are fighting over the midlle ground and radicalising it more and more towards the right' ('Land, wo Links und Rechts sich um die Besetzung der Mitte streiten, die Mitte immer mehr nach rechts hin radikalisieren') (E 3, p. 403).

One feature of the years 1969 to 1976 was the importance which the interview assumed in Böll's work. This came about partly through his position in the West German and international PEN, which entailed frequent appearances on television and radio. But in addition Böll gave no fewer than three substantial interviews between 1971 and 1976, which appeared in book form: *Im Gespräch: mit Heinz Ludwig Arnold, Drei Tage im März* (conversations with Christian Linder), and *Eine deutsche Erinnerung* with René Wintzen, which first appeared in French as *Une mémoire allemande*. Other major occasions on which he discussed his political and literary ideas were with Dieter Wellershoff on *Gruppenbild mit Dame* (1971), with Karin Struck in 1973, and with Manfred Durzak in 1975 on *Die verlorene Ehre der Katharina Blum*. A whole volume of the collected works of 1977–8 is devoted to a selection of interviews, and a further posthumous volume is in preparation. Böll regarded these interviews as a means both of exploiting the media to put across his point of view, and of clarifying his own thoughts (Lengning, 1972, p. 110). It was in these years also that Böll's international reputation was firmly established, partly through his non-literary activities, partly through the award of the Nobel Prize for Literature in 1972. As he pointed out in his address in Stockholm, his German predecessors had been at odds with their country of birth: Nelly Sachs (1966) had had to flee from the Holocaust and was a citizen of Sweden; Hermann Hesse (1946) had left Germany before the First World War and was Swiss; Thomas Mann (1929) had emigrated on the advent of Hitler and died in Switzerland. The last German prize-winner to end his days in Germany was Gerhart Hauptmann, who had received the award five years before Böll was born (E 2, pp. 622f.). And yet at home, as with Brandt's award the previous year, the nationalist press reacted with dismay and disgust. Franz Josef Strauss accused the Swedish Academy of interfering in the Federal elections. Springer's *Bild* reported the award only briefly; his *Die Welt*, on the other hand, found space for a long article by H. Joachim Maitre which sought to demonstrate that the Nobel Prize usually went to minor writers, that it was a political, often left-wing award, and that both these categories applied to Böll (*Die Welt*, 20.10.1972). *Gruppenbild mit Dame* had just been translated into Swedish; it and *Die verlorene Ehre der Katharina Blum* were widely translated and in the latter case the film by Volker Schlöndorff was a further popularising factor. Böll received honorary doctorates from a number of universities, including Dublin and Birmingham in 1973, and in 1974 he was elected an honorary member of the US Academy of Arts and Letters. He travelled abroad at the expense of the West German government, first visiting the United States in 1972. He frequently contrasted the schizophrenia of official German policies towards writers and artists, which attacked them as subversives at home but were happy to reap the credit which they brought the Federal Republic abroad. When in 1974 a 'German Month' in London included an exhibition of political posters by Böll's friend Klaus Staeck, among them one which showed Strauss as a butcher, political pressure was put on the Goethe Institute to ban Staeck from participation in future enterprises of this kind. Böll responded by announcing that in that case he was no longer willing to 'represent German culture abroad' (I, pp. 313–20).

It was now that his relations with his Church came to a head. In the past Böll had frequently accused the Catholic Church of placing its material interests above its responsibilities towards the poor and the hungry. He now defined these accusations more precisely. Cardinal Döpfner had equated the fate of the Church with that of the free-market economy (E 3, p. 309). The Church had joined in with the CDU in opposing Brandt's treaties with Eastern Europe (Limagne, pp. 187f.). Böll's contribution to a Festschrift for the liberal theologian Karl Rahner was so hostile to the Church — he contrasted the support given to striking workers by bishops in France, Spain, Belgium and Brazil with the German bishops' hostility to organised labour — that the book was suppressed (E 3, pp. 242ff; cf. p. 538). The peculiarly German relationship between Church and State was illustrated in 1975 when the Bishop of Münster asked the Minister of Education in North-Rhine-Westphalia to remove the theologian Professor Horst Herrmann from his teaching post because of his unorthodox statements, a right which was given the Church by the Concordat of 1933; Böll commented on the case and wrote a postscript to Herrmann's book (E 3, pp. 300ff., 307ff.). But for Böll the most flagrant way in which the Church identified itself with the State was in its right to receive 10 per cent of its members' income tax, which turned the Church, as he put it, into a 'share-holder' in the capitalist economy (I, pp. 146, 556f.). In 1970 he ceased for a time to pay his church tax in an attempt to force the Church authorities to send in the bailiffs and demonstrate their materialism — which they did (I, pp. 248, 452). In January 1976 he and his wife officially left the Church, while remaining practising Catholics — his quarrel was not with the religion but with the institution (Limagne, p. 187).

In 1969 Böll wrote a second stage-play, *Aussatz* ('Leprosy'), which was first performed on 7 October 1970 in Aachen. A radio version had previously been broadcast on 6 June. It had little more success than *Ein Schluck Erde*. Its structure resembles that of Böll's early novels, an extended exposition being followed by a brief develop-ment. This in turn is the classic analytical form of Sophocles' Oedipus Trilogy and many naturalist plays of the turn of the century. It is a kind of detective story — the detective story plot is paradigmatically analytical. Before the play begins the principal event has already taken place, the suicide of a young priest with the allegorical name Christian; in the course of the first three acts the motives for his suicide and the authorities' attempt to disguise these motives are revealed. Christian was unable to reconcile his loyalty to his Church with his belief in individual humanity; a platonic affair with a young parishioner brought the conflict to a head.

The play is fundamentally an attack on institutions: the Catholic Church once more, but also the police authorities, the medical establishment and even the Communist Party of the GDR. Böll introduces elements of the cheap thriller. One of Christian's friends is Schneider, who was sent to the West from the GDR as a secret agent, first being shot in the hand to make his escape through the mine-fields appear genuine; once in the West, however, he gave himself up and joined both the Catholic Church and the CDU. In the last two acts he, together with Kumpert, another priest, and Tobser, a police inspector who has been unofficially pursuing his investigations, are placed in an isolation ward. The official version is that the suicide was not Christian but an unknown person with leprosy. Christian, Kumpert, Tobser have been betrayed by the institutions they serve; Schneider hopes to return to the GDR, although he knows that the authorities there will imprison him. Loyalty is 'leprosy' — Kumpert hopes to break out of the isola-tion ward and 'infect' the population at large. Böll used the meta-phor of leprosy on a number of occasions at this time: Hans Schnier's religiosity was 'leprosy' (E 2, p. 449); the intellectuals who showed any sympathy for Ulrike Meinhof were being treated like

171

lepers (E 2, p. 576).

Böll's next major work, the novel *Gruppenbild mit Dame*, appeared in the early summer of 1971, and was serialised in the *Frankfurter Allgemeine Zeitung* between July and November of that year. Its success was immediate. Within six months it had sold 150,000 hard-cover copies and when Böll was awarded the Nobel Prize a year later it returned to the bestseller lists. It may well have tipped the scales in Böll's favour with the Nobel Prize committee; Michael Ratcliffe, reviewing the English translation, described it slightly maliciously as 'a Nobel prize novel if ever I saw one' (*The Times*, 3.5.1973). In Germany its critical reception was mixed. Karl Korn called it 'a mature masterpiece' ('ein reifes Meisterwerk') (Lengning, 1972, p. 116); Marcel Reich-Ranicki dismissed it as 'a weak book' ('ein schwaches Buch') (Reich-Ranicki, 1971); Reinhard Baumgart was unsure how to describe it, but saw it as a kind of summary of all that Böll had hitherto achieved (Baumgart, 1971). Of greater weight were the opinions of two other critics. Helmut Heißenbüttel was almost fulsome in his praise: 'Böll, one might say, has reached a literary peak to which his previous works showed he was already on the way. He is at the point where terms like masterpiece no longer have any real meaning or rather — like many of the words in the text of his story — might only turn up with their initial letters, such as P for pain, T for tears or H for happiness' ('Böll hat, so könnte man sagen, einen literarischen Standort erreicht, zu dem er mit den vorhergehenden Arbeiten bereits auf dem Weg war, auf dem Weg schien. Er ist dort, wo Vokabeln wie Meisterwerk keinen rechten Sinn mehr haben oder aber — wie manche Wörter im Text seiner Erzählung — nur noch mit dem Anfangsbuchstaben auftauchen könnten, so S. für Schmerz, T. für Tränen, oder G. für Glück') (Heißenbüttel, 1971). What gives Heißenbüttel's opinions some authority is that he is one of the more avant-garde, anti-realist writers of West Germany. But the East German critic and academic Hans-Joachim Bernhard, writing in the opposite tradition, was equally enthusiastic, praising the 'spontaneous action on behalf of a wronged individual' ('spontane, einer unrecht behandelten einzelnen Person geltende Aktion') and 'the potential for proletarian solidarity' ('die Potenzen proletarischer Solidarität') as a 'supreme example of the presentation of tendencies in the direction of socially relevant action by the humanist counter-forces' ('Höhepunkt in der Darstellung von Tendenzen zu einem gesellschaftlich relevanten Wirken der humanistischen Gegenkräfte'), although he was also uneasy at the way in which in the novel members of the Communist Party seemed to leave the movement at times of crisis (Bernhard, 1972). As with the Festschrift of 1967, in which Adorno and Lukács formed a coalition, *Gruppenbild mit Dame* united the two poles of critical opinion.

In terms of topicality the novel has little to do with the activities of the Baader–Meinhof group, but rather more with the non-violent, imaginative forms of protest and resistance devised in the early stages of the student movement. The booming economy had developed an insatiable hunger for prestige office accommodation. At the same time there was an acute shortage of housing for poorer families. Fortunes were to be made only from the former, however, and perfectly habitable inner-city blocks of flats were allowed to deteriorate, then pulled down and replaced by office towers. 'Hausbesetzungen' ('squats'), later punningly called 'Instandbesetzungen' ('squatting plus renovation') were a means of protest and resistance (cf. E 3, p. 463). The housing shortage and the primitive conditions in which foreign workers were forced to live were topics of Rolf Hochhuth's comedy *Die Hebamme*, which appeared in the same year as *Gruppenbild mit Dame*, and of some of Günter Wallraff's reports. One of the strands of the novel concerns the efforts of the Hoyser family to evict Leni Gruyten from her spacious old flat in order to redevelop the site, and the successful resistance to these efforts by a form of non-violent guerrilla warfare conducted by a 'commune' consisting of a bizarre group of people: a music critic, the proprietor of a flower shop, a civil servant, a rich capitalist, Turkish and Portuguese refuse collectors, a Russian ex-prisoner of war and a retired graveyard worker. The scene in which the plans are laid is, we are told, reminiscent of that of the conspiracy in St Petersburg in October 1917. In order to thwart the bailiffs Leni's friends organise a massive traffic jam by blocking off the street where she lives with refuse lorries. A newspaper report describes it as a 'happening' (R 5, p. 349). Böll had been disappointed at the reception of *Ende einer Dienstfahrt*; in the interview with Dieter Wellershoff he stressed his view of the practicality of the form of resistance proposed in *Gruppenbild mit Dame* (I, p. 128). A further topical motif was that of 'Leistungsverweigerung', the refusal to join the rat race. Leni's son Lev has to be examined by a psychiatrist because he would rather be a refuse collector than go to university. These were the years of the 'drop-outs' and 'hippies'; a few months later one of Böll's admirers, the East German Ulrich Plenzdorf, published a story which centred on a teenage drop-out, *Die neuen Leiden des jungen W*. The theme is foreshadowed in Böll's work by the short satire 'Anekdote zur Senkung der Arbeitsmoral', his most Hebelesque story, which he wrote to be read at a trades union rally on 1 May 1963, but it also

173

goes back to the satire 'Es wird etwas geschehen'. It was one of the issues which particularly infuriated Helmut Schelsky, who attacked Alexander Mitscherlich and others for their rejection of the 'achievement-oriented society' ('Leistungsgesellschaft'), and quoted Böll's 1973 words to *Newsweek*: 'What bothers you most about German society? — Without doubt, this cursed Leistungsprinzip: the "success" or "achievement" principle. It is murderous, simply murderous, and self-destroying' (*Newsweek* 22.1.1973; Schelsky, 1975, pp. 244–81).

In the Wellershoff interview Böll introduced a term which has proved fruitful in discussions of his work, that of 'Fortschreibung'. All his works, whether short stories, novels, essays, reviews, were a continuous process, a refinement and broadening of his craft as a writer and also a development of themes and contents (I, p. 120). Thus the graveyards where Fred Bogner of *Und sagte kein einziges Wort* and the narrator of 'Es wird etwas geschehen' found solace and silence and time to remember the past are an important motif in *Gruppenbild mit Dame*. Leni works during the war making wreaths for a funeral business; she and Boris find refuge in graveyard vaults in the closing of the war; when their son Lev comes in conflict with the State Grundtsch offers to hide him in the vaults where he was born. Böll is drawing a parallel between the fascist reign of terror and contemporary West German capitalism. Leni's father Hubert Gruyten made a living after the war clearing out bomb-ruined houses, as did Fendrich's employer in *Das Brot der frühen Jahre*. Pelzer made his fortune from stealing the gold fillings from the teeth of corpses on the battlefield, a motif which Böll used in the early story 'In der Finsternis'. Eating and drinking were always of potentially ritualistic significance for Böll; restaurants are a frequent location in his works from *Der Zug war pünktlich* down to *Ende einer Dienstfahrt*, while the individual act of breaking bread is thematic in *Das Brot der frühen Jahre* and *Billard um halbzehn*. A central event of *Gruppenbild mit Dame* is Leni's first meeting with Boris when he arrives at the plant nursery to work as a Russian prisoner of war and she offers him a cup of 'real' coffee; the Nazi Kremp at once knocks the cup out of her hands, whereupon she calmly pours a second. But the innumerable cups of coffee, tea, glasses of sherry or beer which the Author receives from the various people he interviews in the course of his researches make the motif into a leitmotiv.

Böll stressed the importance for the novel of the theme of 'Abfall', refuse (I, pp. 127f.). Again he was building on some of the ideas expressed earlier, in his Frankfurt lectures, for example. In *Gruppenbild mit Dame* it ranges from the physiological to the sociological.

Sister Rahel teaches Leni complete acceptance of her bodily secre-
tions; in this way she is able to live a life of integrity in every sense
(by contrast Greck, the inhibited lieutenant of *Wo warst du, Adam?*,
suffered from chronic constipation — Böll, we remember, read his
Freud before the war in a second-hand bookshop in Bonn). Society,
however, is not able to come to terms with its 'refuse': the refuse
collectors are its pariahs, only foreign workers would be willing to
perform this job, and Leni herself is 'treated like dirt' for consorting
with them. A contrasting element is that of pornography. The late
1960s witnessed an enormous upsurge in the availability and distri-
bution of sexually explicit films and magazines in West Germany, as
older, more repressive laws were repealed. Böll did not regard this as
a genuine liberation: pornography itself exploited the women it
depicted and he found the mentality of its supporters humourless
and perverse (E 2, pp. 496–9; I, pp. 172f.). *Gruppenbild mit Dame*
touches frequently on taboos: excrement, menstrual fluids, orgasm,
prostitution, but the allusions to the 'pornography wave' are all
negative. Böll had earlier attacked his Church for discounting the
physical side of love; pornography falls into the opposite trap; the
spiritual and the material were for Böll one.

Of particular interest is the motif of the nuns and their convent.
Again it goes back to Böll's early writings. Ilona of *Wo warst du,
Adam?* originally intended to become a nun, but her yearnings for a
husband and children induced her to return to the world, where she
is murdered. Her outlook and prayer to console God for the wicked-
ness of his world, impresses Feinhals; it is that of the convent, pure
inwardness. One of the characters of 'Nicht nur zur Weihnachtszeit'
becomes a monk, withdrawing from restorative society. In *Und sagte
kein einziges Wort* the monks in the procession are 'photogenic',
incurring the suspicion of superficiality and hypocrisy; but their
liturgical chants are one of the few things that correspond to the
mongol child's purer reality — again withdrawal is viewed posi-
tively. In *Haus ohne Hüter* the church of the nuns is one of Albert's
favourite haunts. However, Bolda is an ex-nun and films with nuns
in them are suitable only for adults, Martin finds; they belong, in
terms of the novel, to the Establishment. By *Billard um halbzehn* Böll's
attitude had changed considerably. The monks of St Anthony's
Abbey sang Nazi songs and took part in celebrations of the summer
solstice. Even after the war they are more ready to forgive the Nazis
than become reconciled with the Communist East. In *Ansichten eines
Clowns* the Catholic college where Hans Schnier's brother Leo is
training for the priesthood is again a negative symbol. Böll goes
further still in *Gruppenbild mit Dame*. Leni was educated in a school

run by nuns. It was there she met Sister Rahel, a Jew who was gradually demoted while the Nazis were in power until she died of starvation in the cellars of the convent; the Church has 'repressed' its mission of 'feeding the hungry'; like the young priest in *Aussatz*, she was betrayed by the institution to which she belonged. When roses spring from the grave where her ashes are buried the Church merely feels embarrassed by the 'miracle'. The Author's researches take him to Rome, where he interviews other nuns, and at the close of the novel he has persuaded one of them, Klementina, to leave her convent and return with him to Germany, where she involves herself with the action to help Leni. In the context of Böll's work as a whole this is an important development, confirming the greater aggressivity of his stance. It is reflected also in the development of the theme of community from *Ende einer Dienstfahrt*: Leni, unlike the Bogners or the Brielachs, but like the Gruhls, is not alone; she has helpers.

The 'idea' behind the novel was one which had occupied Böll almost since the beginning of his career as a writer, 'the fate of a German woman at the end of her forties . . . who has burdened herself and been burdened by the whole weight of this history between 1922 and 1970' ('das Schicksal einer deutschen Frau von etwa Ende Vierzig . . . , die die ganze Last dieser Geschichte zwischen 1922 und 1970 mit und auf sich genommen hat') (I, p. 120). Leni is the central figure of the novel, central in various senses: sociologically she is surrounded by capitalists, intellectuals, writers, foreign workers, civil servants, all of whom fall in love with her; geographically she brings together Germany, Russia (her lover Boris), Turkey (her lover Mehmet), Portugal (her lodgers the Pinto family), even Ireland (her reading of Yeats); politically her life includes a brief marriage to the Nazi Alois Pfeiffer, a flirtation with the Communist Party — and one of her friends is a Rhineland separatist; literarily she has read and quotes from Kafka, Brecht, Hölderlin, Trakl and Yeats. And yet in the end we know relatively little of her, never encountering her directly. 'My heroine is not to have an image' ('Meine Heldin soll kein Image haben'), Böll said (Courts, 1971). In some ways she resembles Leen Cunigan in *Haus ohne Hüter* and Edith Fähmel in *Billard um halbzehn*, who by their absence take on mythical significance. Wellershoff suggested she was a Rhenish madonna (I, p. 133), and the notion gave its title to a volume of essays on the novel (Matthaei, 1975). In the text she is variously compared to 'Sleeping Beauty' and the 'Fair Lilofee'. But unlike *Haus ohne Hüter* and *Billard um halbzehn*, *Gruppenbild mit Dame* is the story of a *search* for the elusive female, and it falls into a literary category of the time exemplified in such novels as Uwe Johnson's

Mutmassungen über Jakob (1959) — one review was entitled 'Conjectures on the tin years. Did Johnson and Grass collaborate?' ('Mutmaßungen über die Blechjahre. Haben Johnson und Grass mitgeschrieben?') (Röhl, 1971) —, Christa Wolf's *Nachdenken über Christa T.* (1967) and Ulrich Plenzdorf's *Die neuen Leiden des jungen W.* In each of these three works the central figure is dead, the novel is the self-conscious attempt to reconstruct, re-present the dead. In Böll's novel Leni is far from dead, but certainly elusive. Allegorical implications abound. The stages of her father's career coincide with those of the development of Germany: he married above his station in 1919, studied from 1919 to 1924, enjoyed relative prosperity from 1924 to 1929 (the Stresemann years), went through enormous difficulties between 1929 and 1933, enjoyed meteoric success up to 1943 (Stalingrad), when he was imprisoned for fraud; after 1945 he was a modest labourer, but he died in 1949, the year the Federal Republic was founded. Leni herself was once awarded the title of the 'most German girl of the school' (R 5, p. 29); this is one of the novel's ironies, but if she does incorporate something of the spirit of Germany then associations of Germany as the 'Land der Mitte' the land which mediates between East and West, emerge. She is also described as 'so marvellously proletarian' ('so herrlich proletarisch') (p. 305). Sociologically this is hardly true; the epithet refers rather to her rejection of the bourgeois values of property and achievement. The German proletariat has been sadly abused by ideologies in the course of the twentieth century; Leni's favourite poem is Yeats's 'A Coat'; she abjures all ideology: 'For there's more enterprise / in walking naked' (p. 344).

Gruppenbild mit Dame has frequently been compared to *Ende einer Dienstfahrt* (I, pp. 153, 324ff.): the 'happening' motif has already been mentioned; both novels are narrated by an extra-diegetic narrator, as Böll's earlier works were not. More revealing, however, is the parallel with the techniques used in *Entfernung von der Truppe*, the seemingly rambling construction, the introduction of documents, the post-modernist rejection of aesthetic autonomy. However, just as Böll could never accept the most radical manifestations of modernism, so he refused to accept that the novel was 'dead' (Courts, 1971), and he gave a spirited defence of imaginative literature on many occasions (I, pp. 276ff.; E 3, pp. 34ff.). *Gruppenbild mit Dame* is one of the most imaginative novels he wrote, abounding in invention both of characters and events: the fictitious workers with literary names thought up by Hubert Gruyten; the detailed description of wreath-making; Pelzer's profiteering by recycling coffins, wreaths, inscriptions; the Hoysers' ultra-modern office block, whose inmates are slaves to the over-sensitive air-conditioning system. At the same time it deliberately breaks with the literariness of the earlier novels, to such an extent that it was dismissed by some critics as being badly written (Reich-Ranicki, 1971; Durzak, 1972). The opening sentence refers to a 'first section' of the novel, but we never encounter a second. The multiplicity of characters prompted Joachim Kaiser and Hans Schwab-Felisch to draw up a dramatis personae — the English translation provides one — and this might have helped Helmut Heißenbüttel, who confused Margret Schlömer and Marja van Doorn. The language used is clumsy and ugly. Sometimes Böll is consciously parodying scientific jargon, as when the narrator refers to himself throughout in the third person as 'Verf.', the abbreviation used in academic biographies to distinguish the author from his subject. But as a whole the style is slovenly and very unliterary, in stark contrast to the language of Böll's early novels, the sometimes obtrusive metaphors of *Das Brot der frühen Jahre* or the liturgical rhythms of *Billard um halbzehn*. This is one way in which Böll abandons modernist aestheticism. When terms such as 'tears', 'laughter', 'suffering', 'happiness' are first given their dictionary definitions and thereafter used in abbreviated form, this is a Brechtian 'alienation device', designed to activate the reader and to open up the fiction of the text on to his own reality.

A major feature of *Gruppenbild mit Dame* is the profusion of narrative levels it contains. There are two story levels, the inner one the biography of Leni Gruyten, the outer the story of the writing of this biography. On the face of it this is a modernist technique, found in numerous twentieth-century novels, Gide's *Les Faux-Monnayeurs* and Mann's *Doktor Faustus*, for example. But whereas the modernist use of the technique is designed to stress the autonomy of the artistic process, to create the illusion of a self-reflecting work of art, Böll takes the opposite direction. His narrator's researches lead him to intervene in the story he is researching: he contributes to the fund for Leni; more significantly still he persuades Klementina to leave her convent. At least from *Haus ohne Hüter* onwards the figure of the artist plays an increasingly important part in Böll's novels: the poet Rai Bach, who ceased to write poetry when he found the Nazis exploiting it, the architect family of Fähmels and the clown Hans Schnier. On flimsy evidence Durzak believes the Author in *Gruppenbild mit Dame* to be a journalist, and goes on to accuse Böll of failing to motivate his researches on Leni Gruyten (Durzak, 1972, p. 182). Vogt sees him more as a Günter Wallraff (Vogt, 1978, p. 105). The Author is a writer, the expenses which he incurs are to be set off against tax, one of Böll's preoccupations, as we have seen, and his development from apparently neutral documentarist to active participant implies Böll's conviction that the aesthetic stance is inadequate. To a certain extent the pattern is repeated on the level of the various subsidiary narrators, the sources whom the Author consults for his researches, at least some of whom join the action to help Leni. All these narrators have their corresponding narratees, the Author himself in the case of the intra-diegetic narrators, but he too explicitly addresses himself to his readers, the 'more or less patient reader' (R 5, p. 54) or even 'the gentle reader' ('der geneigte Leser') (p. 229) of eighteenth- and nineteenth-century fiction.

It is this last, deliberately archaic phrase which gives an important clue to the status of the narrative of *Gruppenbild mit Dame*. Böll has abandoned the notion of the autonomy of the modernist literary artefact, the fiction that the novel simply 'is'. Direct references to the reader's contemporary world are numerous, frequently even trivial, as when the Author has to pause in his researches to watch the Clay–Frazier boxing match. Like the post-modernist architect Böll has at his disposal the whole range of historical styles and techniques. His novel 'quotes' eighteenth-century narrative. It also 'quotes' the fashionable documentary novel of the late 1960s which eschewed fiction as politically inadequate. As in *Entfernung von der Truppe* a number of 'documents' are reproduced: military regulations, accounts of life at the front, the report of a psychiatrist on the character of Leni's son Lev. Böll identified his sources to Durzak (Durzak, 1972, pp. 179f.) otherwise it is not obvious which of the documents are factual and which fictitious. By mingling document and fiction Böll is stressing both the fictionality of document and the factuality of fiction — as he put it in one of his earliest essays, 'reality *is* fantastic' ('das Wirkliche *ist* phantastisch') (E 1, p. 75). A comparable literary predecessor is Clemens Brentano's Romantic novel *Godwi*, subtitled 'a novel run riot' ('ein verwilderter Roman') as Böll's might have been and which similarly plays with narrative conventions, an epistolary novel, in which the editor of these 'documents' himself becomes a character in a novel which has yet another author. The Brentano model and the documentary model are opposite extremes, the one proclaiming the supremacy of imagination, the other that of empirical reality; Böll's position is a synthesis of the two. The novel's ending is revealing. New developments begin — the relation between the Author and Klementina, the story of Lev — but they are left incomplete, and the final pages simply present the reader with a further set of documents for his consideration. Böll himself admitted he could have gone on for ever (I, p. 174); if it is 'the rough version of a novel' ('Roman . . . im

Rohzustand'), as Durzak claims (Durzak, 1972, p. 177), its completion is deliberately left to the reader.

In 1972 Böll published his first and only collection of poems, a slim volume of nine. Two of them had appeared in 1965 under the pseudonym Victor Hermann — Böll must have been especially unsure about the reception they might have. Most of the others had also appeared at intervals elsewhere. They are occasional pieces. One is dedicated to Peter Huchel, who had just been allowed to leave East Germany, and is a comment on the division of Germany. Another satirises the West German air force's Starfighters, which were notorious for their tendency to crash out of control. Three, including the longest, are on Cologne. 'Gib Alarm!' ('Sound the alarm!'), dedicated to Ulrich Sonnemann, concerns the poet's and Sonnemann's critics, the 'rabbits baring their teeth', the 'sparrows practising dive-bombing', which are more dangerous than hyenas and jackals. The other poems are more private: 'Meine Muse' ('My muse'), which takes up several key motifs from his more central works, 'Engel' ('Angel'), and 'später herz später' ('later my heart later'). This is not 'great poetry', and it has nothing to do with the modernist, hermetic verse favoured by West German writers after the war; rather it is, in the phrase of Volker Hage, 'Poetry for readers' ('Lyrik für Leser') (Hage, 1980), unpretentious, readable and usable poetry written in free rhythms. In this respect it is of its time, the late 1960s and 1970s. Its careful attention to style and rhythm demonstrates that the slovenliness of style in *Gruppenbild mit Dame* and *Die verlorene Ehre der Katharina Blum* was deliberate. Böll continued to publish occasional poems. In 'sieben Jahre und zwanzig später', a gloss on Ingeborg Bachmann's poem 'Früher Mittag', the Nazi 'hangmen' of the original have become Springer's *Bild* and *Die Welt*. He composed poems for the birthdays of his friends Walter Warnach, Joseph Beuys and Alexander Solzhenitsyn, and one for Peter-Jürgen Boock, a former member of the Red Army Faction, who had been given an especially harsh prison sentence because, although he had abandoned terrorism and had appealed to his former comrades to do likewise, he had refused to testify against them. In May 1985 he wrote a poem for his grandchild Samay, moving in its anticipation of his own death two months later.

Die verlorene Ehre der Katharina Blum (1974) is the most directly polemical of all Böll's major works and to a certain extent it represents the culmination of the development which began with *Ansichten eines Clowns*. Böll himself described it as a 'Pamphlet', whose literary qualities were of secondary importance, a minor work between more important books (I, p. 343). It was serialised in four instalments in *Der Spiegel* between July and August 1974, the first time that *Der Spiegel* had serialised a literary work and an indication of the controversial nature of the material. The hardcover edition sold 150,000 copies in six weeks, a pirate edition was published in Austria, and the school edition published in England in 1980 has been one of the most popular texts for sixth-formers. Volker Schlöndorff made an internationally successful film of it, which was premiered in October 1975. It is clearly of more than just topical interest. The story of a helpless woman being bullied by police, press and public inevitably strikes a sympathetic chord. Böll suggested the theme had something of the classical tragic myth about it (I, pp. 334f.): Katharina finds herself forced to choose between her lover and society — whichever way she turns she must inevitably become 'guilty'.

The target of the polemic is made explicit in the author's preface, which parodies the traditional disclaimer: 'Characters and plot of this story are free inventions. If the depiction of certain journalistic practices should have resulted in similarities with the practices of *Bild* newspaper, these similarities are neither intended nor coincidental but inevitable' ('Personen und Handlung dieser Erzählung sind frei erfunden. Sollten sich bei der Schilderung gewisser journalistischer Praktiken Ahnlichkeiten mit den Praktiken der "Bild"-Zeitung ergeben haben, so sind diese Ahnlichkeiten weder beabsichtigt noch zufällig, sondern unvermeidlich') (R 5, p. 385). Böll was pursuing his feud with the Springer press which went back to 1967 and the persecution of the students, although one can trace the theme of incompetent or unscrupulous journalists at least to *Ansichten eines Clowns*. *Katharina Blum* continues the line taken in the *Spiegel* article on Ulrike Meinhof. Böll frequently said that as a prominent writer he himself had the means to defend himself against unscrupulous reporting which other victims might lack; for a time he employed an assistant to read the popular press in search of examples of such victims, and one outcome was this story (I, p. 390). Katharina is arrested by the police after giving refuge to a wanted man. The gutter press takes up the case, they delve into her past, interview those who know her, distort their statements to make it appear she has a Communist past and a cold, calculating character. She becomes the object of threatening, anonymous telephone calls and obscene letters; the reporter Tötges forces his way into the hospital where her mother lies dying; when later he obtains a private interview with Katharina he has the effrontery to begin by suggesting they have sex together, whereupon she shoots him dead — it is only at this point that she has become guilty of a serious crime. In West Germany, where the press laws are more liberal than elsewhere, most of these journalistic activities are legal if scarcely legitimate; Böll was accused in Springer's *Die Welt* of making out a case for greater restrictions (Zehm, 1974). But what is in some ways more disturbing about the gutter press in his story is the way it is ready to take on defenceless people like Katharina rather than the more powerful and dangerous industrialists like Sträubleder, a 'Christian employer' reminiscent of Hans Schnier's father, who makes uplifting speeches at Christian congresses and has for some time been privately pestering Katharina for sexual favours. Sträubleder has friends who can manipulate the mass media; when the *Newspaper* starts to look into the background of Katharina's secret admirer, a telephone call from Lüding suffices to call them off the trail. The so-called free press is in fact manipulated by capital. Böll does make it clear the he is not attacking the press in general. The title *Newspaper* ('Zeitung') was chosen not to indicate *all* newspapers, but because it was the only title he could find which did not already exist. When Katharina is distressed by the lies about her in the *Newspaper* she is advised by a friendly policewoman to read the reports in the other journals, which are more neutral and preserve her anonymity. She replies, however, that this does not help as all her friends read the *Newspaper* — something which indicates both the power of the Springer-owned press and the conservative character of Katharina and her friends. A subsidiary theme of the story is the close cooperation between press and police. In 1972 Böll attacked the way in which the police allowed press photographers to infringe human dignity by taking pictures, for example, of a naked Andreas Baader being arrested (E 2, pp. 574f.). And as we have seen, he himself had cause to complain of this cooperation, when in 1974 news that his son's flat in Berlin had been searched appeared in the Springer press before it had actually happened. One ironic effect of his story was that Springer's newspaper *Die Welt* ceased to publish a bestseller list, which would have been topped by *Katharina Blum*. Böll was delighted at the popular response, believing that it must mean a greater critical awareness with regard to *Bild* (I, p. 344).

The story is thus only indirectly related to the question of urban terrorism. Neither Katharina nor Ludwig Götten, her lover, is a terrorist. The latter, it turns out, is merely a deserter from the army who had run off with the regimental cash-box. The deployment of police resources is made to appear disproportionate and even counter-productive, as he panics when surrounded by police and uses a firearm. The case of Peter Paul Zahl may have been in Böll's mind, who panicked in similar circumstances in December 1972, was sentenced to four years imprisonment which on appeal were increased to fifteen, although Zahl's case was much more directly political than Götten's (Engelmann, 1978; cf. VG, p. 269). Böll himself stated that the only direct connection between his story and the Baader–Meinhof complex was in Katharina's giving refuge to a wanted man, as Peter Brückner had done for Ulrike Meinhof (I, p. 335; on Brückner see Raddatz, 1978).

Götten is *not* a terrorist. But, like Böll's *Spiegel* article, the story was at once misrepresented on the right. Writing in *Die Welt* Hans Habe, one of the principal actors in the earlier campaign against Böll, described the story as 'the tale of the pure and innocent housekeeper who, only because she loves a pure and innocent terrorist, is driven to murder by the popular press' ('die Mär von der blütenreinen Hausangestellten, die, nur weil sie einen blütenreinen Terroristen liebt, von der Boulevardpresse zum Mord getrieben wird' (Habe, 1974, p. 252); in America Tötges would have been awarded the Pulitzer Prize for investigative reporting (p. 257). Habe was reluctant to call the book 'an incitement to violence' ('eine Aufforderung zu Gewalt') (p. 254). Others were less so, notoriously the CDU parliamentary chairman Karl Carstens, later to become Federal President, when in December 1974 he appealed to the German people to abjure terrorism, singling out 'the poet Heinrich Böll, who only a few months ago under the pseudonym of Katharina Blüm [sic] wrote a book which represents an incitement to violence' ('den Dichter Heinrich Böll, der noch vor wenigen Monaten unter dem Pseudonym Katharina Blüm ein Buch geschrieben hat, das eine Rechtfertigung von Gewalt darstellt'); this statement inspired one of Klaus Staeck's more memorable posters (Schröter, 1982, p. 107). Carstens presumably had not read the book; Peter Hofstätter certainly had when he contributed an essay on it to a collection of pieces on the origins of contemporary terrorism as seen from the point of view of the CSU (Hofstätter, 1978); even in 1983 Karl Steinbruch accused Böll of having encouraged terrorism with his book (FT, pp. 309f.).

The question of violence is indeed central to the story, as the subtitle indicates: 'How violence can arise and where it can lead' ('Wie Gewalt entstehen und wohin sie führen kann'). It was not the first time that Böll had taken up the theme. *Haus ohne Hüter* ends with a fight between Albert and Gäseler, as Martin's grandmother boxes Schurbigel's ears and punches Pater Willibrord in the chest; at the end of *Billard um halbzehn* there is an attempted assassination. Neither of these actions is presented as more than one of impotent rage at the continued presence of former Nazis in leading positions in West German life; but the subtitle of *Die verlorene Ehre der Katharina Blum* might equally apply there. The latent violence in Walter Fendrich's character has already been noted. Manfred Durzak pointed out parallels between *Das Brot der frühen Jahre* and *Katharina Blum* in terms of the love story (I, pp. 334f.); but Katharina is, or becomes, an 'angry young woman' just as Fendrich is an angry young man. Her initial violence is directed at objects rather than people, when she sets about demolishing her flat in frustration. The theme of violence is a leitmotiv of Böll's speeches and essays from the late 1960s onwards. In his address on the award of the Georg Büchner Prize he had quoted Büchner's letter from Strasburg to his family in April 1833 in which Büchner had countered the accusations of violence levelled at the young with the rhetorical question, 'are we not in an eternal state of violence?' The princes of 1833 would grant no democratic rights unless forced to do so. Böll himself never advocated violence, as he was accused of doing. On the contrary, in his speech against the Emergency Legislation he declared that it was politically senseless to attempt to overturn the structure of West German society by force (E 2, p. 289), in 1970 he quoted with approval Che Guevara's admission that he had been unable to shoot at two unarmed soldiers when they passed by his ambush, and appealed to both police and terrorists to follow this example (E 2, pp. 469f.), and in 1972 he publicly repudiated the violent tactics of the Meinhof group as being possibly appropriate in South America but suicidal in the Federal Republic (I, pp. 225f.). He did, however, as did Büchner, point out on numerous occasions that violence is not confined to those who oppose the status quo. The West's cultural heritage was full of violence: the Old Testament, the *Odyssey*, the *Nibelungenlied*, the *Asterix* comics (E 3, p. 233); German history contained a succession of terrorisms, from the Thirty Years War down to National Socialism (Kesting, pp. 79f.). Indeed the terrorism of the Nazis is concealed in the text in one interesting phrase. By coincidence the press photographer Schönner is murdered only a few days after Katharina shoots Tötges. When she is asked by the police whether she killed Schönner too her somewhat puzzling reply is: 'Yes, why not him too after all?' ('Ja, warum eigentlich nicht den auch?') (R 5, p. 388). The phrase was one which had gone through Böll's mind in July 1934 when he examined his collection of cigarette cards after the purge of the SA by Hitler and wondered why, for example, Göring and Himmler had survived (E 3, p. 294). But there were other, less obvious forms of violence, such as the power held by banks and stock-markets, where political processes could be manipulated against the will of the people (E 2, pp. 605f.). And there was the violence contained in the language of *Bild*'s headlines, designed to steam-roller the reader into accepting what he could not be persuaded to believe (E 2, p. 577).

When Katharina shoots Tötges we undoubtedly understand her action, without, however, thereby approving it. Unlike the *Newspaper* Böll's text invites us to meditate on violence, its nature and its origins, not to indulge in it. The title at once influences our state of mind. The first part may be an echo of Friedrich Schiller's story 'Ein Verbrecher aus verlorener Ehre' ('A criminal from lost honour') — Böll first denied it, later admitted there might have been an unconscious association (I, pp. 327f.) — but in any case the term 'lost honour' is archaic. The dual title is also archaic, one which, like the phrase 'gentle reader' in *Gruppenbild mit Dame*, takes the reader back to the eighteenth century, with its *Pamela or: Virtue Rewarded*, its *Minna von Barnhelm oder: Das Soldatenglück* or its *Der Hofmeister oder: Vorteile der Privaterziehung*. This post-modernist quotation of earlier literary forms implies a didactic stance (*How* violence arises) and simultaneously parodies the didactic stance. It invites an intellectual rather than an emotional response. All of the formal devices used by Böll in his text have this purpose. Once more *Entfernung von der Truppe* offers parallels. To the child's painting book of the earlier story corresponds the metaphor of 'damming and draining' which the narrator of *Die verlorene Ehre der Katharina Blum* employs — and indeed Böll used the term 'Malvorlage' from *Entfernung von der Truppe* to describe the later work (I, p. 389). Like *Ende einer Dienstfahrt* and *Gruppenbild mit Dame* it has an extra-diegetic narrator, one who is more obtrusive than in the former, but less personalised than in the latter. As a mediator between the reader and the story he not only provides information which would otherwise be inaccessible, he also defuses tension at important junctures and performs a distancing function similar to the 'alienation devices' of Brecht (Giles, 1984). His language is almost more slovenly than that of the narrator of *Gruppenbild mit Dame*. Habe noted this feature of the text but attributed it to Böll's literary bankruptcy (Habe, 1974, pp. 254–6); in fact it is a deliberate device to prevent the text becoming an aesthetic and therefore irrelevant artefact. The narrator's pedantic concern for accuracy, which on occasion leads him to state that an event occurred 'at approximately 19.04' (R 5, p. 386), is both another distancing device and a contrast with the *Newspaper*'s blatant disregard for facts. This pedantry is mirrored on a different level, when Katharina in her statements to the police insists on the difference between 'tender' ('zärtlich') and 'impertinent' ('zudringlich'), between 'kindly' ('gütig'), 'nice' ('nett') and 'good-natured' ('gutmütig'). And the most fundamental device of all, the narrator betrays the climax of the story, the killing of Tötges, at the outset. Like Brecht, Böll is concerned not with *what* happened, but with *how* it happened.

The violence in the novel does not emanate from the protagonists. Blorna's threat to throw a Molotov cocktail at Sträubleder's house is dismissed by his wife as 'spontaneous, petty-bourgeois, romantic anarchism' ('spontan-kleinbürgerlich-romantischen Anarchismus') (p. 460). The true terrorists are the anonymous members of the public who abuse Katharina through telephone and letter-box. Their ideological backing comes from the *Newspaper* — it is not just a pun to say that the latter 'does violence' to the facts. The 'structural violence' in society (cf. p. 452) might better be described as its authoritarianism, its demand that the individual conform to certain conservative expectations. This is one of Böll's oldest themes. Where his story goes further than before is in its presentation of woman as victim of these conservative expectations. In this, as in so much else, Böll was a keen observer of contemporary social developments.

The new feminist movement began in West Germany almost at the same time as the student movement and the Extra-Parliamentary Opposition, when it has been said the participating women found that their menfolk were expecting them to make the coffee and do the washing up, while they themselves conducted the discussions (Möhrmann, 1981). From 1971 onwards much of the movement's activities centred on the repeal of 'Paragraph 218', aiming to liberalise the abortion laws; their success was short-lived, when the Constitutional Court ruled in 1975 that the legislation proposed by Brandt's government was unconstitutional. Böll had little sympathy for the pro-abortion movement (I, pp. 453f.). In the course of the late 1960s and the 1970s, however, he increasingly spoke out against the machismo of society and the Catholic Church's hostility to women. The latter, for example, was the tenor of his article on the Papal encyclical 'Humanae Vitae' in 1968 (E 2, pp. 299–302); some years later he spoke of the 'absurdity' of male pretensions, especially in war, condemning Hemingway's cult of manliness in particular (I, pp. 542ff.). His mother appears to have been a dominant influence in his image of woman (I, p. 542) and motherliness is a vital component of his feminine ideals at least up to *Gruppenbild mit Dame* — Karin Struck, whose own feminism is largely embodied in the biological phenomenon of motherhood, found this aspect of the novel especially fascinating (I, pp. 251ff.). Just how radically different *Katharina Blum* is can be gauged from a comparison with *Das Brot der frühen Jahre* and *Ansichten eines Clowns*. In these earlier works both Hedwig and Marie are seduced by the male protagonist and happily abandon all ambitions for academic qualifications and a career. Katharina is a single woman, living on her own, independent both financially and sexually. She has a well-paid job which she carries out efficiently, she divorces her husband and repulses the advances of wealthy Sträubleder because both of them lack 'tenderness' ('Zärtlichkeit'), but she invites Ludwig Götten to spend the night with her although she has known him only a few hours. Marcel Reich-Ranicki, in an almost unbelievable *fehlleistung*, declared that unlike Böll's previous heroes, who were the victims of society, Katharina suffered from her own frigidity (Reich-Ranicki, 1979 a, p. 31). Böll makes it very clear how hostile male society, illustrated no doubt unconsciously by Reich-Ranicki, is towards the independent woman. Not even in church can Katharina be safe from molestation, she cannot go alone into pubs or cafés and she finds herself forced to go for long lonely drives across the country if she does not wish to stay at home. And once she is the object of the gutter press society vents its indignation at her independence by subjecting her to the most infamous indignities.

Not that she is a militant revolutionary. Walter Jens saw her as a 'pure, pious and helpless soul' ('reine, fromme und hilflose Seele') (Jens, 1974, p. 250), Habe as a 'pure and innocent housekeeper' ('blütenreine Hausangestellte') (Habe, 1974, p. 252), Christian Linder found 'angelic qualities' ('Engelhaftigkeit') in her character (I, p. 386). It is true that the name Katharina means 'the pure one'. Böll, however, tried to stress her more questionable qualities: she was a conformist, had benefited from the Economic Miracle, would end as a successful businesswoman running a hotel (I, p. 386). Someone who, like all her friends, reads *Bild* is hardly an angelic figure. In fact the truly emancipated woman of the story is Trude Blorna, she too a professional woman but one who is enlightened politically and is able to restrain her foolish husband when he wants to throw bombs. By contrast, because Katharina is 'unpolitical', lacking in revolutionary awareness, she is affected so profoundly by the experience of injustice at the hands of the Establishment. And like the Gruhls and like Leni Gruyten, she is not alone in her hour of need but finds others gathering round to help her, friends and colleagues in the restaurant trade in this case. This, however, is the last of Böll's works to present solidarity as a defence against the inhumanity of society. *Fürsorgliche Belagerung* is much more pessimistic on this score.

One year after *Die verlorene Ehre der Katharina Blum* Böll published

187

the short satire *Berichte zur Gesinnungslage der Nation*. The two works are connected inasmuch as they both attack McCarthyism in the Federal Republic, the witch hunts directed at those who might remotely be associated with left-wing radicalism. In the former the witch hunts were almost entirely the work of the press. The latter has more in common with Peter Schneider's novel . . . *schon bist du ein Verfassungsfeind*, which appeared in the same year. The State itself is shown to be engaged in spying on its citizens, keeping dossiers on their reading habits and details of their private behaviour: taking the uncle of a relative of Ulrike Meinhof to the railway station or feeding a dog belonging to a relative of Gudrun Ensslin, possessing books by Sartre or Wallraff — all that is regarded as highly incriminating. The title is an ironic allusion to the Federal Chancellor's annual 'Report on the state of the nation'; the secret services, from whom Böll's 'reports' emanate, are concerned with the state of the nation's ideological firmness. The 'reports' themselves are from three sources, each belonging to a different secret service. The satire has two main elements. In the first place there is the evident exaggeration. When it appears that matches are about to be rationed because if used in sufficient quantities they could cause explosions, there is an out-break of panic buying. Similarly parmesan cheese becomes the object of suspicion when it emerges that it too can be an ingredient of explosives. And in the second place it soon turns out that the three services are actually spying on one another, acting partly as *agents provocateurs*, founding spurious 'radical' committees joined only by themselves and their rivals. In fact the only plot they uncover is that of a right-wing theology student, who is planning to blow up a Cardinal for his progressive views. When in the end they discover the truth they are unrepentant and their final joint recommendation takes Böll's readers back a quarter of a century to the short story 'Mein trauriges Gesicht' (1950). There the narrator, living in some unspecified fascistoid society, found himself arrested for looking melancholy when cheerfulness had been officially ordained. Here the secret services recommend that resources be set aside for the 'physi-ognomical registration of attitudes' ('physiognomische Erfassung von Gesinnung') (R 5, p. 498), secret cameras which will photo-graph the look on people's faces during demonstrations and the like, in order to determine their loyalty to the constitution.

Böll described the writing of the text in some detail (I, pp. 658f.). The names adopted by the secret agents, the terms used by them to refer to the objects of their observations he found in the dictionary of the Brothers Grimm. The literary models were Juvenal, Aristo-phanes, and especially the *Epistolae virorum obscurorum* or *Dunkelmänner-*

briefe of 1515/17. The latter is a satirical work of German humanism directed against the reactionary scholasticism and obscurantism of its day, manifested not least in the barbarity of its language. Böll's satire likewise is an appeal on behalf of contemporary humanism. It implies a stark contrast with the optimism of 1969. The SPD state has become a quasi-totalitarian one. It is true that the secret service does not identify with the party in power — indeed one of them admits that it would be no great pity if the present Chancellor (Helmut Schmidt) were to be blown up. But the anti-radicals legislation has opened the door for contemporary 'viri obscuri', whose barbaric language is taken directly from the putatively progressive left. In *Ende einer Dienstfahrt* and *Gruppenbild mit Dame* avant-garde art in the shape of the 'happening' was progressive and a potential for social change. In *Berichte zur Gesinnungslage der Nation* the avant-garde has been taken over by the reaction: Rotgimpel, a former member of the APO, now a secret service agent, specialises in 'Ignition Art', which he performs with the help of 60,000 matches in Catholic Churches and East Asian embassies alike. In *Die verlorene Ehre der Katharina Blum* there is a similarly ironic reference to the avant-garde in Frederich Le Boche's 'One minute piece of art', the blotting paper with Sträubleder's blood on it after Blorna has punched him on the nose. Böll had become more sceptical about the avant-garde as a vehicle of change.

8

Mourning and Resistance
(1976–1985)

One of the journalistic slogans of the mid-1970s was that of the *Tendenzwende*, the change in direction that literature and society seemed to take after the upheavals associated with 1968. Instead of politically committed literature, writers, it was claimed, were turning inwards once more, were concerned with their own personal, existential, private problems (Reich-Ranicki, 1979; Kreuzer, 1981; Roberts, 1982). Nicolas Born's novel *Die erdabgewandte Seite der Geschichte* (1976), in which disappointment with the outcome of the 1968 movement is explicitly coupled with a retreat into the private domain, was widely regarded as a symptom of this development, as were the later novels of Peter Handke. Even where external, social reality was less radically excluded, it seemed to be viewed in more subjective terms than documentary literature had allowed. A flood of autobiographies appeared on the market from 1975 onwards, many of them depicting daily life under the Nazis as having been remarkably harmless. A film on the life of Hitler was an enormous popular success and ushered in what some critics feared was a 'Hitler wave' which did not clarify but rather obscured the evils of National Socialism.

Journalistic slogans have only limited usefulness. East German scholars have stressed the continuities between 1968 and the 1970s (Bernhard, 1977). Günter Wallraff, for example, was still writing documentary literature in the 1980s — his *Ganz unten*, an account of the exploitation of foreign workers in West Germany, was a best-seller in 1985. The Werkkreis Literatur der Arbeitswelt, a group of worker-writers, was only founded in 1970. Böll used the term *Tendenzwende* almost invariably with scorn: Peter Weiss's political autobiography, *Die Ästhetik des Widerstands*, a political novel which seeks a link between art and revolutionary commitment and whose first volume appeared in 1975, ought to have ushered in a real change of direction, he said, whereas the *Tendenzwende* the media were offering was one for opportunists (E 3, p. 429). Erich Kuby's *Mein Krieg* (1975) was 'a genuine relief' in the context of the

self-justifications of former Nazis Leni Riefenstahl and Arno Breker
(E 3, p. 287). He praised Peter Handke's *Wunschloses Unglück* in 1973,
but this account of the life and death of Handke's mother is the
author's most socially 'relevant' text. However, in 1977 he described
the 'so-called new inwardness' ('sogenannte neue Innerlichkeit') as
'so to speak an eternal current in literature' ('ein sozusagen ewiger
Strom in der Literatur'), denying that it was necessarily an alarming
development: the distinction between committed and uncommitted
literature was never a clear-cut one (Riese, pp. 21f.). Böll's own
development in the last ten years of his life is much more complex
than the term *Tendenzwende* can convey. This is partly because, as we
have seen, he never fully accepted the premises of, for example, the
documentarists. Marcel Reich-Ranicki's attempt to set *Die verlorene
Ehre der Katharina Blum* in the context of a new subjectivity, by
suggesting that Katharina suffers from frigidity rather than social
pressures, is revealingly perverse; Manfred Durzak's claim that the
same story is more subjective than *Das Brot der frühen Jahre* because
we never see Katharina and Ludwig together (I, pp. 321ff.), likewise
misses the point. Both *Die verlorene Ehre der Katharina Blum* and
Berichte zur Gesinnungslage der Nation are as committed and polemical
as anything Böll wrote. And after 1976 Böll continued to intervene
on behalf of those oppressed by whatever system: Wolf Biermann,
expatriated by the GDR authorities in 1976 (E 3, pp. 414f.), Rudolf
Bahro, the East German dissident imprisoned by the same authorities in 1979 (*Die Zeit*, 18.5.1979), the Slovenian writer Edvard
Kocbek (E 3, pp. 238f., 371), and the victims of West Germany's
anti-radicals legislation. There was a brief moment at the end of
1977 when the hysteria over the Schleyer kidnapping was at its
height and he evidently felt that any further intervention on his part
would be counter-productive (Riese, p. 36), but even then he denied
that this was resignation (ibid., p. 5). If anything his journalism
intensified. Together with Günter Grass and Carola Stern he
founded the periodical *L'76 Demokratie und Sozialismus* in 1976 (the 'L'
referred to the Czech journal *Literární Listy*, banned in 1968); it
briefly ceased to appear when the publishers were sold off by their
trade union owners, but was revived in 1980 as *L'80*. He was
co-editor of various pamphlets in the series *rororo aktuell*: *Briefe zur
Verteidigung der Republik* (1977), *Briefe zur Verteidigung der bürgerlichen
Freiheit* (1978), *Kämpfen für die sanfte Republik* (1980), *Zuviel Pazifis-
mus?* (1981) and *Verantwortlich für Polen* (1982). One of the last images
that Germans had of Böll before his death was of a frail figure with a
stick taking part in the blockade of the American nuclear base at
Mutlangen, hardly a man who had resigned or was devoting himself

to his own inner life. And yet there are, naturally enough, developments to be registered in his outlook and activities. He too did eventually write an autobiography of sorts; his turning away from the city in favour of the countryside, his support for the ecology party, the Greens, his open declaration of a new German patriotism were moves which, while logical in the context of his known views, were not altogether expected; and the literary direction taken by his last two novels, *Fürsorgliche Belagerung* (1979) and *Frauen vor Flußlandschaft* (1985) is in considerable contrast with that of their immediate predecessors.

It is therefore an over-simplification to characterise the later 1970s as years of introspection, whether in the literary or in the socio-political domain. The impetus of the student movement was not really lost at all. There was a direct link between the APO, which organised demonstrations against the Emergency Laws, and the pressure groups of the later 1970s which were set up to oppose the building of nuclear power-stations (Riese, pp. 22f.). The difference was that where the student movement aimed at a global reform of society, objectives in its aftermath were more limited ones. Concern for the environment might be one, the rights of women another, the peace movement yet another.

Economic problems relating to the oil crisis had weakened the SPD's attractiveness to the electorate, and in the Federal elections of October 1976 the party lost ground considerably. However, although the CDU/CSU had become the strongest party in parliament once more, the FDP agreed to continue the coalition, one with the narrowest of majorities, just eight seats. Böll's support for the SPD had been lukewarm; in view of the fact that almost 49 per cent of the voters had been prepared to accept the ultra-conservative Alfred Dregger as Minister of the Interior and Karl Carstens as Foreign Minister, the result of the election was not, he felt, reassuring; the real victor was Franz Josef Strauss, leader of the CSU, which had scored a massive success in Bavaria (E 3, pp. 404ff.).

The year 1977 witnessed the most serious threat to parliamentary democracy the Federal Republic had experienced. Ulrike Meinhof had committed suicide in prison in May 1976. In April 1977, almost five years after their arrest, judgment was at last pronounced in the trial against the other chief members of the Red Army Faction: Andreas Baader, Gudrun Ensslin and Jan Carl Raspe each were sentenced to life imprisonment. But the third phase of terrorism had already begun. Earlier that month Siegfried Buback, the Federal Republic's chief public prosecutor, was murdered, along with his chauffeur and a motor mechanic. At the end of July Jürgen Ponto, the chairman of the Dresdner Bank, was murdered by his god-daughter and others when he resisted a kidnapping attempt. A month later a rocket attack on the Federal Prosecutor's office in Karlsruhe was foiled. And on 5 September Hanns-Martin Schleyer, the president of the West German employers' federation, was kidnapped; his driver and three bodyguards were murdered. The kidnappers demanded the release of Baader, Ensslin, Raspe and eight other prisoners. The government refused to give in. On 13 October a Lufthansa airliner on its way from Majorca to Frankfurt was hijacked by Palestinians demanding the release of all their 'comrades' in West German gaols. After landing at various airports, in the course of which the pilot was shot dead, the aircraft was taken to Mogadishu, Somalia, where it was stormed on the 18 October by the West German anti-terrorist squad GSG 9. The hijackers were killed, all the passengers and the remaining crew were liberated. On the same day, however, it emerged that in spite of the extreme precautions taken in a maximum security prison built specially to house them, Baader, Ensslin and Raspe had had radios and guns smuggled into their cells, and had been able to communicate with one another; on hearing the news of the end of the hijacking, they had all committed suicide in such a way as to make it appear like murder. The following day Schleyer's body was found in Mulhouse; he had been shot in the head.

Isolated acts of terrorism have continued down to the present, but the situation of 1977 has not been repeated. At the height of it politicians like Strauss appeared in public only behind bullet-proof glass barriers. The theatre director Claus Peymann almost lost his post in Stuttgart for having pinned a letter from Gudrun Ensslin's mother on the theatre noticeboard. Camus' play *Les Justes* was taken off theatre programmes because it showed a political assassination (Kesting, p. 80). It was even rumoured that Mozart's *Die Entführung aus dem Serail* had been cancelled because of its title — 'Entführung' is also the word for hijacking. Public hysteria of this kind was not helpful, Böll, and many others, believed. It led to ever more repressive legislation: the law passed in the middle of the Schleyer affair, which enabled the Minister of Justice to isolate prisoners from all contact with the outside world, the anti-terrorism laws of February 1978 which gave the police wide-ranging powers to search buildings and set up road blocks and made it easier to exclude from trials lawyers suspected of conspiracy with their clients. The film *Deutschland im Herbst* (1978), a joint venture by some of West Germany's best-known directors, is an impressive documentation of the atmosphere of the time. An episode directed by Volker Schlöndorff used a scenario by Böll, *Die verschobene Antigone*: there had been public protests over the decisions of the Mayor of Stuttgart to allow Gudrun Ensslin to be buried in the cemetery there; a production of Sophocles' *Antigone*, it too the tragedy of a conflict over the right to honourable burial, has to be postponed as the theme is too topical (H, pp. 609ff.).

The Schleyer kidnapping led to a revival of the accusations of 'sympathy with the terrorists' levelled against Böll and others, notably Grass and the Protestant theologian Helmut Gollwitzer. The magazine *Quick* published a photograph of the four corpses in Cologne surmounted by a photograph of Böll; *Bild* urged him to leave Germany in sackcloth and ashes; the CSU parliamentarian Spranger called him a 'cause of terrorism', the *Neue Ruhr-Zeitung* accused him of paving the way for terrorism. Anonymous telephone calls led to police searches of flats belonging to him or to his family, in one case of a flat he had not used for years. Böll had immediately and unambiguously condemned the kidnapping and any kind of 'secret satisfaction' which the left might feel at the plight of Schleyer, who had been prominent in opposing the demands of the trade unions (E 3, pp. 459ff.). Together with Heinrich Albertz, Helmut Gollwitzer and Kurt Scharf he had publicly appealed to the kidnappers to abandon 'the murderous exchange of human life for human life' (Wagenbach, 1979, p. 309). He defended himself in an interview on Bavarian television on 28 September: the campaign of slander had begun in the 'serious' Springer newspapers, from there it had gone into the popular press, and right-wing politicians were grasping the opportunity for popularity by taking up the cause (I, pp. 684ff.). Ten minutes before it was due to be transmitted the programme was postponed, because viewers, incited to do so by *Bild*, had protested against Böll's being allowed to appear on television at all, and in order to give the opposing side the opportunity to reply — a spurious argument, as Böll pointed out, since he was the one who had been maligned. The collected interviews include no fewer than four which Böll gave on the subject between 28 September and 18 December (I, pp. 684ff.). In addition he took part in a public discussion in Paris on 21 March 1978 with the Bavarian Minister of Culture Hans Maier (CSU) on the topic, 'The Federal Republic: Ideal democracy or police-state?' (I, pp. 713ff.). Böll's protests against the searching of his property by the police led the chairman of the Police Federation in North-Rhine-Westphalia to protest in turn that they were only doing their duty (E 3, pp. 547f.), to which Böll replied that he had never attacked the police and had every sympathy with them in difficult times (I, pp. 483f.). In Paris he stated that if the Federal Republic were to become a police-state, it would not be the fault of the police but of the politicians who passed laws whose execution they could not control (I, p. 718). Some aspects of the novel *Fürsorgliche Belagerung* become clearer in this light.

How the terrorism of the Red Army Faction could come about in a prosperous and apparently stable Federal Republic was a question that exercised Böll and his compatriots, especially once the hysteria had died down. The discussion with Hans Maier in Paris is revealing. Maier accused Böll of going no further back than the Third Reich in his understanding of history: he was so afraid of neo-Nazism that he failed to see that the weakness of the Weimar Republic had enabled the Nazis to come to power; strong laws against extremist parties were designed to prevent the Federal Republic from going the way of its democratic predecessor. Maier pointed at the illegal activities of left-wing groups during the student movement, when the windows of the American Embassy were broken in the course of demonstrations, or when professors were prevented from speaking if their arguments were held to be hostile to the students. Böll replied that the notion that democracy in West Germany was or ever had been under threat from the left was simply ludicrous; rather the repeated refusal by the political establishment to accept the moral commitment of the younger generation when they opposed atomic weapons, the American involvement in Vietnam, the Federal Government's support for the Shah, had inevitably led to frustrations; they had been betrayed by Adenauer, who had released hundreds of convicted Nazis from prison, and by the Catholic Church which had refused to contemplate any ideals other than those of the free market economy. Earlier, refuting Maier's claim that he ignored the instability of the Weimar Republic, Böll had found the attacks on intellectuals ominously reminiscent of the early 1930s (I, p. 686). In 1975 Michael Baumann, a founder member of the Movement of 2 June, who had left the group but was in hiding, wanted by the police, published his own account of the origins of violence, *Wie alles anfing*. The book was banned, bookshops raided for copies and its publishers prosecuted. Böll attacked the banning in a review of 1976: on the contrary, all schools should put it on the syllabus (just as he had earlier supported the dissemination of Ulrike Meinhof's *Bambule*); the violence had begun with the shooting of Ohnesorg, the attempted assassination of Dutschke and the terrorism of the Springer press (E 3, pp. 318ff.).

At the end of 1977 he reviewed *Die Reise*, the posthumous autobiography of Bernward Vesper, an erstwhile member of the Red Army

Faction and for a time married to Gudrun Ensslin. In his review he suggested that one of the causes of urban terrorism in Germany was the post-war failure to recognise the extent to which the Nazis had debased traditional values. Taking issue with the neo-conservative Alfred Dregger, who had declared: 'We must orient ourselves on experiences which point beyond Hitler and on basic values which Hitler could falsify but not refute' ('Wir müssen uns an Erfahrungen orientieren, die über Hitler hinausweisen, und an Grundwerten, die Hitler zwar verfälschen, aber nicht außer Kraft setzen konnte'), Böll retorted: 'I ask, myself included, whether this refusal to con- front the total repeal of all basic values is not after all *one* of the causes of such destruction and self-destruction as Bernward Vesper indulged in. Then all of us, whether directly guilty or not, would be Hitler's Children, not only the terrorists' ('Ich frage und frage mich mit, ob in dieser verweigerten Konfrontation mit der totalen Au- ßerkraftsetzung aller Grundwerte nicht doch *eine* der Ursachen für Zerstörung und Selbstzerstörung liegt, wie Bernward Vesper sie betrieb. Dann wären wir alle, ob direkt schuldig oder nicht, Hitler's Children, nicht nur die Terroristen') (E 3, p. 499). Terrorism was a result of the failure to accept the consequences of the Third Reich. Bernward Vesper, son of the Nazi poet, Will Vesper, is probably the only terrorist who could justify the title of Jillian Becker's book on the Baader–Meinhof group, *Hitler's Children*, to which Böll was alluding in his review, a title which is ambiguous, nowhere ex- plained in the text and which was probably adopted by the author as a money-spinning catch-phrase (Becker, 1977). It nevertheless caught on. Invited to comment on it in the same year, Böll replied: 'The terrorists are not Hitler's children, they are the children of fathers who were allowed too easily, or who allowed themselves too easily to change over from a terrorist dictatorship to a parliamentary democracy. This diagnosis does *not* apply to all the persons of the scene, for example it does not apply to Ulrike Meinhof or Gudrun Ensslin' ('Die Terroristen sind nicht die Kinder Hitlers, sie sind die Kinder von Vätern, denen es zu leicht gemacht worden ist, oder die es sich zu leicht gemacht haben, aus einer terroristischen Diktatur in eine parlamentarische Demokratie überzuwechseln. Diese Fest- stellung trifft *nicht* auf alle Personen der Szene zu, zum Beispiel nicht auf Ulrike Meinhof und Gudrun Ensslin') (Bauer, p. 110). The 'social commitment' of the latter two, which the Springer press had refused to recognise, was something he had already stressed (I, p. 571). Later he was to suggest that the desire to get rid of the material ruins from the war had left his generation too little time to instil positive values in the younger generation — and even the terrorists were looking for values (Vormweg, pp. 88ff.).

In another conversation of 1977 Böll pointed out that terrorism was not just a German phenomenon (Riese, p. 37). The IRA in the United Kingdom, the Palestinians in the Middle East, the Basque separatists in Spain were all active at the time; the following year Aldo Moro was kidnapped by the Red Brigades in Italy and later murdered. Nor did Böll even regard it as the chief problem of West German society. Neo-Nazism *was* a specifically German problem. As an East German colleague put it, for a German the debate on fascism was 'an endless road' ('ein Weg ohne Ende') (Kleinschmid, 1979, p. 228). As late as 1975 another major trial of war criminals began in Düsseldorf, when former members of the staff of the Majdanek concentration camp were brought to justice, thirty years after the end of the Third Reich and when many of them were too old to stand trial. A number of scandals relating to the failure to come to terms with the past aroused Böll's concern in the later 1970s. In November 1976 Hans-Ulrich Rudel, Germany's most highly decorated airman of the Second World War, who had subsequently been actively involved with neo-Nazi organisations, was the guest of honour at a reunion meeting of Hitler's Wehrmacht. When General Krupinski was challenged on this he replied that as long as Herbert Wehner, the SPD's parliamentary chairman, a former Communist, was in the Federal Parliament he did not see why he should not invite Colonel Rudel. Eventually Krupinski and another general were dismissed but the affair had created the impression that the new Bundeswehr was not entirely dedicated to principles of democracy (E 3, pp. 418–24). In 1977 a brawl between Communists and neo-Nazis resulted in prison sentences only for the former (E 3, pp. 542, 434ff.). The prime minister of Baden-Württemberg, Hans Filbinger, was forced to resign in 1978 when Rolf Hochhuth brought to light that as one of Hitler's naval judges he had passed a death sentence for looting in 1943, and similar sentences on three naval deserters as late as 1945 (VG, pp. 142ff.). The American television series *Holocaust* was shown in West Germany in January 1979, was widely viewed and hotly debated — it seemed that for many this was the first inkling that Jews had been persecuted by Germans in the Third Reich. Böll rightly denied that post-war German literature had ignored the topic; but he suggested that it was an occasion to reconsider firstly the artificial division between popular and serious literature, the former of which was evidently able to get through where the latter failed, and secondly the achievements of school history lessons (Lodemann, p. 64); elsewhere he pointed out that people could have informed themselves on the background twenty years previously through the Germania Judaica archives in Cologne, of which he had been a co-founder (VG, pp. 137f.). The recession led to an upsurge in hostility to foreign workers, especially the large Turkish community in West Berlin. Terms such as 'pure blood' and 'German blood' began to circulate once more (EZ, p. 58). Böll's continued interest in the fate of the Jewish community was documented in a piece of historical research on the Jews of the village of Drove, near Düren, which he published in 1982 (EZ, pp. 94–117).

In 1977 he also celebrated his sixtieth birthday. The city of Cologne honoured its most famous living citizen with an official reception (VG, pp. 18ff.) and the occasion was marked by the publication of the first five volumes of a collected edition of his works; a further five appeared in 1978. Earlier in the same year another collection of essays had come out, *Einmischung erwünscht*. In 1978 the Fischer Bücherei brought out an anthology of writings selected by Böll, *Mein Lesebuch*, which offers an interesting insight into his wide-ranging interests, literary, political, theological. Besides excerpts from Virginia Woolf, Camus and Dostoevsky, the New Testament and documents of the Third Reich, Rosa Luxemburg and Teresa of Avila, we find a marked interest in South America, which reminds the reader of the optimism Böll expressed when Salvador Allende came to power in Chile and his bitterness when democracy was overthrown in that country with the help of the CIA (I, p. 167; E 3, pp. 518ff.). It was around this time that Böll began to express unease about the image which was being forced on him, the responsibilities he was being expected to shoulder. He spoke of the 'disintegration' of public opinion, of the failure of society to create a moral forum, so that in its place writers were being set up as 'moral authorities', as the 'conscience of the nation' (I, pp. 417ff.). There was schizophrenia in the attitude of the conservative elements in society towards writers; on the one hand they were expected to express an opinion on public affairs, on the other they were immediately condemned when the opinions they expressed did not conform to expectations. The notion that writers could be their country's conscience was simply undemocratic (Riese, p. 7; Kesting, pp. 67–85).

Fürsorgliche Belagerung, his next important work of fiction, was published in the summer of 1979 and had such an extraordinarily mixed reception that within a year no fewer than four articles had appeared which analysed the reviews (anon., 1979; anon., 1979; Vormweg, 1980; Heißenbüttel, 1980). The conservative Marcel Reich-Ranicki complained that reading it had been a torture

(Reich-Ranicki, 1979b); the social democrat Heinrich Vormweg called it 'an extraordinary book' (Vormweg, 1980, p. 85); Hans Maier, Böll's debating opponent in Paris, approved of it (cit. ibid.); and the liberal Wolfram Schütte found it a 'catastrophic failure' (Schütte, 1979). F. C. Delius's novel *Ein Held der inneren Sicherheit* (1981) contains a hidden *hommage* to *Fürsorgliche Belagerung*, when it mentions Fritz Tolm, the central figure of Böll's novel, as one of the industrialists' leaders (Delius, 1981, p. 77). In content *Fürsorgliche Belagerung* pursues Böll's most recent interests, those manifested in *Die verlorene Ehre der Katharina Blum* and *Berichte zur Gesinnungslage der Nation*, and modifies attitudes adopted in works from *Ende einer Dienstfahrt* onwards; in form and technique, however, it represents a return to the Böll of the 1950s and is especially reminiscent of *Billard um halbzehn*.

The novel is set in November 1978, but its events relate directly to those of the autumn of 1977. Fritz Tolm has just been elected chairman of the industrialists' federation. He, his family and other important businessmen are being guarded day and night against a threatened assassination or kidnapping attempt by terrorists, who include Tolm's former daughter-in-law Veronica and the man she is living with, Heinrich Bewerloh. There are thus reminiscences of Jürgen Ponto and Hanns-Martin Schleyer. The threat is no empty one: Tolm's predecessor Pliefger was almost killed by a bomb hidden in his birthday cake. The measures taken for their protection are grotesquely comprehensive but, Tolm feels, ultimately useless – the killers will strike in a place where nobody is expecting it, and indeed in the end the threat is averted only when Veronica gives herself up — as Ulrike Meinhof and Gudrun Ensslin refused to do. Moreover they have negative consequences: family life crumbles when there is always a police officer at the door; whole communities suffer when someone as prominent as Tolm's daughter Sabine lives among them. Total security leads precisely to its opposite: all of the main characters of the novel are insecure, dominated by *Angst*. It also involves total surveillance — the upshot is a totalitarian state and the fulfilment of one of the terrorists' aims, to demonstrate the undemocratic nature of West German society. Two simultaneous suicides take place: Bewerloh's when arrested by the police in Turkey, and that of Kortschede, an industrialist friend of Tolm's. Tolm's insistence on attending Bewerloh's funeral rather than that of Kortschede, will, he realises, mean that he will have to resign his office — one of the most striking visual effects of the film *Deutschland im Herbst* was the repeated cutting between the state funeral of Hanns-Martin Schleyer and the 'alternative' funerals of the suicides of Stammheim. As in *Die verlorene Ehre der Katharina Blum* Böll shows his concern over the power of the gutter press and its close and mutual cooperation with the police. Fritz Tolm is the liberal proprietor of a newspaper chain — there *are* newspapers other than those owned by the Springer concern — but he is about to be taken over by his less scrupulous rival. And in the novel it appears that the press, which is becoming concentrated in fewer and fewer hands, is collaborating with the police to suppress information which the public has a legitimate right to know, namely the pessimistic assessment of the future by a prominent industrialist who has just committed suicide, while allowing information on individuals' private lives to be published which is of no legitimate interest to the public.

Fürsorgliche Belagerung also belongs to a large group of novels which deal with the aftermath of the student movement, from Peter Schneider's *Lenz* (1973) to Peter Renz's *Vorläufige Beruhigung* and Uwe Timm's *Kerbels Flucht* (1980). In 1980 Böll and Vormweg discussed the novel in the context of the gulf between the generations which seemed to have opened up; the term 'satellite children' ('Satellitenkinder') used in the novel (cf. FB, pp. 51, 177) was, according to Böll, a keyword to describe this gulf: to Tolm his children seem to live on the moon (Vormweg, p. 88). Rolf Tolm and his friends represent the generation whose lives have been destroyed by the anti-radicals legislation, and Rolf's career illustrates Böll's own development from *Ende einer Dienstfahrt* onwards. Rolf was imprisoned for setting fire to cars as a protest gesture; the Gruhls went on trial for burning a military jeep. Today he abjures all violence, even that directed at objects. He has withdrawn to the countryside into a kind of 'inner emigration', one marked by contempt rather than active resistance towards the authorities. His brother Herbert, an environmentalist, is planning a protest against cars which will involve the use of a number of articulated lorries to block key points in the city, just as Leni was saved from eviction by a similar stratagem in *Gruppenbild mit Dame*. But Herbert is persuaded by his mother Käthe to desist, since the lives of innocent people might be placed at risk if ambulances, for example, were unable to get through. Böll was alarmed at the way the relatively harmless 'happenings' of the early days of student protest turned into bank robberies, kidnappings and murder — Fritz Teufel, who on one notorious occasion disrupted the formal proceedings of his trial by appearing in orange trousers and a violet shirt and refused to stand up for the judge until he could be persuaded that doing so would 'help to unravel the truth' (*Der Spiegel*, 1.1.1968, p. 38), appeared to him initially as 'a lovable anarchist' (I, p. 698). The direct action he had been advocating ten years earlier is now rejected; in fact it is the police who intend to use road blocks to capture the terrorists — 'happenings' have been taken over by the Establishment.

Ludwig Götten in *Die verlorene Ehre der Katharina Blum* was not a terrorist. In *Fürsorgliche Belagerung* Böll took up the accusation of his critics that he was thereby trivialising the actual threat to society from those who had declared war on it. Heinrich Bewerloh and Veronica Zelger are a genuine threat. Rolf has no more time for them than for the Establishment they profess to hate. Part of Böll's contribution to the terrorism debate is the common mentality he finds in the terrorists and their opponents. The age, says Tolm, is that of both Bewerloh and Amplanger, Tolm's putative successor and a far more ruthless capitalist than he could ever be. Bewerloh would have made an excellent banker, Tolm believes. The cold, calculating rationality with which the one side accumulates wealth is mirrored by that which enables the other to construct booby-traps, and that in turn is mirrored by the former's ability to frustrate them. The most terrifying person in the novel is the seven-year-old child of Veronica and Heinrich, Holger I, who turns out to be a 'bomb', trained to set fire to Tolmshoven; his parents have destroyed all spontaneity in him — and the destruction of spontaneity is one of the effects of the security precautions to which the Tolms have to submit. Spontaneity is a key concept in the novel, as it was in *Ansichten eines Clowns*. Tolm's relationship to his wife Käthe began when he met her in a military hospital during the war and at once resolved to spend the night with her. His daughter Sabine is having an illicit relationship with the policeman who is supposed to be guarding her, which began in a quite unpremeditated moment. By contrast her marriage has become as mechanical as the pornography which governs the high society in which she and her husband live, and her husband always anxiously enquires whether she has remembered to take the Pill.

Was terrorism a right-wing or a left-wing phenomenon? A further key concept in the novel is that of 'Treue', fidelity to a person or an idea. Sabine is unfaithful to her husband, and we are invited to sympathise with her. The terrorists, by contrast, are 'faithful unto death', as Rolf reflects (FB, p. 230); they are unable to give up, once they have begun. Veronica has to struggle with her conscience before she is 'unfaithful' to Bewerloh and surrenders to the police. 'Honour' and 'fidelity' were two of the Germanic virtues abused by the Nazis; the motto of the SS was 'Our honour is our fidelity' ('Unsere Ehre ist die Treue') (FT, p. 92). Böll is implying remnants of fascist ideals in the terrorists' mentality (Vormweg, p. 96). They

201

are therefore not so far removed from capitalists like Bleibl and his friends, who sing Nazi songs from time to time. The failure to come to terms with the Nazi past is once more apparent.

Terrorism *is* a threat. At least as serious is the threat to the environment posed by the industrial establishment itself. At its most inhumane level technological 'progress' is represented by the motorway which faceless bureaucrats have pointed straight into the city and which destroys people's peace, nerves, sleep with the uninterrupted noise of its traffic. As Sabine's husband invariably describes sex in terms of car driving, we are invited to view this mechanisation of life, which Böll elsewhere described as a 'manifestation of fascism' (I, p. 171), as on a par with pornography. But the onward march of the coal mines is at least as important as the motorway. The Tolms have had to move once before to make way for coal mining. Eickelhof, their late-nineteenth-century villa, and the whole of the surrounding area including the village of Iffenhoven where Käte was born, have been rased in the cause of industry. And in due course Tolmshoven is due to go the same way. The vast illuminated power-stations which are coming ever closer represent a threat at least as tangible as that of the terrorists. The novel's ending makes the connection explicit. For doomed Tolmshoven is indeed destroyed — by the child Holger I, acting under instructions from his father Bewerloh, and aided, presumably unwittingly, but certainly appropriately by a press photographer, a successor of Tötges in *Katharina Blum*, who enables him to elude the security cordon.

The destruction of the environment is an external factor. Böll also diagnoses an inner disintegration of German society. Failure to recognise that Nazism discredited traditional values is one of the breeding-grounds of the present disorder. Tolm himself tried to counter the 'nihilisation by Nazism' by promoting liberal values after the war, but failed (p. 174). In *Fürsorgliche Belagerung* the ruling classes are characterised by social cynicism and moral degeneracy. Sabine's husband owes his wealth to the exploitation of cheap labour in Eastern Europe and the developing countries. The trade unions have thrown in their lot with the employers, as has the Church. A dominant leitmotiv of the first half of the novel is the phrase: 'All around chaos, disintegration' ('Ringsum Chaos, Auflösung') (cf. VG, p. 123). Brecht's dialectics of order — 'Disorder is where nothing is in the proper place. Order is where in the proper place there is nothing' ('Wo nichts am rechten Platz liegt, da ist Unordnung. Wo am rechten Platz nichts liegt, ist Ordnung') (Brecht, 1961, p. 17) — are illustrated in *Fürsorgliche Belagerung*. The terrorists attempt to create chaos; society tightens up security measures until total order prevails; the result is a moral vacuum. Bleibl's succession of wives, the Fischers' social life — these are the most obvious manifestations of decadence. Orgies which take place under the protection of security men (FB, p. 176) were not Böll's invention; nor was the incident in which Heinrich Schmergen, sitting peacefully in a bus and reading a book about Fidel Castro, suddenly notices that the other passengers are staring at him so full of hostility that he gets off in fear of his life (FB, pp. 409f.; cf. E 3, pp. 475f.). As in *Die verlorene Ehre der Katharina Blum* terrorism is not the exclusive province of 'terrorists'. When Rolf and Katharina first came to live in Hubreichen after Rolf had been released from prison they were met by stone-throwing and threats of arson. Veronica's father has had to give up his medical practice because of his daughter's reputation.

The novel is thus as topical as anything that Böll wrote. And yet, by comparison with *Ansichten eines Clowns*, for example, it is more indirect, more fictional in its treatment of West German political realities. There are no references to contemporary political figures, other than obliquely to Holger Meins, who died in prison on hunger strike on 9 November 1974, and even more obliquely to Holger Börner, prime minister of the state of Hesse (p. 118). SPD and CDU are mentioned only in passing. Geographical locations are largely fictionalised, although identifiable as the area north-west of Cologne. The narrative techniques used by Böll are closer to the modernist ones of the novels of the 1950s than to the post-modernist ones of *Entfernung von der Truppe* or *Gruppenbild mit Dame*, so that in *Fürsorgliche Belagerung* Böll has written a novel which for all its topicality is more autonomous than its immediate predecessors.

In its treatment of time, for example, *Fürsorgliche Belagerung* approaches the compactness of *Billard um halbzehn*. Böll's longest novel after *Gruppenbild mit Dame*, it compresses its narrated time into under seventy-two hours — possibly even forty-eight hours, as Stephen Smith believes (Beth, 1980, pp. 101f.; cf. Reid, 1983, p. 135). More than three-quarters of the text takes place in the afternoon and evening of the first day; as in Böll's early novels, the narrative is expanded into the past by means of recollection. The atmosphere is one of timelessness, emphasised in the motif of ritual. In *Billard um halbzehn* this consisted of billiards-playing or Heinrich Fähmel's 'paprika breakfast'; in *Fürsorgliche Belagerung* it is the ceremony of fetching the milk, Sabine with her daughter Kit, Rolf with his son Holger. There follows an acceleration, as things begin to happen, people arrive, the plot builds up to a climax, decisions are taken, Bleibl's to return to his first wife, Veronica's to give herself up,

Roickler's, Hubert's and Sabine's to stop living a lie. Tolm, like Heinrich Fähmel before him, resolves to give up his attempt to compromise with the Establishment; the burning of Tolmshoven sets the seal on this decision, and is comparable to Heinrich Fähmel's cheerful destruction of his own abbey, at least in effigy, at the close of the earlier novel.

The other formal similarity between *Fürsorgliche Belagerung* and the novels of the 1950s is the narrative point of view adopted. The post-modernist extra-diegetic narrators of *Gruppenbild mit Dame* and *Die verlorene Ehre der Katharina Blum* have given way once more to a modernist limited perspective technique. Each of the twenty-one chapters has its own separate focaliser — there are eleven of these in all — and again with each successive chapter opening Böll keeps the reader in suspense as to the identity of the focaliser. Focalisers include not only the principal characters, but also, for example, Holzpuke, the policeman in charge of security operations, who is presented in a wholly sympathetic light, as if Böll were doing his best to show that he was not attacking the police, who are making the best of a bad job, but rather those in charge of them. By contrast we are given no insight into the minds of Bewerloh, the unreconstructed terrorist, or Amplanger, Tolm's unscrupulous rival: the narrative technique underlines their common mentality. The use of independent focalisers is the formal equivalent of the isolation in which the characters live, each in his own armoured cell; the sense of community which was such an important aspect of *Gruppenbild mit Dame* has been lost once more. 'Berührungsängste', fear of contact, was diagnosed by Böll as one of the threats to people's lives, vividly illustrated in the way politicians at the time of the Schleyer kidnapping were making speeches from behind bullet-proof glass (I, pp. 707f.). And although at the end of the novel the principal characters appear to be congregating in the village of Hubreichen, the community which they may be about to form there will be a much more inward-looking one than that which helped the Gruhls in *Ende einer Dienstfahrt* or Leni in *Gruppenbild mit Dame*. Tolm expresses the hope 'that a socialism must come, must win' ('daß ein Sozialismus kommen muß, siegen muß') (FB, p. 414), but it is in the context of the novel a desperate one. *Fürsorgliche Belagerung* is much more melancholy than anything Böll had written since 1963.

One possibly post-modernist aspect, however, is worth pointing out. Böll himself called his novel a 'Krimi' (Raddatz, 1979). It consciously parodies the 'thriller' of the variety exemplified in Frederick Forsyth's *The Day of the Jackal*, in which the hired assassin comes closer and closer to his victim in spite of all the security precautions taken to frustrate him. Not until the final page of Böll's novel do we know whether Tolm will survive the threats on his life, nor do we know who, if anyone, will be the assassin. Böll presents us with a series of red herrings. The reader's suspicion first falls on the butler, a traditional suspect in the genre, then on the latter's girlfriend, whose hobby is archery. A bicycle seems likely to be used — and promptly Erna Breuer resolves to cycle to Hubreichen. Tolm imagines that his grandson may have been trained to butt him in the chest, causing a heart attack; Holger eventually arrives from Beirut and butts his grandfather — but only in the stomach. Finally Veronica herself succeeds in evading the security forces — but having proved her point she gives herself up. Böll too is 'proving a point': total security is impossible, the attempt to fulfil it is counter-productive. The attack will always come from the quarter from which it is least expected. Nobody thought of arson — but that is what Holger has been trained to commit; Sabine is indeed 'abducted' — but she goes willingly, and with the policeman who was sent to guard her. Parody is one means by which modernist literary detachment can be pierced; it provokes Böll's readers to a more critical attitude.

The federal elections of 1980 restored the SPD/FDP coalition's majority to forty-five, almost entirely because the CDU/CSU's candidate for chancellor was Franz Josef Strauss, who appeared too extreme to many conservative voters outside his home state of Bavaria. The shift of allegiance was, however, primarily to the FDP. As the international recession worsened the coalition soon found itself in serious disagreement over economic policies, and in October 1982 the smaller party defected to the CDU/CSU, with whom they had been in coalition throughout the 1950s and much of the 1960s. Helmut Schmidt was replaced as chancellor by the CDU leader Helmut Kohl. Looking back, Böll singled out two major mistakes made by the SPD in office: one was the anti-radicals legislation; the other was the failure to make proper use of the media — even those parts of it which had been friendly towards the SPD had been cowed by conservative pressures and the party had not attempted to stop the witch hunt against intellectuals in 1977 (EZ, pp. 139f.; FT, p. 9). To legitimise the change of government elections were brought forward to March 1983. They confirmed the new coalition in office. The SPD was heavily defeated, but with twenty-seven seats the new Greens Party was represented in the Federal Parliament for the first time.

The Greens Party had been founded out of various ecological groups in October 1979. One of the central issues of West German society in the latter half of the 1970s and beyond was the threat to the environment posed by nuclear power-stations and the concomitant problem of waste disposal, the acid rain which was destroying forests at an alarming rate, and the general destruction of the landscape by industrial progress, which is a central motif of *Fürsorgliche Belagerung*. In February 1975 the site of a planned nuclear reactor was occupied by protestors at Wyhl on the Upper Rhine; violent demonstrations took place in October and November 1976 at a similar site at Brokdorf on the Lower Elbe, and again in March 1977 at Grohnde on the Weser and on the site of a nuclear waste disposal project at Gorleben on the Elbe.

Böll's concern for the environment dates back at least to 1969, when he commented on the memorandum published by the Soviet physicist Andrey Sakharov warning on the dangers to the world posed by industrialisation and the arms race (E 2, pp. 347–53). He referred to Sakharov's words again during the 1972 election campaign, pinpointing man's 'exploitation of the landscape' as a major issue confronting the political parties (E 2, pp. 609–12). Commenting on the Brokdorf and Wyhl demonstrations in 1976 he stressed how important it was to rescue the concept of 'soil' from the taint of Nazism: culture began with the tilling of the earth, not with its destruction; today mankind was confronted with two mutually exclusive values, 'earth' and 'growth' (E 3, p. 417). As early as 1961, however, his play *Ein Schluck Erde* had attempted to rehabilitate the notion of 'soil', prompting *Der Spiegel* to entitle an article on him 'Bread and soil' ('Brot und Boden') (anon., 1961), punning on the Nazi ideology of 'blood and soil'. He frequently returned to this theme. In his address to a conference in Recklinghausen on the topic 'Our cultural emergency — culture in democracy' ('Unser kultureller Notstand — Kultur in der Demokratie') in October 1977, he praised the efforts of young socialists to save trees from being felled and old houses from being pulled down: they had helped to create a new awareness of the value of conservation (E 3, pp. 462ff.). The unbridled pursuit of economic growth was irresponsible — cancer too was a growth (Vormweg, pp. 12f.); it was necessary to redefine the concept of labour in order to create jobs for everyone — 'There is little work but plenty to be done' ('Es gibt wenig Arbeit, aber viel zu tun') (ibid., p. 134). *Gruppenbild mit Dame* had already questioned the notion of 'achievement' ('Leistung'). Elsewhere he expressed the belief that the traditional parties were incapable of dealing with these problems and that perhaps a new political party needed to be founded (Riese, pp. 23f.).

Böll's friend Beuys stood for the Federal Parliament in 1980 on behalf of the Greens and it is not difficult to see them as a political grouping which would have great attraction for Böll. Its insistence on the limits to growth, its rejection of the 'achievement society', its refusal to take seriously the solemn rituals of established society, the strong anarchist component in it — all of these features replicate strands in Böll's outlook. It is true that in *Fürsorgliche Belagerung* the environmentalists Herbert Tolm and his friends are negative figures to Tolm himself, not least because they are lacking in humour, and Böll never had much time for dogmatic theories untempered by humour (E 1, pp. 355ff.). But the destruction of the landscape, the inhospitability of the cities are important themes in that novel. When the social–liberal coalition ended in 1982 Böll hoped that the SPD and the Greens would overcome their mutual dislike (EZ, p. 71), and he wrote a preface to *Um Hoffnung kämpfen* by the Greens' leader Petra Kelly, which was published by his son in 1983 (EZ, pp. 76ff.). In his last recorded interview he spoke of the vital importance of the Greens, seeing them as 'an expression of everything that in the Sixties represented changes and protest, protest aiming at changes' ('der Ausdruck für alles das, was Veränderungen und Protest, Protest mit dem Ziel von Veränderungen, in den sechziger Jahren dargestellt hat') (Limberg, p. 10).

What is perhaps unexpected about Böll's concern for the environment is that he had hitherto been regarded primarily as a city-dweller; the city is the scene of his major works from *Und sagte kein einziges Wort* to *Die verlorene Ehre der Katharina Blum* with the exception of *Ende einer Dienstfahrt*. But by 1977 Cologne was only his second place of residence and he lived primarily in a village in the Eifel (Vormweg, p. 84); in 1982 he even gave up his house in Cologne (EZ, p. 28). Cologne had become 'alien' to him, he said; the neighbourliness and community of street life had been destroyed by traffic; pedestrian precincts were artificial; civilisation was dominated by the motor car — he himself had one — and the motor car was 'an instrument of isolation' (Vormweg, pp. 73–85; cf, E 2, pp. 585–94). Parallel to his disengagement from the city went a growing interest in villages, one expressed for example in his piece on the Jews of Drove, Kreis Düren (EZ, pp. 94ff.). Böll had come a long way from the hostility expressed towards rural locations in early stories such as 'Die Botschaft' or 'Ein Hemd aus grüner Seide'.

Not the least of the Greens' attractions for Böll was their involvement in the peace movement (EZ, p. 233), the other main preoccupation of his last years. The new peace movement in West Germany and elsewhere began after the dual decision of the NATO Foreign and Defence Ministers in Brussels in December 1979, to modernise nuclear forces and at the same time negotiate with the Soviet Union on a reduction of the same forces (Sandford, 1986). Böll's interest was scarcely surprising; he had consistently opposed the re-militarisation of Germany in the 1950s and a major thrust of his writings is directed against war and weapons. The new weapons he believed lessened security rather than increasing it (EZ, p. 188). In 1981 he attacked the absurdity and dishonesty of seeking a 'balance' of armaments when both sides were over-armed; it was alarming that pacifism was associated with Communism — the Federal Republic ought to be proud of its numerous conscientious objectors, just as it should be proud of the numbers of foreigners seeking refuge with it (VG, pp. 187–93). In 1982 he reviewed Vilma Sturm's *Mühsal mit dem Frieden*, returning to his attacks on the Catholic Church in Germany for its unconditional support of NATO (EZ, pp. 30–3). In the same year he contributed three episodes to a film *Krieg und Frieden*; an intercontinental nuclear war has taken place, some American and Soviet astronauts have survived in space but have no future since there is nowhere for them to land; another scene depicts a nuclear bunker in Germany — when the sister of one of its inmates arrives she is shot for fear she might bring radiation with her (EZ, pp. 42ff.). At a conference organised by the Karl Renner Institute in Vienna in 1982 he spoke on the 'images' of other peoples which literature and the media constructed and which made wars possible: clichés of 'the Jew', 'the foreigner', 'the Communist'. It was the last of these clichés which was now a major threat to peace; the primitive anti-Communism of President Reagan kept in power such inhuman dictators as Duvalier in Haiti and Pinochet in Chile (EZ, pp. 49ff.). In his 1983 review of Franz Alt's *Frieden ist möglich* he pointed out that the Federal Republic had the greatest density of nuclear arms in the world; again he attacked the Catholic hierarchy for its policies of support for rearmament; a majority of the Catholic population was against it (EZ, pp. 118ff.). Reviewing André Glucksmann's *Philosophie der Abschreckung* in 1984, which attempted to justify the arms race with reference to, among other things, Aquinas's theory of the just war, he found the slogan 'rather dead than red' inhumane and lacking in credibility: millions in Eastern Europe evidently did not agree, and even Solzhenitsyn and others who had been imprisoned under the extreme conditions of the Gulag had preferred life to suicide (FT, pp. 141ff.). It was over this issue that Böll found himself in disagreement with some of the Soviet dissidents who had been allowed to emigrate from the Soviet Union, partly with Böll's help. Their experience of Soviet-style socialism had engendered in them a hatred for any kind of socialism.

Mourning and Resistance (1976–1985)

In 1977 he tried to defend Solzhenitsyn, who was attacking the West for its decadence and unwillingness to stand up to the Soviet Union (Vormweg, pp. 27ff.). In 1983 he found Vladimir Bukovski's book *Dieser stechende Schmerz der Freiheit* full of incomprehensible attacks on the revolutionaries in South and Central America. The US support of dictatorships in the Philippines, in Paraguay, Haiti, Nicaragua would, Böll believed, drive the population of these countries eventually into the hands of the Soviet Union, just as in Cuba and Angola democratic socialism had been frustrated by the hostility of the United States (EZ, pp. 222ff.). This review provoked a remarkable attack on Böll from the *émigré* poet Naum Korshavin in 1984 (FT, pp. 313ff., 189ff.). Ironically enough, from 1973 onwards Böll's books were no longer available in the Soviet Union, partly because in that year the Soviet Union signed the Universal Copyright Convention and would for the first time have had to pay to publish them, partly because of Böll's criticism of its policies over dissidents (Hüttel, 1981).

In October 1981 300,000 people demonstrated in Bonn against the decision to deploy Cruise and Pershing missiles in West Germany; it was the biggest demonstration the country had ever seen. Böll was one of those who addressed the gathering; he insisted that he and his friends were not anti-American, as was being claimed by their opponents; on the contrary, he would never forget the liberation by the Americans and their literature; but the Reagan administration was not to be identified with the American people, and the CDU was more monolithic in its support of the NATO decision than the Americans (VG, pp. 257ff.). The following year even more people came to demonstrate in Bonn and in October 1983 the numbers reached half a million. Böll was a speaker again on the latter occasion; he viewed the arrival of the Greens in parliament and the presence of Willy Brandt at the demonstration as hopeful signs (EZ, pp. 233ff.). Earlier that year he had taken part in the attempt to blockade the American air-base at Mutlangen near Schwäbisch Gemünd; he was attacked by, among others, Colonel Heinz Kluss for 'undemocratically' using force where arguments had not prevailed; Böll replied that he and the other blockaders were not endangering democracy, on the contrary they were practising democracy; civil *obedience* had been the crime of Rudolf Höss, Klaus Barbie and Adolf Eichmann (EZ, pp. 176ff., 240ff.). Afterwards he claimed to have been impressed by the notes of encouragement which American servicemen had passed through the fence, containing the words 'Don't yield' (EZ, pp. 165, 184), and he criticised the misleading reports on the blockade published by *Bild* (EZ, pp.

209

184ff.). In spite of all these efforts the first of the missiles arrived in West Germany in November. The demonstrations continued and Böll continued to support the movement, pinning his hopes on a possible change of government in 1987 (FT, pp. 72, 199f.). In March 1984 along with Günter Grass and other writers, he took part in a debate with Bundeswehr officers on the question at what point a soldier had the duty to disobey orders (Raddatz, p. 43). Böll's position on armaments was more radical than that of Grass: while the latter was in favour of increasing the West's supply of conventional weapons at the expense of the new nuclear weapons, Böll was against any kind of increase.

In all these ways Böll remained actively involved in attempts to preserve the world as a humane place. Indeed the theme of 'resistance' ('Widerstand') is a leitmotiv of the articles and reviews he wrote in his last years. He repeatedly referred to Werner von Trott zu Solz's book *Widerstand heute* (1958), an extract from which closes his reader of 1978. 'Resistance today must consist in making use of one's liberty' ('Widerstand muß heute darin bestehen, von seiner Freiheit Gebrauch zu machen'), he declared in 1983 (FT, pp. 133ff.). It was wrong to see resistance only in the context of totalitarian states, whether in honouring the men of 20 July 1944 or those who were resisting oppression in Czechoslovakia and the Soviet Union. Resistance was an 'element of life' (FT, p. 166). He attacked the hypocrisy of the Catholic Church, which had encouraged people to resist parliament over the liberalisation of abortion but in the matter of nuclear arms was appealing to them to respect parliamentary majorities (FT, pp. 66f.; cf. also EZ, pp. 170ff., 204ff., 215ff.; FT, pp. 61ff., 73ff.).

And yet there is also a strong component of melancholy in Böll's pronouncements during the last years of his life. This is partly because they are so critical of the contemporary Federal Republic. The new cable television he regarded as a 'plague' (FT, pp. 21, 205), one which would reduce the citizen's critical faculties — he even wrote an Orwellian satire on this topic entitled 'Kain oder Kabel' ('Cain or cable') (EZ, pp. 124ff.). The increasing hostility of West Germans to foreigners and refugees he found depressing (FT, pp. 27ff., 39ff., 120). He commented bitterly on the scandal when it emerged in 1983 that the Flick concern had been paying considerable sums to political parties in exchange for tax concessions (EZ, pp. 148ff.; FT, pp. 43ff., 76, 113f.). In 1984 when Peter Boenisch, a columnist of *Bild* and one of those who had been active in the vendetta against intellectuals in the 1970s, became the new conservative government's press officer, Böll selected twenty-seven of

Boenisch's columns from the years 1970 to 1983, printing them in facsimile and commenting on them (*Bild Bonn Boenisch*); they make predictably depressing reading with their philistine joviality and their reactionary tenor — that Böll felt it worth the effort is more remarkable than the pieces themselves. The state of the world, he said in 1982, was a very melancholy one (Limagne, p. 196), and the following year, under the impact of the change of government in Bonn, he foresaw 'a new variant of inner emigration, one that has been prepared by the wave of new inwardness' ('eine neue Variante der inneren Emigration, die durch die Welle neuer Innerlichkeit vorbereitet ist'), which he himself, however, refused to adopt (EZ, pp. 181, 184). In the last interview he gave before his death he complained: 'daily another piece of freedom withers' ('es stirbt täglich Freiheit weg') (Limberg, p. 10).

The component of melancholy is compounded by the necessarily backwards-looking nature of the autobiographical writings which played an increasingly important part in his literary output. The publication of the two volumes of early works *Das Vermächtnis* (1981) and *Die Verwundung* (1983) may be seen as a further symptom. With advancing age he began to reflect on his own past. He claimed that only from 1970 did he begin to dream of the war, and these dreams always included the fear of being caught by the Nazis (E 3, pp. 311ff.). In 1977 he spoke of the increasing fascination which the years before 1939, even pre-1933 held for him (Kesting, p. 67). But the public's curiosity about or nostalgia for the past did not pass him by and he was invited to describe, for example, the first years after the war (E 3, pp. 51ff.) or the experience of the Currency Reform (FT, pp. 53ff.). One difficulty in writing a classical autobiography (I, p. 379) was the autobiographical mode of the time; Böll feared falling into the 'veteranism' of old soldiers at their annual reunions (E 3, p. 293). Congratulating Walter Jens on his sixtieth birthday, he spoke of old soldiers' boasting, which Plautus had pilloried in his comedies, and with self-irony saw himself as a young man looking at himself as he was today, someone who 'no longer understands the times' (EZ, p. 35). His two major autobiographical writings attempt to get over the difficulty by the self-conscious use of literary patterns: *Buddenbrooks* and *David Copperfield* in the case of *Was soll aus dem Jungen bloß werden?* (1981) and the *Märchen* and thriller patterns of the 'Brief an meine Söhne' of 1985.

Interviewers suggested he had become pessimistic. Böll denied it: they were confusing pessimism with melancholy (Kesting, p. 74; Limagne, p. 196; cf. also EZ, p. 181). 'Man has the right, indeed almost a duty to mourn' ('Der Mensch hat ein Recht auf Trauer, fast sogar die Pflicht dazu'), he said to Kesting. The Mitscherlichs' book *Die Unfähigkeit zu trauern* had appeared in 1967. Böll entitled his 1984 review of Vassily Grossman's *Leben und Schicksal* 'Die Fähigkeit zu trauern', and this was the title given by his editors to the posthumous collection of his essays which appeared in 1986. If 'resistance' is one of the leitmotivs of these later years, another is 'mourning': 'The inability to mourn' described the later character of *Der Spiegel* (EZ, p. 69); cable television would be a permanent distraction from mourning and meditation (EZ, p. 129); Uwe Johnson's greatness consisted in his 'patience and mourning' (FT 71); and Germans preferred football to 'mourning for their Jewish fellow-citizens' (FT, p. 121).

Böll was not alone in his concern about the direction his country seemed to be taking. Many of his preoccupations were shared, for example, by Grass, who was lampooned by Hellmuth Karasek in, of all places, *Der Spiegel* as 'the professional nonconformist', ever ready to make a statement on 'the German forests, world peace, the army, relations with the GDR, Nicaragua, the end of the world' (FT, pp. 310–12). Böll wrote an indignant letter to *Der Spiegel*: the periodical which had been notorious for 'meddling', for 'non-conformism' and which was now conforming to the new conservativism and urging acceptance of what the government said (FT, pp. 115f.). But there is a further element involved, one which Böll emphasised ever more strongly in view of possible misunderstandings, that of patriotism. When *Bild* or CDU voters urged him to emigrate, because they regarded him as unpatriotic, he was deeply wounded. The constitution of the Federal Republic was 'probably the best constitution a state could have in the twentieth century' ('wahrscheinlich die bestmögliche Verfassung, die ein Staat sich im 20. Jahrhundert geben konnte') (E 2, p. 575; Riese, p. 11); but it was his right and his duty as a writer and a citizen to test the theory against the practice. The highest form of patriotism, he said in 1975, was to write in the language of one's own country; a writer who wrote in German was 'more German than any politician' (I, p. 432). In his discussion with Hans Maier on the causes and nature of terrorism he returned to this theme: politicians ignored the 'patriotic' element in post-war German literature, because they looked only for unquestioning support (I, pp. 727f.). In 1982 he spoke of 'our patriotism': 'The Federal Republic is really *our* country, there is no other for us, it is an astonishing country with a still remarkable degree of stability, a country too in which in spite of rising unemployment the number of conscientious objectors is rising — that is politically and historically a flattering phenomenon — for a German state' ('Die Bundesrepublik ist ja wirklich *unser* Land, es gibt kein anderes für uns, ein erstaunliches Land von immer noch bemerkenswerter Stabilität, ein Land auch, in dem trotz steigender Arbeitslosigkeit die Zahl der Wehrdienstverweigerer steigt — das ist politisch und geschichtlich ein schmeichelhaftes Phänomen — für einen deutschen Staat') (EZ, p. 81). There was undoubtedly an element of patriotism in the peace movement, in the recognition that the Americans and the German government appeared ready to turn Germany into a nuclear desert; the refusal to be dictated to by the Americans goes back to the Vietnam demonstrations of the 1960s. It was a patriotism quite different from that of the neo-Nazis — as Böll's pride in the number of conscientious objectors clearly indicates.

Honours and controversy continued to pursue him at the end of his life. When in 1979 the news was leaked that he, Grass and Siegfried Lenz had turned down a *Bundesverdienstkreuz*, one of the Federal Republic's highest honours, the *Frankfurter Allgemeine Zeitung* wrote a malicious commentary, to which the three made angry replies (25.5.1979, p. 23; 30.5.1979, p. 25). Böll later said that if it had been offered him in 1977 during the campaign against him by the right-wing media he would have accepted it, but by 1979 it was too late (Kopelew/Vormweg, p. 9). On the 29 April 1983 he was made an honorary citizen of Cologne, only the fifth person to be given this honour (one of his predecessors was Konrad Adenauer). The citation had originally included a reference to his non-literary commitment, but the more conservative city fathers objected. In his address Böll alluded to the debate and suggested that his fiction, like Goethe's, Kleist's, Hebel's and Brecht's, was more subversive than his essays (EZ, pp. 83–90). In October 1984 the French Minister of Culture, Jack Lang, made him a commander in the Ordre des Arts et des Lettres (FT, pp. 185–7). On 16 July 1985, after a brief stay in hospital he was allowed home, where he quite suddenly died. He had suffered from diabetes for many years. Although the family had requested that the funeral be kept private, it was attended by the Federal President, Richard von Weizsäcker, sitting unobtrusively in the background; in spite of their quarrels it was conducted according to the rites of the Roman Catholic Church. The coffin was carried to the grave by Böll's two surviving sons, René and Viktor, and four friends and colleagues, Lev Kopelev, Caspar Markard, Günter Grass and Günter Wallraff. Writers, politicians, journalists East and West paid tribute to Böll the man, the writer and the critic; a selection of the obituaries were published by Inter Nationes in a commemorative booklet *Heinrich Böll. On his Death* (Bonn 1985). By one of history's ironies, his old adversary Axel Springer died just two months after him.

In the previous few years Böll had published a succession of non-fictional works: the collections of essays and speeches *Vermintes Gelände* (1982) and *Ein- und Zusprüche* (1984) — a posthumous collection *Die Fähigkeit zu trauern* appeared in 1986; conversations with Lew Kopelew and Heinrich Vormweg, *Antikommunismus in Ost und West*, (1982); and with Vormweg alone, *Weil die Stadt so fremd geworden ist* (1985). Two months after his death a final novel appeared, *Frauen vor Flußlandschaft*.

Frauen vor Flußlandschaft once again includes motifs from some of Böll's earlier works. Dr Murke's tormenting of Bur-Malottke is echoed when Grobsch makes Plukanski, the government minister whose speeches he writes, listen to tape-recordings of these speeches. The Nazis who killed their families and then committed suicide at the end of the war, decribed by Marianne in *Billard um halbzehn*, are referred to again here. In the same novel Johanna Fähmel was placed in a mental hospital for her outspoken criticism of the Nazis; here a similar fate befalls Elisabeth Blaukrämer, when she refuses to keep silent about the Nazi war criminal whom she sees forty years after the end of the war. In *Billard um halbzehn* Johanna broke out of her hospital to shoot at an ex-Nazi minister; in *Frauen vor Flußlandschaft* not even that moment of liberation is vouchsafed to Elisabeth, who herself commits suicide. In his great treatise of 1796, *Über naive und sentimentalische Dichtung*, Friedrich Schiller divided 'modern' poetry and literature into two main modes, the elegiac and the satirical; both proceeded from a dissatisfaction with reality. We have seen the importance of the satirical mode in Böll's works. It is particularly pronounced in the shorter works, and finds its most successful expression in stories like 'Nicht nur zur Weihnachtszeit', 'Doktor Murkes gesammeltes Schweigen', *Die verlorene Ehre der Katharina Blum* and *Berichte zur Gesinnungslage der Nation*. The elegiac mode is perhaps less obvious. It is a strong element in the retrospective passages of *Und sagte kein einziges Wort*, *Billard um halbzehn* and *Ansichten eines Clowns*. It becomes the dominant element of *Fürsorgliche Belagerung* and especially of *Frauen vor Flußlandschaft*. *Frauen vor Flußlandschaft* is a novel of mourning. Elisabeth is not allowed to mourn for the Russian officer with whom she was in love; the official version is that the Russians were barbarians who raped her and murdered her family, when in reality her father killed the rest of her family before committing suicide himself; she is sent to an institution which will 'correct' her memories and make her 'happy' — the sexual services of an athletic young man are among the facilities on offer. The novel itself performs the task which Böll's contemporaries have shirked. 'One cannot help being melancholy'

('Man kann nur traurig sein'), says Karl von Kreyl, the young drop-out whose role resembles that of Rolf Tolm in *Fürsorgliche Belagerung* (FF, p. 187).

The action takes place over two days in the late summer of 1984, mainly in the vicinity of the Rhine among the villas of the top politicians, civil servants and bankers of the West German establishment, between Bonn and Bad Godesberg. In 1982, when Böll had left Cologne, he suggested to Vormweg that the Rhine and its most famous city were alien to each other: one turned one's back on Cologne when one looked at the Rhine; this might be the subject of a novel (Vormweg, p. 82). In *Frauen vor Flußlandschaft* a number of women 'look at the Rhine': Erika finds solace in watching the barges pass, she would always wish to return there; Elisabeth was happy on its banks; Heinrich von Kreyl's wife drowned herself in its waters. Metaphorically, they also turn their backs on the Bonn establishment. What Böll called the 'elemental nature-essence of the Rhine' ('Elementar-Naturhafte des Rheins') (ibid.) contrasts with the artificiality, pomp and circumstance of social life. This social milieu carries that of *Fürsorgliche Belagerung* one step further: there it was the world of business, here it is the affairs of state — Böll had come a long way from the milieu of poverty in *Und sagte kein einziges Wort*. The novel begins with preparations for the annual High Mass in memory of Erftler-Blum, the architect of the State, who died more than fifteen years previously (Konrad Adenauer died in 1967); in its course we read of ministers being toppled, others appointed, others resigning; in the end Heinrich von Kreyl rejects the offer of some high office, possibly that of chancellor. Fortunes are being made in 'Heaven Hint Shares', which relate to the American Strategic Defence Initiative; the new missiles are already in place and not one voice from the Church has been raised against them. It is the West Germany of the 1980s which is being described, with its financial scandals and its forged documents. As one of the characters puts it, 'scandals hereabouts are never fully cleared up' ('Skandale hierzulande [werden] nie bis ins letzte aufgeklärt') (FF, p. 92): those with millions to spend on bribes get off scot-free, like the beneficiaries of the Flick affair, whereas those who steal small sums which they believe their own are heavily punished. The Americans are regarded as 'naïve' for having allowed the public to hear about their Watergate scandal at all. Although the name is never stated, the party to which the main political protagonists belong must be the CDU, the party which used the Church as ornamentation as long as it was opportune to do so, the party of the 'charitable ladies', whose charity as in *Und sagte kein einziges Wort* extends only to the deserving, not to the undeserving poor. And it cannot be fortuitous that it is invariably referred to simply as 'the Party', just like the Communist Parties in the Eastern Bloc; the absence of any reference to an alternative implies one-party rule since 1949, although it may be significant that the incriminating 'Klossow documents' were disposed of fifteen years previously, i.e. in 1969, the year the SPD came to power; on the other hand, it seems that in 1977, when 'Number 1' (or Hanns-Martin Schleyer, perhaps) was murdered by terrorists, negotiations over his life were aborted for reasons of state, and in 1977 the SPD was still in power. Böll's view of the Federal Republic as a one-party state, broken only by the brief period of the Brandt administration, is reflected in this final novel.

It is a novel about the State and about the rottenness in the state of the Federal Republic of Germany. Documents relating to 'Number 1' and to the affairs of other businessmen and politicians have been stolen by Bingerle, who is using them for blackmail. The interests of these people, however, are identified with those of the State. It is a state which has been formed in the image of those who created it and which has corrupted them in turn: 'This is the only state we have, there is no other, nor any better one. It has made us, and we have made it' ('Dies ist der einzige Staat, den wir haben, es gibt keinen anderen, auch keinen besseren. Er hat uns gemacht, und wir haben ihn gemacht') (p. 239). On the face of it society is a strange mixture of aristocrats and upwardly mobile opportunists. Counts and more minor nobility abound; but Grobsch and Plukanski were of humble origins. Appearances, however, are deceptive. The true power behind the State is the power of wealth, what Grobsch calls the 'divine right of money' ('Gottesgnadentum des Geldes') (p. 125), which is in the hands of bankers and industrialists, who like to decorate themselves with aristocratic titles. Just as the most sinister person of *Die verlorene Ehre der Katharina Blum* was the industrialist Lüding, who did not actually appear in person, in *Frauen vor Flußlandschaft* it is the finance magnate nicknamed Schwamm who is the true power in the land. He puts in a brief appearance; his nickname ('sponge') is due to his ability to 'absorb' money (p. 14). In the past the old-established bankers were liquidated as Jews; today the 'Aryanisation' process consists of financial takeovers.

The principal women in *Fürsorgliche Belagerung*, Sabine Fischer and Käte Tolm, resembled the homely, motherly figures of Böll's earlier novels; those of *Frauen vor Flußlandschaft* are more akin to the emancipated women of *Die verlorene Ehre der Katharina Blum*. Erika Wubler is more strong-willed than her husband Hermann; she is the one who breaks with the past (in the familiar manner of Böll's novels), refusing to attend the mass for Erftler-Blum, rejecting the role of 'picture-book democrat' (p. 46). Elisabeth Blaukrämer falls out with her husband when she refuses to accept that the Nazi past is over. Eva Plint has left Karl von Kreyl and is now living with Ernst Grobsch; she refuses to put up with disparaging comments on his social origins, but she has dreams of an idealised Cuba to which she would like to emigrate — Cuba and Nicaragua are leitmotivs of the novel. All of these women are sexually emancipated, ready to make advances to men they find attractive, repulsing the advances of men who regard them as 'fair game'. The most progressive character is Katharina Richter, now living with Karl, working as a waitress and domestic servant in order to finance her university course in economics; she is writing a doctoral dissertation on 'Profit maximisation in the Third World' (p. 48). Her analyses of society are rational and clear-sighted.

The importance of women in the novel is underlined by the title. An alternative might have been 'Ghosts' — it is a novel written entirely in dialogue or monologue like a play, and as in Ibsen's drama the unravelling of the past forms an important part of the plot. The principal ghost from the past is Plietsch, one of Hitler's youngest generals, known as the 'bloodhound' (p. 164), whose voice made everyone tremble as it drove men to their deaths; the character is probably modelled on Ferdinand Schörner, whose nickname was 'the bloodhound' (FT, p. 110), although Schörner indubitably died in 1973 at the age of eighty-one. He now calls himself Plonius and has been rehabilitated. Two women commit suicide when they recognise him and nobody will accept their word. Erika Wubler has seen him too and is not allowed to speak his name aloud. But Plietsch is only one of the many ghosts from the past which frequent this society. Plukanski is toppled from his ministerial post when he is found to have done business selling German weapons to Polish partisans during the war. The memory of the gold from the teeth of those murdered in the extermination camps haunted Krengel's wife until she too committed suicide. Karl's mother drowned herself in the Rhine, pursued by faces from the past. Chundt has documents on Blaukrämer's past when he was in charge of a machine-gun unit. The Klossow documents and the Plottger documents have been destroyed: presumably they contained incriminating evidence on similar war crimes. There is a derelict property on the Rhine belonging to the New York descendant of a murdered Jew; all attempts to buy it for whatever price fail: it is to remain a 'monument of shame' ('Denkmal der Schande') (pp. 108ff.).

Clearly *Frauen vor Flußlandschaft* contains many of the ingredients of the cheap novelette: former Nazis appearing in unexpected places, scandals being hushed up, numerous suicides. Karl von Kreyl is being employed by the West German Secret Service to steal the Mercedes stars from cars belonging to prominent diplomats and bankers for a Soviet diplomat whose passion is collecting these objects; the diplomat will then be blackmailed into betraying secrets to the Federal Government. The story is peopled with counts and bastards. The characters are peculiarly flat; their speeches do not so much reveal their personalities as inform the reader on the state of the world — there is something of the baroque *Staatsaktion* about this novel. Katharina, for example, delivers an uninterrupted six-page speech in the presence of three other persons — she even uses the words 'So now we have been banished from court' ('Nun sind wir also vom Hofe verbannt') (p. 203), referring to her dismissal from Blaukrämer's service for boxing Schwamm's ears. Böll is, not for the first time, careless with the arrangement of the story: it is difficult to reconstruct plausibly the chronological sequence of events so as to include the concert at Kapspeter's house, the demolition of his piano, the mass for Erftler-Blum, the deaths of Plukanski and Elisabeth, Blaukrämer's reception and the resignation of Heulbuck within the space of forty-eight hours. Like *Fürsorgliche Belagerung* it has elements of the thriller. The opening chapter confronts the reader with various puzzles. Who are the three people whose names must not be spoken aloud? Who is Bingerle and why has he been imprisoned? What are or were the 'Klossow documents', which were sent to the bottom of a lake fifteen years previously? Who is the mysterious person who has been breaking into the homes of bankers and carefully dismantling their grand pianos? Most of these questions remain unanswered at the end of the novel. Böll was concerned more with the atmosphere of suspicion, intrigue, guilty secrets — the legacy of the West German political failure to come to terms with the Nazi past, his oldest theme. The events described may seem implausible, but when compared with the daily revelations of scandals that were taking place in West Germany at the time they cannot be dismissed. Böll was suggesting that the Federal Republic was an implausible place. As one of his characters puts it: 'truth always sounds implausible, truth is true colportage' ('das Wahre klingt immer unglaubhaft, das Wahre ist die wahre Kolportage') (FF, p. 184).

Böll's second play *Aussatz* already contained elements of 'colportage' — an East German agent, the hushing up of scandals. Böll defended his use of these elements in an interview: 'I sometimes have the impression that reality consists of clichés' ('Ich habe

218

manchmal den Eindruck, daß die Wirklichkeit aus Klischees besteht'). He had chosen the drama form in preference to narrative
because in prose the subject would have become 'too much like
colportage' ('zu kolportagehaft') (Rischbieter, pp. 67, 66). The
stage was appropriate for 'staginess'. This may explain the form of
Frauen vor Flußlandschaft, which is written entirely in dialogue or
monologue. Apart from its length it is outwardly indistinguishable
from the text for a stage play. Long sections of dialogue are a feature
of some of Böll's earlier works. In *Fürsorgliche Belagerung* they are
occasionally so extensive that Böll himself was not always sure who
was speaking (Reid, 1983, p. 138). In his last novel, since the
characters know more than the reader but are not always allowed to
say what they know, Böll's use of the dialogue form contributes to
the atmosphere of suspense and melodrama, which is his novel's key
characteristic. In *Fürsorgliche Belagerung* he made extensive use of
internal focalisation, which in places amounted to a kind of interior
monologue. In *Frauen vor Flußlandschaft* he went one step further. It
was Henry James who enjoined novelists to 'Dramatise, dramatise',
and in his wake the modernist novel aspired to mimesis, showing,
rather than telling in the manner of Dickens or Thackeray (Rimmon-
Kenan, 1983, p. 107). In *Frauen vor Flußlandschaft* the 'narrator' confines himself to setting the scene, describing the appearance of the
characters and their movements. It is possible to detect an attitude
behind his remarks, in the very slight irony with which he describes
Chundt and Kreyl for example. But otherwise Böll has to resort to
monologue, as when Grobsch reveals the truth about Plukanski, the
politician for whom he had to write a dishonest electoral pamphlet.
Böll's last novel is thus as experimental as anything he wrote: a
modernist, 'dramatic' novel, a parody of the cheap novelette, an
elegy on contemporary Germany.

There is one further aspect which makes *Frauen vor Flußlandschaft* a
particularly fitting conclusion to Böll's *oeuvre*. His first independent
publication, *Der Zug war pünktlich*, contained a scene in a brothel
where Andreas and Olina, shedding copious tears, played the piano
to one another, Schubert, Bach, Beethoven. At the end of *Frauen vor
Flußlandschaft* Karl von Kreyl sits down at the piano and plays the
beginning of a Beethoven sonata. But a central motif of this last
novel is the *dismantling* of concert pianos, those with classical associations, pianos which Beethoven or Mozart or Wagner played on. It
began with Karl von Kreyl, who destroyed his own piano on hearing
that his friend Konrad Fluh had been shot by police when on his
way to negotiate with terrorists for the life of 'Number 1'. Since then
three further instruments have been destroyed, each belonging to a

rich banker, each time at night and each has been carefully dismantled and left in a neat pile on the floor. Suspicion falls on Karl himself, but we probably can take his word when he denies responsibility. It is more likely to have been Grobsch, who has nightmares in which he shouts out 'Beethoven doesn't belong to them. Must they take over everything, everything — even Beethoven?' ('Beethoven gehört denen nicht. Soll ihnen denn alles, alles gehören — auch noch Beethoven?') (FF, pp. 118). Grobsch has the sobriquet 'the prole'; he is more genuinely proletarian than Leni Gruyten was. He weeps when he hears Beethoven — like Andreas and Olina. The cultural heritage is one of the many features of West German society that has been taken over by capital. The act of destroying pianos is a form of protest, foreshadowed when Hermann Wubler came back from the war and felt like destroying all the towns and churches that had remained intact — pianos too. It is therefore another manifestation of art itself, the avant-garde, the 'happening', like setting fire to a military jeep in *Ende einer Dienstfahrt*. But the dilemma of the avant-garde remains, as in *Dienstfahrt*, as in *Katharina Blum*. For it is at once taken over by the very cultural establishment at which it is protesting. The banker Krengel asks Karl to demolish his piano in front of an invited audience, as 'an act of the highest spirituality, a kind of protest against the illusions of music, against luxury, hunger, thirst, against war and all manner of misery and all forms of materialism' ('ein Akt höchster Spiritualität, eine Art himmlischen Protest gegen die Täuschungen der Musik, gegen den Luxus, den Hunger, den Durst, gegen Krieg und jegliches Elend und jegliche Form von Materialismus') (p. 191). Krengel is not simply a buffoon; Katharina regards bankers as more sensitive than politicians, and Karl sees tragedy in the fact that they really love art, the art which they debase with their wealth. There is a final twist, when Krengel's bank is taken over and the 'happening' cancelled. His are the last words of the novel: 'In the beginning . . . there was much lead, in the end there shall be lead. That corresponds to my leaden existence' ('Am Anfang . . . war viel Blei, am Ende soll Blei sein. Das entspricht meinem bleiernen Dasein') (p. 254). His 'leaden existence' is probably an allusion to a poem by Böll's favourite poet, Friedrich Hölderlin, 'Der Gang aufs Land', in which the poet refers to the 'leaden age' ('bleierne Zeit'), a phrase which gave the title to Margarethe von Trotta's 1981 film on German terrorism.

Frauen vor Flußlandschaft is prefaced by two stanzas of a poem, not by Hölderlin, however, but by Goethe. It stands not only as an epigraph to the novel but as an epitaph to the novelist himself:

Wanderers Gemütsruhe

Übers Niederträchtige
Niemand sich beklage;
Denn es ist das Mächtige,
Was man dir auch sage.

In dem Schlechten waltet es
Sich zu Hochgewinne,
Und mit Rechtem schaltet es
Ganz nach seinem Sinne.

(**Traveller's Serenity**. Let no one complain about malice; for whatever they tell you, it is the real power in the land. It rules amid evil to its own great advantage, and it manipulates the law just as it pleases.)

The poem is from the *Buch des Unmuts* (Book of ill-humour) in Goethe's *Westöstlicher Divan*, and is one of those in which Goethe struck back at his critics, the Matthias Waldens, the Georg Ramsegers, the Marcel Reich-Ranickis of his day. It has a third stanza, which Böll did not quote:

> Wandrer! — Gegen solche Not
> Wolltest du dich sträuben?
> Wirbelwind und trocknen Kot,
> Laß sie drehn und stäuben.

(Traveller! Did you really wish to oppose such calamity? Leave them to it, whirling the whirlwind and scattering the dry dung.)

Böll's Goethe was not the Olympian Goethe, the poet aloof from the petty preoccupations of his time. Böll was one who did 'oppose' the 'malice' and the 'evil' of his time.

In this study I have deliberately concentrated on Böll's 'contemporaneity'. This is how he believed writers should be read (Hoven, 1985). Critics may ask how much of his works will survive. One answer might be that they will survive as long as the issues with which they deal continue to be of interest, and I hope that this book may have contributed in some small way to the understanding of these issues. Again and again critics have dismissed Böll as *passé*. The reading public has never agreed; within a few days of his death his books had practically sold out. This may of course have to do with the more archetypal themes of his works which he outlined in his Frankfurt lectures: love, home, breaking bread. To deal with these would, however, require a quite different book.

Bibliography

I. Works by Böll

Editions and codes used

Werke. Romane und Erzählungen, Bernd Balzer (ed.), 5 vols., Cologne, n.d. [1977] (R 1–5)

Werke. Essayistische Schriften und Reden, Bernd Balzer (ed.), 3 vols., Cologne, n.d. [1978] (E 1–3)

Werke. Hörspiele, Theaterstücke, Drehbücher, Gedichte I, Bernd Balzer (ed.), Cologne, n.d. [1978] (H)

Werke, Interviews I, Bernd Balzer (ed.), Cologne, n.d. [1978] (I)

Querschnitte. Aus Interviews, Aufsätzen und Reden von Heinrich Böll, Viktor Böll and Renate Matthaei (eds.), Cologne 1977 (Q)

Mein Lesebuch Frankfurt on Main, 1978 (ML)

Fürsorgliche Belagerung, Roman, Cologne, 1979 (FB)

Was soll aus dem Jungen bloß werden? Oder: Irgendwas mit Büchern, Bornheim, 1981 (J)

Vermintes Gelände. Essayistische Schriften 1977–1981, Cologne, 1982 (VG)

Das Vermächtnis, Erzählung, Munich, 1984 (VM)

Die Verwundung und andere frühe Erzählungen, Bornheim-Merten, 1983 (VW)

Ein- und Zusprüche. Schriften, Reden und Prosa 1981–1983, Cologne, 1984 (EZ)

Bild Bonn Boenisch, Bornheim-Merten, 1984

Frauen vor Flußlandschaft. Roman in Dialogen und Selbstgesprächen, Cologne, 1985 (FF)

Die Fähigkeit zu trauern. Schriften und Reden 1983–1985, Bornheim-Merten, 1986 (FT)

Codes for conversations and interviews not included in the collected works

Bauer = Alexander Bauer, ' "Die Terroristen sind nicht die Kinder Hitlers . . ." Dialog mit dem deutschen Literatur-Nobelpreisträger Heinrich Böll', in *AION. Sezione Germanica, Studi Tedeschi*, 20, 1977, no. 3, pp. 109–16

Courts = Gert Courts, 'Meine Heldin soll kein Image haben. Publik-Gespräch mit Heinrich Böll anläßlich seines neuen Romans "Gruppenbild mit Dame" ', in *Publik*, 13.8.1971, p. 27

Bibliography

Hoven = 'Die Lust am Lesen. Literatur im Unterricht: Wie Heinrich Böll darüber dachte', in *Die Zeit*, 18.10.1985, p. 49

Kesting = '"Ich bin kein Repräsentant!" Heinrich Böll im Gespräch mit Hanjo Kesting', in *die horen*, 25, 1980, no. 120, pp. 67–85

Kopelew/Vormweg = Heinrich Böll / Lew Kopelew / Heinrich Vormweg, *Antikommunismus in Ost und West. Zwei Gespräche*, Munich, 1984

Lenz = '"Ich habe nichts über den Krieg aufgeschrieben". Ein Gespräch mit Heinrich Böll und Hermann Lenz', in *Literaturmagazin 7. Nachkriegsliteratur*, Reinbek, 1977, pp. 30–74

Limagne = '"Glauben Sie an die Sünde?" Ein Gespräch mit Joseph Limagne', in Franz Sutter (ed.), *Das Tintenfaß, Magazin für Literatur und Kunst*, no. 8, Zurich, 1983

Limberg = Margaret Limberg, '"Es stirbt täglich Freiheit weg". Das letzte groß, Interview mit Heinrich Böll', in *Die Zeit*, 26.7.1985, pp. 9–10

Lodemann = 'Heinrich Böll: Kein Märchen', in *Die Zeit*, 9.3.1979, p. 64

Raddatz = Heinrich Böll, "Wehrkraftzersetzung"', in *Die Zeit*, 2.3.1984, p. 43

Riese = Heinrich Böll / Hans-Peter Riese, 'Schriftsteller in dieser Republik. Gespräch über Selbstverständlichkeiten', in *L' 76*, no. 6, 1977, pp. 5–37

Rischbieter = Henning Rischbieter, 'Gespräch mit Heinrich Böll über sein neues Stück "Aussatz"', in *Theater 1969*, Velber, 1969, pp. 66–8

Selbstinterview = 'Geduld und Ungeduld mit der deutschen Sprache', in *Welt der Literatur*, 2, 1965, p. 601

Vonnegut = 'Heinrich Böll and Kurt Vonnegut: In Conversation: "We were all Nazis in a way"', in *The Listener*, 4.7.1985, pp. 16–17

Vormweg = Heinrich Böll / Heinrich Vormweg, *Weil die Stadt so fremd geworden ist . . . Gespräche*, Bornheim-Merten, 1985

Wallmann = '"Der Autor is immer noch versteckt". Jürgen P. Wallmann im Gespräch mit Heinrich Böll', in *die horen*, 27, 1982, no. 126, pp. 127–35

Later poems and their date and place of publication

'Für Hans Werner Richter (und Toni natürlich)', 1979, and 'Für Walter Warnach zum 70. Geburtstag', in Heinrich Böll / Klaus Staeck, *Gedichte Collagen*, Munich, 1981

'Für Beuys zum 60.', in *Die Zeit*, 8.5.1981, p. 38

'Für Alexander S. zum 65. Geburtstag', ibid., 16.12.1983, p. 45

'Für Peter-Jürgen Boock', ibid., 13.7.1984, p. 35

'Für Samay', in *L'80*, no. 36, December, 1985, p. 19

Major translations of Böll's works in English

(*Note*: in most cases American and English editions came out in the same year)

Bibliography

The Train was on Time (*Der Zug war pünktlich*), tr. Leila Vennewitz, London, 1973

Traveller, If You Come to Spa (*Wanderer, kommst du nach Spa . . .*), tr. Mervyn Savill, London, 1956

Children are Civilians too (*Auch Kinder sind Zivilisten* and other stories), tr. Leila Vennewitz, London, 1973

And Where Were You, Adam? (*Wo warst du, Adam?*), tr. Leila Vennewitz, London, 1974

And Never Said a Word (*Und sagte kein einziges Wort*), tr. Leila Vennewitz, London, 1978

The Unguarded House (*Haus ohne Hüter*), tr. Mervyn Savill, London, 1957

The Bread of Those Early Years (*Das Brot der frühen Jahre*), tr. Leila Vennewitz, London, 1976

Irish Journal (*Irisches Tagebuch*), tr. Leila Vennewitz, New York, 1967

Billiards at Half Past Nine (*Billard um halbzehn*), tr. Patrick Bowles, London, 1961

The Clown (*Ansichten eines Clowns*), tr. Leila Vennewitz, London, 1965

Absent Without Leave and Other Stories (*Entfernung von der Truppe, Als der Krieg ausbrach, Als der Krieg zu Ende war*, and 18 other stories), tr. Leila Vennewitz, London, 1967

The End of a Mission (*Ende einer Dienstfahrt*), tr. Leila Vennewitz, London, 1968

Group Portrait with Lady (*Gruppenbild mit Dame*), tr. Leila Vennewitz, London, 1973

The Lost Honour of Katharina Blum, or, How Violence Develops and Where it can Lead (*Die verlorene Ehre der Katharina Blum*), tr. Leila Vennewitz (London 1975)

Missing Persons and Other Essays, tr. Leila Vennewitz, London, 1977

The Safety-Net (*Fürsorgliche Belagerung*), tr. Leila Vennewitz, London, 1982

What's to Become of the Boy?, or, Something to do with Books (*Was soll aus dem Jungen bloß werden?*), tr. Leila Vennewitz, London, 1984

A Soldier's Legacy (*Das Vermächtnis*), tr. Leila Vennewitz, London, 1985

The Casualty (*Die Verwundung*), tr. Leila Vennewitz, London, 1986

II. Secondary Sources

The following does little more than list those works cited in the text; for a more exhaustive bibliography of works on Böll the reader is referred to Lengning (1972 and later), Beth (1980) and Schröter (1982).

Adorno, Theodor W. (1954), 'Standort des Erzählers im zeitgenössischen Roman', in *Noten zur Literatur*, Frankfurt on Main, 1958, pp. 61–72

Amery, Carl (1963), *Die Kapitulation oder Deutscher Katholizismus heute*, Reinbek, 1963

Andersch, Alfred(1951), 'Christus gibt keinen Urlaub', in *Frankfurter Hefte*, 6, 1951, pp. 939–41

—— (1976), 'Es gibt keine Kulturdebatte oder Allenthalben fassungsloses Entsetzen. Ein Gedicht macht sich selbständig — Eine Diskussion in Dokumenten und Fußnoten', in *Das Tintenfaß*, 12, 1976, no. 26, pp. 265–97

anon. (1959), 'Böll. Die Turnlehrertheologie', in *Der Spiegel*, 13, 1959, no. 19, pp. 52–4

—— (1961), 'Böll. Brot und Boden', ibid. 15, 1961, no. 50, pp. 71–86

—— (1979), 'Katastrophal mißglückt', ibid., 13.8.1979, p. 137

—— (1979), '"Eine glatte Fünf für Marcel Reich-Ranicki". Rezension der Rezensionen des neuen Böll-Romans', in *Die Neue*, 4.9.1979

Arntzen, Helmut (ed.) (1964), *Gegen-Zeitung. Deutsche Satire des 20. Jahrhunderts*, Heidelberg, 1964

Barzel, Rainer (1959), *Rettet die Freiheit. Gründungskongress am 20.2.1959 in Köln*, chairman of the committee "Rettet die Freiheit" (ed.) (n.p., n.d.)

Baudelaire, Charles (1863), 'Le peintre de la vie moderne', in *Oeuvres complètes*, Y.-G. Le Dantec (ed.), Paris, 1954, pp. 881–920

Bauer, Arnold (1952), 'Der restaurative Stil', in *Die Literatur*, 1, 1952, no. 1

Baum, Georgina (1959), *Humor und Satire in der bürgerlichen Ästhetik*, Berlin/GDR, 1959

Baumgart, Reinhard (1971), 'Potpourri und Inventur. Über Heinrich Böll "Gruppenbild mit Dame"', in *Der Spiegel*, 2.8.1971, p. 104

Becker, Jillian (1977), *Hitler's Children. The Story of the Baader–Meinhof Gang*, London, 1977

Becker, Jürgen, and Wolf Vostell (eds.), (1965), *Happenings, Fluxus Pop Art Nouveau Réalisme, Eine Dokumentation*, Reinbek, 1965

Benn, Gottfried (1934), 'Lebensweg eines Intellektualisten', in *Gesammelte Werke*, Dieter Wellershoff (ed.), vol. 8, Wiesbaden, 1968, pp. 1885–1934

—— (1980), *Briefe an F.W. Oelze 1950–1956*, Wiesbaden, 1980

Bering, Dietz (1978), *Die Intellektuellen. Geschichte eines Schimpfwortes*, Stuttgart, 1978

Bernhard, Hans Joachim (1970), *Die Romane Heinrich Bölls. Gesellschaftskritik und Gemeinschaftsutopie*, Berlin/GDR, 1970

—— (1972), 'Der Clown als "Verf."', in *Neue deutsche Literatur*, 20, 1972, no. 4, pp. 157–64

—— (1977), 'Positionen und Tendenzen in der Literatur der BRD Mitte der siebziger Jahre', in *Weimarer Beiträge*, 23, 1977, no. 12, pp. 53–84

Bertermann, Hanne-Christa (1958), *Heinrich Böll. Ein Bücherverzeichnis*, Dortmund, 1958

Beth, Hanno (ed.) (1980), *Heinrich Böll. Eine Einführung in das Gesamtwerk in Einzelinterpretationen*, 2nd edn., Königstein/Ts, 1980

Böll, Alfred (1981), *Bilder einer deutschen Familie. Die Bölls*, Bergisch Gladbach, 1981

Bräunig, Werner (1965), 'Rummelplatz', in *Neue deutsche Literatur*, 13, 1965, no. 10, pp. 7–29

Brecht, Bertolt (1930), 'Das moderne Theater ist das epische Theater. Anmerkungen zur Oper *Aufstieg und Fall der Stadt Mahagonny*', in *Schriften zum Theater, Über eine nicht-aristotelische Dramatik*', Frankfurt on Main, 1957, pp. 13–28

—— (1961), *Flüchtlingsgespräche*, Frankfurt on Main, 1961

Brückner, Christine (1954), *Ehe die Spuren verwehen. Roman*, Gütersloh, 1954

Büchner, Georg (1833), *Sämtliche Werke und Briefe*, Werner R. Lehmann (ed.), vol. 2, Hamburg, 1971

Conard, Robert C. (1969), 'Two Novels about Outsiders: The Kinship of J. D. Salinger's *The Catcher in the Rye* with Heinrich Böll's *Ansichten eines Clowns*', in *University of Dayton Review*, 5, 1969, no. 3, pp. 23–7

—— (1981), *Heinrich Böll*, Boston, 1981

Coupe, W. A. (1964), 'Heinrich Böll's *Und sagte kein einziges Wort* — An Analysis', in *German Life and Letters*, 17, 1963/4, pp. 238–49

Dahrendorf, Ralf (1965), *Gesellschaft und Demokratie in Deutschland*, Munich, 1965

Delius, Friedrich Christian (1981), *Ein Held der inneren Sicherheit. Roman*, Reinbek, 1981

Doderer, Klaus (1953), *Die Kurzgeschichte in Deutschland, ihre Form und ihre Entwicklung*, Wiesbaden, 1953

Drews, Jörg (ed.) (1980), *Vom "Kahlschlag" zu "movens". Über das langsame Auftauchen experimenteller Schreibweisen in der westdeutschen Literatur der fünfziger Jahre*, Munich, 1980

Durzak, Manfred (1971), *Der deutsche Roman der Gegenwart*, Stuttgart, 1971

—— (1972), 'Heinrich Bölls epische Summe? Zur Analyse und Wirkung seines Romans "Gruppenbild mit Dame"'', in *Basis*, 3, 1972, pp. 174–97

Endres, Elisabeth (1980), *Die Literatur der Adenauerzeit*, Munich, 1980

Engelmann, Bernd (1978), 'Die Kontaktsperre des Peter Paul Zahl', in Freimut Duve et al. (eds.), *Briefe zur Verteidigung der bürgerlichen Freiheit*, Reinbek 1978, pp. 72–8

Enzensberger, Hans Magnus (1962), 'Poesie und Politik', in *Einzelheiten II*, Frankfurt on Main, n.d., pp. 113–37

—— (1968), 'Gemeinplätze, die Neueste Literatur betreffend', in *Kursbuch* no. 15, 1968, pp. 187–97

Frank, Joseph (1958), 'Spatial form in modern literature', in Mark Shorer, Josephine Miles, Gordon McKenzie (eds.), *Criticism. The Foundations of Modern Literary Judgment*, New York, 1958, pp. 379–92

Friedrich, Hugo (1956), *Die Struktur der modernen Lyrik. Von Baudelaire bis zur Gegenwart*, Hamburg, 1956

Giles, Steve (1984), 'Narrative transmission in Böll's *Die verlorene Ehre der Katharina Blum*', in *Modern Languages*, 65, 1984, pp. 157–63

Grass, Günter (1968), 'Uber Ja und Nein', in *Die Zeit*, 20.12.1968, pp. 22–3

Bibliography

Grenzmann, Wilhelm (1953), *Deutsche Dichtung der Gegenwart*, Frankfurt on Main, 1953

Grosser, Alfred (1974), *Geschichte Deutschlands seit 1945. Eine Bilanz*, Munich, 1974

Grützbach, Frank (ed.) (1972), *Heinrich Böll: Freies Geleit für Ulrike Meinhof. Ein Artikel und seine Folgen*, Cologne, 1972

Habe, Hans (1974), 'Requiem auf Heinrich Böll', in Heinrich Böll, *Die verlorene Ehre der Katharina Böll. Mit Materialien und einem Nachwort des Autors*, Cologne, 1984, pp. 251–8

Hage, Volker (ed.) (1980), *Lyrik für Leser. Deutsche Gedichte der siebziger Jahre*, Stuttgart, 1980

Hagelstange, Rudolf (1963), *Die Puppen in der Puppe. Eine Rußlandreise*, Munich, 1965

Heise, Wolfgang (1964), 'Hegel und das Komische', in *Sinn und Form*, 16 1964, pp. 811–30

Heißenbüttel, Helmut (1971), 'Wie man dokumentarisch erzählen kann. Zwei Stimmen zu Heinrich Bölls neuem Roman', in *Merkur*, 25, 1971, pp. 911–14

—— (1980), 'Erzählung von einem sentimentalen Wirrkopf und Trottel? Heinrich Bölls *Fürsorgliche Belagerung*', in *Freibeuter*, no. 4, 1980, pp. 157–61

Hermand, Jost (1982), 'Unbewältigte Vergangenheit. Westdeutsche Utopien nach 1945', in Jost Hermand et al. (eds.), *Nachkriegsliteratur in Westdeutschland 1945–49. Schreibweisen, Gattungen, Institutionen*, West Berlin, 1982, pp. 102–28

Hillgruber, Andreas (1978), *Deutsche Geschichte 1945–1975. Die 'deutsche Frage' in der Weltpolitik*, Frankfurt on Main, 1978

Hinderer, Walter (1971), 'Zur Situation der westdeutschen Literaturkritik', in Manfred Durzak (ed.), *Die deutsche Literatur der Gegenwart. Aspekte und Tendenzen*, Stuttgart, 1971, pp. 300–21

Hofer, Walther (ed.) (1957), *Der Nationalsozialismus. Dokumente 1933–1945*, Frankfurt on Main, 1957

Hoffmann, Leopold (1973), *Heinrich Böll. Einführung in Leben und Werk*, 2nd edn., Luxemburg, 1973

Hofstätter, Peter (1978), 'Wie Gewalt entsteht und wohin sie führen kann', in Heiner Geissler (ed.), *Der Weg in die Gewalt. Geistige und gesellschaftliche Ursachen des Terrorismus und seine Folgen*, 2nd edn., Munich, 1978, pp. 163–74

Hohoff, Curt (1957), 'Der Erzähler Heinrich Böll', in *Merkur*, 11, 1957, pp. 1208–10

Hüttel, Martin (1981), 'Böll in der Sowjetunion', in *L'80*, no. 18, May 1981, pp. 98–107

[Inter Nationes] (1985), *Heinrich Böll. On his Death*, Bonn, 1985

Jansen, Peter (1984), *The New German Film*, Munich, 1984

Janssen, Werner (1985), *Der Rhythmus des Humanen bei Heinrich Böll. ". . . die Suche nach einer bewohnbaren Sprache in einem bewohnbaren Land"*, Frankfurt on Main, 1985

Jens, Walter (1961), *Deutsche Literatur der Gegenwart. Themen, Stile, Tendenzen*, Munich, 1961

—— (1962), *Statt einer Literaturgeschichte*, 5th edn., Pfullingen, 1962.

—— (1974), review of *Die verlorene Ehre der Katharina Blum*, in Heinrich Böll, *Die verlorene Ehre der Katharina Böll. Mit Materialen und einem Nachwort des Autors*, Cologne, 1984, pp. 243–50

Jeziorkowski, Klaus (1968), *Rhythmus und Figur. Zur Technik der epischen Konstruktion in Heinrich Bölls "Der Wegwerfer" und "Billard um halbzehn"*, Bad Homburg, 1968

Jünger, Ernst, (1920), *In Stahlgewittern*, 21st edn., Berlin, 1941

—— (1922), *Der Kampf als inneres Erlebnis*, in *Werke*, vol. 5, Stuttgart, 1960

—— (1949), *Strahlungen*, Tübingen, 1949

Kaiser, Joachim (1971), 'Mitleidiger Naturalismus und mystische Vision', in *Süddeutsche Zeitung*, 31.7.1971

Kalow, Gert (1955), 'Heinrich Böll', in Hermann Friedmann and Otto Mann (eds.), *Christliche Dichter der Gegenwart. Beiträge zur europäischen Literatur*, Heidelberg, 1955, pp. 426–35

Kleinschmid, Harald (1979), '"Ein Weg ohne Ende". Zur Reaktion der DDR auf "Holocaust"', in *Deutschland Archiv*, 12, 1979, pp. 225–8

Kloss, Günther (1976), *West Germany. An Introduction*, London, 1976

Kogon, Eugen (1947), *Der SS-Staat*, Stockholm, 1947

Korn, Karl (1953), 'Eine Ehe in dieser Zeit', in *Frankfurter Allgemeine Zeitung*, 4.4.1953 (Literaturblatt)

Kreuzer, Helmut (1981), 'Neue Subjektivität. Zur Literatur der siebziger Jahre in der Bundesrepublik Deutschland', in Manfred Durzak (ed.), *Deutsche Gegenwartsliteratur. Ausgangspositionen und aktuelle Entwicklungen*, Stuttgart, 1981, pp. 77–106

Kröll, Friedhelm (1977), *Die "Gruppe 47", Soziale Lage und gesellschaftliches Bewußtsein literarischer Intelligenz in der Bundesrepublik*, Stuttgart, 1977

—— (1982), 'Literaturpreise nach 1945. Wegweiser in die Restauration', in Jost Hermand et al. (eds.), *Nachkriegsliteratur in Westdeutschland 1945–49. Schreibweisen, Gattungen, Institutionen*, West Berlin, 1982, pp. 143–64

Lehnardt, Eberhard (1984), *Urchristentum und Wohlstandsgesellschaft. Das Romanwerk Heinrich Bölls von "Haus ohne Hüter" bis "Gruppenbild mit Dame"*, Berne, 1984

Lengning, Werner (1972), *Der Schriftsteller Heinrich Böll. Ein biographisch-bibliographischer Abriß*, 3rd edn., Munich, 1972

Lettau, Reinhard (ed.) (1967), *Die Gruppe 47. Bericht. Kritik. Polemik. Ein Handbuch*, Neuwied, 1967

Linder, Christian (1986), *Heinrich Böll. Leben und Schreiben 1917 bis 1985*, Cologne, 1986

Lukács, Georg (1983), 'Es geht um den Realismus', in Hans-Jürgen Schmitt (ed.), *Die Expressionismusdebatte. Materialien zu einer marxistischen Realismuskonzeption*, Frankfurt on Main, 1973, pp. 192–230

Majut, Rudolf (1960), 'Der deutsche Roman vom Biedermeier bis zur

Gegenwart', in Wolfgang Stammler (ed.), *Deutsche Philologie im Aufriß*, 2nd edn., vol. 2, West Berlin, 1960, col. 1356–794

Mannzen, Walter (1952), 'Literarische Restauration — literarische Opposition', in *Die Literatur*, 1, 1952, no. 5

Martini, Fritz (1961), 'Heinrich Böll: "Billard um halbzehn"', in *Moderna Språk*, 55, 1961, no. 1, pp. 27–38

Matthaei, Renate (ed.) (1975), *Die subversive Madonna. Ein Schlüssel zum Werk Heinrich Bölls*, Cologne, 1975

Mayer, Hans (1967), *Zur deutschen Literatur der Zeit. Zusammenhänge, Schriftsteller, Bücher*, Reinbek, 1967

Michel, Karl Markus (1968), 'Ein Kranz für die Literatur. Fünf Variationen über eine These', in *Kursbuch*, no. 15, 1968, pp. 169–86

Mitscherlich, Alexander and Margarete (1967), *Die Unfähigkeit zu trauern. Grundlagen kollektiven Verhaltens*, Munich, 1967

Möhrmann, Renate (1981), 'Feministische Trends in der deutschen Gegenwartsliteratur', in Manfred Durzak (ed.), *Deutsche Gegenwartsliteratur. Ausgangspunkte und aktuelle Entwicklungen*, Stuttgart, 1981, pp. 336–58

Motekat, Helmut (1957), 'Gedanken zur Kurzgeschichte. Mit einer Interpretation der Kurzgeschichte "So ein Rummel" von Heinrich Böll', in *Der Deutschunterricht* (Stuttgart), 9, 1957, no. 1, pp. 20–35

Müller, Hans Dieter (1968), *Der Springen-Konzern. Eine kritische Studie*, Munich, 1968

Nägele, Rainer (1976 a), *Heinrich Böll. Einfuhrung in das Werk und in die Forschung*, Frankfurt on Main, 1976

—— (1976 b), 'Aspects of the Reception of Heinrich Böll', in *New German Critique*, 7, 1976, pp. 45–68

Neumann, Robert (1955), 'Mit fremden Federn II', in *Die Parodien. Gesamtausgabe*, Munich, 1962

O'Connor, Frank (1963), *The Lonely Voice. A Study of the Short Story*, Cleveland, 1963

Ohff, Heinz (1973), *Anti-Kunst*, Düsseldorf, 1973

Pache, Walter (1970), 'Funktion und Tradition des Ferngesprächs in Bölls *Ansichten eines Clowns*', in *Literatur in Wissenschaft und Unterricht*, 3, 1970, pp. 151–68

Peitsch, Helmut (1982), 'Politisierung der Literatur oder "geistige Freiheit"? Materialien zu den Literaturverhältnissen in den Westzonen', in Jost Hermand et al. (eds.), *Nachkriegsliteratur in Westdeutschland 1945–49. Schreibweisen, Gattungen, Institutionen*, West Berlin, 1982, pp. 165–207

——, and Hartmut Reith (1983), 'Keine "innere Emigration" in die "Gefilde der Literatur". Die literarisch-politische Publizistik der "Gruppe 47" zwischen 1947 und 1949', in Jost Hermand et al. (eds.), *Nachkriegsliteratur in Westdeutschland. 2: Autoren, Sprache, Traditionen*, West Berlin, 1983, pp. 129–62

Plard, Henri (1960), 'Böll le constructeur. Remarques sur "Billard um halbzehn"', in *Etudes germaniques*, 15, 1960, pp. 120–43

Bibliography

[Plenzdorf, Ulrich] (1973), 'Diskussion um Plenzdorf', in *Sinn und Form*, 25, 1973, pp. 219–52

Plievier, Theodor (1948), *Stalingrad. Roman*, Munich, 1958

Poser, Therese (1962), 'Heinrich Böll: Billard um halbzehn', in Rolf Geissler (ed.), *Möglichkeiten des modernen deutschen Romans. Analysen und Interpretationsgrundlagen*, Frankfurt on Main, 1962, pp. 232–55

Prodaniuk, Ihor (1979), *The Imagery in Heinrich Böll's Novels*, Bonn, 1979

Raddatz, Fritz J. (1978), 'Staatstreue — Untertanengeist oder Mut zur Kritik?', in Freimut Duve et al. (eds.), *Briefe zur Verteidigung der bürgerlichen Freiheit*, Reinbek, 1978, pp. 57–71

—— (1979), 'Vom Überwachungs-Staat', in *Die Zeit*, 3.8.1979, 'LITERATUR', p. 37

Reich-Ranicki, Marcel (1962), 'Hüben und drüben — Heinrich Böll', in *Die Zeit*, 1.6.1962, p. 13

—— (1963), *Deutsche Literatur in West und Ost, Prosa seit 1945*, Munich, 1963

—— (ed.) (1968), *In Sachen Böll. Ansichten und Aussichten*, Cologne, 1968

—— (1971), 'Nachdenken über Leni G.', in *Die Zeit*, 6.8.1971, pp. 13–14

—— (1979 a), *Entgegnung. Zur deutschen Literatur der siebziger Jahre*, Stuttgart, 1979

—— (1979 b), 'Nette Kapitalisten und nette Terroristen', in *Frankfurter Allgemeine Zeitung*, 4.8.1979

—— (1985), 'Dichter, Narr, Prediger', in *Frankfurter Allgemeine Zeitung*, 18.7.1985, p. 19

Reid, J. H. (1967), 'Time in the Works of Heinrich Böll', in *Modern Language Review*, 62, 1967, pp. 476–85

—— (1973), *Heinrich Böll. Withdrawal and Re-emergence*, London, 1973

—— (1974), 'Böll's Names', in *Modern Language Review*, 69, 1974, pp. 575–83

—— (1979), 'Back to the Billiards Table? — Heinrich Böll's *Fürsorgliche Belagerung*', in *Forum for Modern Language Studies*, 19, 1983, pp. 126–41

—— (1986), 'Heinrich Böll. From Modernism to Post-Modernism and beyond', in Keith Bullivant (ed.), *The Modern German Novel*, Leamington Spa and New York, 1987

Richter, Hans Werner (ed.) (1961), *Die Mauer oder Der 13. August*, Reinbek, 1961

—— (ed.) (1962), *Almanach der Gruppe 47 1947–1962*, Reinbek, 1962

—— (1986), *Im Etablissement der Schmetterlinge. Einundzwanzig Portraits aus der Gruppe 47*, Munich, 1986

Rimmon-Kenan, Shlomith (1983), *Narrative Fiction: Contemporary Poetics*, London, 1983

Roberts, David (1982), 'Tendenzwenden. Die sechziger und siebziger Jahre in literaturgeschichtlicher Perspektive', in *Deutsche Vierteljahresschrift für Literaturwissenschaft und Geistesgeschichte*, 56, 1982, pp. 290–313

Röhl, Klaus Rainer (1971), 'Mutmaßungen über die Blechjahre. Haben Johnson und Grass mitgeschrieben?', in *Konkret*, 12.8.1971

Sandford, John (1976), *The Mass Media of the German-speaking Countries*,

London, 1976

—— (1986), 'The New Peace Movement in West Germany', in Moray McGowan and Malcolm Pender (eds.), *Contemporary German Studies*, no. 2, Glasgow, 1986, pp. 18–33

Schäfer, Hans Dieter (1981), *Das gespaltene Bewußtsein. Deutsche Kultur und Lebenswirklichkeit 1933–1945*, Munich, 1981

Schäfermeyer, Michael (1984), *Thomas Mann: Die Biographie des Adrian Leverkühn und der Roman "Doktor Faustus"*, Frankfurt on Main, 1984

Schelsky, Helmut (1975), *Die Arbeit tun die anderen. Klassenkampf und Priesterherrschaft der Intellektuellen*, Munich, 1977

Scherpe, Klaus R. (1982), 'Erzwungener Alltag. Wahrgenommene und gedachte Wirklichkeit in der Reportageliteratur der Nachkriegszeit', in Jost Hermand et al. (eds.), *Nachkriegsliteratur in Westdeutschland 1945–49. Schreibweisen, Gattungen, Institutionen*, West Berlin, 1982, pp. 35–102

Schonauer, Franz (1961), *Deutsche Literatur im Dritten Reich. Versuch einer Darstellung in polemisch-didaktischer Absicht*, Olten, 1961

—— (1977), 'Sieburg & Co. Rückblick auf eine sogenannte konservative Literaturkritik', in Nicolas Born and Jürgen Manthey (eds.), *Literaturmagazin 7. Nachkriegsliteratur*, Reinbek, 1977

Schröter, Klaus (1982), *Heinrich Böll mit Selbstzeugnissen und Bilddokumenten*, Reinbek, 1982

Schütte, Wolfram (1979), 'Lauter nette Menschen', *Frankfurter Rundschau*, 4.8.1979

Schwab-Felisch, Hans (ed.) (1962), *Der Ruf. Eine deutsche Nachkriegszeitschrift*, Munich, 1962

—— (1971), 'Wie man dokumentarisch erzählen kann. Zwei Stimmen zu Heinrich Bölls neuem Roman', in *Merkur*, 25, 1971, pp. 914–16

Schwarz, Wilhelm Johannes (1967), *Der Erzähler Heinrich Böll. Seine Werke und Gestalten*, Berne, 1967

Stresau, Hermann (1964), *Heinrich Böll*, West Berlin, 1964

Ulshöfer, Robert (1958), 'Unterrichtliche Probleme bei der Arbeit mit der Kurzgeschichte', in *Der Deutschunterricht* (Stuttgart), 10, 1958, no. 6, pp. 5–35

Unseld, Siegfried (1955), 'An diesem Dienstag. Unvorgreifliche Gedanken über die Kurzgeschichte', in *Akzente*, 2, 1955, pp. 139–48

Vogt, Jochen (1978), *Heinrich Böll*, Munich, 1978

Vormweg, Heinrich (1980), 'Entlarvende Belagerung', in *Merkur*, 34, 1980, pp. 84–7

Wagenbach, Klaus (ed.) (1979), *Vaterland, Muttersprache. Deutsche Schriftsteller und ihr Staat von 1945 bis heute*, West Berlin, 1979

Wagner, Richard (1848), *Die Musikdramen*, Munich, 1978

Waidson, H. M. (1959), *The Modern German Novel. A Mid-Twentieth-Century Survey*, London, 1959

Walser, Martin (ed.) (1961), *Die Alternative oder Brauchen wir eine neue Regierung*, Reinbek, 1961

Bibliography

Watt, Roderick (1985), '"Wanderer, kommst du nach Sparta": History through Propaganda into Literary Commonplace', in *Modern Language Review*, 80, 1985, pp. 871–83

Weninger, Heinz (1952), 'Warum denn immer noch Trümmerliteratur', in *Die Literatur*, 1, 1952, no. 11, p. 7

Widmer, Urs (1966), *1945 oder die "Neue Sprache". Studien zur Prosa der jungen Generation*, Düsseldorf, 1966

Wiegenstein, Roland H. (1953), review of *Und sagte kein einziges Wort*, in *Frankfurter Hefte*, 8, 1953, pp. 474–6

Wildermuth, Rosemarie (ed.) (1978), *Heute — und die 30 Jahre davor*, Munich, 1978

Wirth, Günter (1968), *Heinrich Böll. Essayistische Studie über religiöse und gesellschaftliche Motive im Prosawerk des Dichters*, Cologne, 1969

—— (1972), 'Tradition "Im Futteral". Bemerkungen über Böll und Stifter', in *Sinn und Form*, 24, 1972, pp. 1018–41

Witte, Bernd (1983), 'Schmerzton. Ingeborg Bachmann. Perspektiven einer feministischen Literatur', in *die horen*, 28, 1983, no. 4, pp. 76–82

Wölfel, Kurt (1960), 'Epische Welt und satirische Welt. Zur Technik des satirischen Erzählens', in *Wirkendes Wort*, 10, 1960, no. 2, pp. 85–98

Zehm, Günter (1974), 'Heinrich der Grätige. Macht Bölls neue Erzählung Stimmung für ein restriktives Pressegesetz?', in *Die Welt*, 16.8.1974

Ziltener, Walter (1980), *Die Literaturtheorie Heinrich Bölls*, Berne, 1980

Ziolkowski, Theodore (1962), 'The Odysseus theme in recent German fiction', in *Comparative Literature*, 14, 1962, pp. 225–41

Index

I. Works by Heinrich Böll

Index

II. General Index

236

Index

Index

Index

Index